Make the Right Call!
A User's Guide

Make the Right Call gives you, the baseball enthusiast, an easy and entertaining way to familiarize yourself with the game's intricate rules. We have laid out the book to guide you through several of the elements that govern the game. These components are presented in the text as follows:

Official Rules of Baseball.

The complete rules as drafted by the Official Playing Rules Committee and used by professional baseball umpires.

The Case Book of the Official Playing Rules Committee.

The Case Book material interprets and elaborates on the language of the Official Rules, providing insight into the Rules Committee's intent when drafting the Official Rules.

AMERICAN LEAGUE UMPIRES RULES AND REGULATIONS

The handbook used by American League (AL) umpires contains rules drafted by the American League. In cases where the AL rules differ from or expand upon the Official Rules, the AL rule has been included.

INSTRUCTIONS TO NATIONAL LEAGUE UMPIRES

The handbook used by National League (NL) umpires contains rules drafted by the National League. In cases where the NL rules differ from or expand upon the Official Rules, the NL rule has been included.

In certain circumstances, the Official Playing Rules Committee has drafted approved rulings and specific penalties to be used by umpires as they rule on special game situations.

APPROVED RULING: Instructs the umpire on the correct means to resolve a questionable game situation.

PENALTY: Instructs the umpire on the correct penalty to be imposed upon the infraction of one of the Official Rules.

We hope this book enhances your enjoyment of the game by taking you out of the stands and onto the field—enabling you to **Make the Right Call**.

Mitchell Rogatz
Publisher

125TH ANNIVERSARY

Make The Right Call ™

TRIUMPH BOOKS
CHICAGO

The Official Playing Rules Committee:

William A. Murray, Chairman
Bill White
John McHale
Bill Giles
Tom Grieve
Pat Gillick
Robert Brown, M.D.
Joseph J. Buzas
Jimmy Bragan
George Sisler, Jr.

Amateur Baseball Advisory Members:

Raoul Dedeaux
Ronald Tellefsen

Diagrams: John P. Coyne and Janet L. Rogatz

Design & Typography: Monica Rix Paxson

Editorial: Yvonne M. Ingalls and Brian M. Reid

Front Cover Photo Copyright © L.C. Lambrecht/Major League Baseball Photos.

This book is available in quantity at special discounts for your group or organization.
For further information contact:

Triumph Books, Inc.
644 South Clark Street
Chicago, IL 60605
Tel: (312) 939-3330, Fax: (312) 663-3557

10 9 8 7 6 5 4 3 2 1

Table of Contents

A User's Guide . . . i

1.00 Objectives of the Game . . . 1

The Game
The Objective
The Winner
Playing Field Dimensions
Club Discretion
Pitcher's Mound Dimensions
Home Base Dimensions
Base Dimensions

Pitcher's Plate Dimensions
Players' Benches
Ball Dimensions
Bat Dimensions
Bat Handle
Uniforms
Home and Away Colors
Player Names

Catcher's Mitt
First Baseman's Glove
Fielders' Gloves
Pitcher's Glove
Batting Helmets
Logos

2.00 Definitions of Terms . . . 17

3.00 Game Preliminaries . . . 31

Before the Game
Baseball Supply
Altering the Ball
Player Substitutions
Substitute Runners
Pitcher Substitution
Umpire Notification

Substitution Announcement
Lack of Substitution
    Announcement
Fraternization
Game Postponement
Playing Field Fitness
Calling "Time"

Ground Rules
Clearing Field
Individuals Allowed on Field
Spectator Interference
Team Benches
Police Protection

4.00 Starting and Ending a Game . . . 55

Pre-Game Activities
Umpires Take Charge
Starting the Game
Starting Positions
Batting Order
Base Coaches
Coach's Box
Team Conduct
Ejections

Bench Conduct
How a Team Scores
Regulation Game
Called Game
Scoring in a Regulation Game
Called Game Becomes
    Suspended Game
Suspended Games
Resuming Suspended Games

Exact Point of Suspension
Doubleheaders
Second Game
Playing Field Lights
Forfeited Game—General
Forfeited Game
Forfeited Game
Report of Forfeit
Protesting Games

5.00 Putting the Ball in Play — Live Ball . . . 83

Umpire Calls "Play"
Ball in Play
Delivery to Batter
Offense's Objective
Defense's Objective

Scoring a Run
Changing Sides
Thrown Ball Hits Coach or
    Umpire
Advancing Runners

Ball Lodged in Mask
Calling "Time"
Fielder Steps into Bench
Resuming Play

Make the Right Call

6.00 The Batter . . . 93

Batting Order	Three-Foot Line	Umpire to Remain Silent
Batter's Box	Stealing Home	Becoming Runner Without
Legal Batting Position	Batter's Illegal Action	Liability
Legal Time at Bat	Switching Batter's Boxes	Becoming Runner With Liability
Batter is Out	Batting Out of Turn	Ball Lands in Shrubbery
Bat Hits Ball Twice	Improper Batter Becomes	Designated Hitter
Deflecting Foul Ball	Proper	Designated Hitter Terminated

7.00 The Runner . . . 113

Title to a Base	Obstruction	Overrunning First Base
Touching Bases in Order	Play on Obstructed Runner	Missing Home Base
One Runner per Base	No Play on Obstructed Runner	Interference
Baserunner Advancement	Interference with Batter	Confusing Fielders
Without Liability	Runner is Out	Coach Assists Runner
All Runners Advance Without	Runner is Tagged	Appeal Plays
Liability	Failure to Retouch Base	Successive Appeals
Wild Throw by Pitcher	Force Play	"Fourth Out"
Ball Lodged in Umpire's	Runner Touched by Fair Ball	Fielder's Space
Equipment	Running Bases in Reverse	Following Runner Status

8.00 The Pitcher . . . 141

Legal Pitching Delivery	Pitcher's Prohibitions	Illegal Pitch
The Windup Position	Foreign Substances	Feinting Pitch
The Set Position	Warm-Up Pitches	Intent of Pitcher
Complete Stop	Delay by Pitcher	Visit to the Mound
Illegal Pitch	Balk by Pitcher	Visit Concluded

9.00 The Umpire . . . 161

Umpire Appointment	Field Umpires	Additional American League
Umpire Authority	Final Determination	and National League
Judgment Decisions	Reporting Violations	Guidelines for Umpires
Consulting Another Umpire	Penalties	
Jurisdiction of the Umpire	General Instructions	
Umpire-In-Chief		

10.00 The Official Scorer . . . 183

Official Scorer Appointment	Safe Hits	Double or Triple Play
Scorer Judgment Calls	Oversliding Base	Letting Foul Fly Fall
Scorer's Authority	Last Base Safely Touched	Pitcher and Catcher
Respect and Dignity	Game Ending Hits	Wild Pitches and Passed Balls
Official Scorer Report	Stolen Bases	Bases on Balls
Fielder Records	Wild Throw	Strikeouts
Pitcher Records	Double or Triple Steal	Earned Runs
Passed Balls	Muffed Throw	No Earned Run
Grand Slam	Caught Stealing	Relief Pitcher
Umpire Names	Sacrifice Bunt	Count on Batter
Player Listings	Sacrifice Fly	Winning and Losing Pitchers
Box Score	Putouts	Multiple Relievers
Batting Out of Turn	Other Automatic Putouts	Shutout
Runs Batted In	Assists	Saves
Scorer's Judgment	Double and Triple Plays	Statistics
Base Hits	Errors	Percentage Records
Unnatural Bounce	Wild Throws	Minimum Standards
No Base Hit	Missed Throw	Hitting Streaks
Runner Interference	No Error Charged	

Index . . . 215

Objectives of
The Game

	1.00	Objectives of the Game.

The Game 1.01 Baseball is a game between two teams of nine players each, under direction of a manager, played on an enclosed field in accordance with these rules, under jurisdiction of one or more umpires.

The Objective 1.02 The objective of each team is to win by scoring more runs than the opponent.

The Winner 1.03 The winner of the game shall be that team which shall have scored, in accordance with these rules, the greater number of runs at the conclusion of a regulation game.

Playing Field Dimensions 1.04 THE PLAYING FIELD. The field shall be laid out according to the instructions below, supplemented by Diagrams No. 1, No. 2 and No. 3.

The infield shall be a 90-foot square. The outfield shall be the area between two foul lines formed by extending two sides of the square, as in Diagram 1. The distance from home base to the nearest fence, stand or other obstruction on fair territory shall be 250 feet or more. A distance of 320 feet or more along the foul lines, and 400 feet or more to center field is preferable. The infield shall be graded so that the base lines and home plate are level. The pitcher's plate shall be 10 inches above the level of home plate. The degree of slope from a point 6 inches in front of the pitcher's plate to a point 6 feet toward home plate shall be 1 inch to 1 foot, and such degree of slope shall be uniform. The infield and outfield, including the boundary lines, are fair territory and all other area is foul territory.

It is desirable that the line from home base through the pitchers plate to second base shall run East-Northeast.

It is recommended that the distance from home base to the back-stop, and from the base lines to the nearest fence, stand or other obstruction on foul territory shall be 60 feet or more. See Diagram 1.

When location of home base is determined, with a steel tape measure 127 feet, 3 3/8 inches in desired direction to establish second base. From home base, measure 90 feet toward first base; from second base, measure 90 feet toward first base; the intersection of these lines establishes first base. From home base, measure 90 feet toward third base; from second base, measure 90 feet toward third base; the intersection of these lines establishes third base. The distance between first base and third

Objectives of the Game

*Playing
Field
Dimensions
(Diagram 1)*

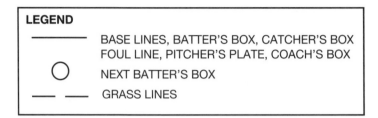

LEGEND

———	BASE LINES, BATTER'S BOX, CATCHER'S BOX FOUL LINE, PITCHER'S PLATE, COACH'S BOX
◯	NEXT BATTER'S BOX
— – —	GRASS LINES

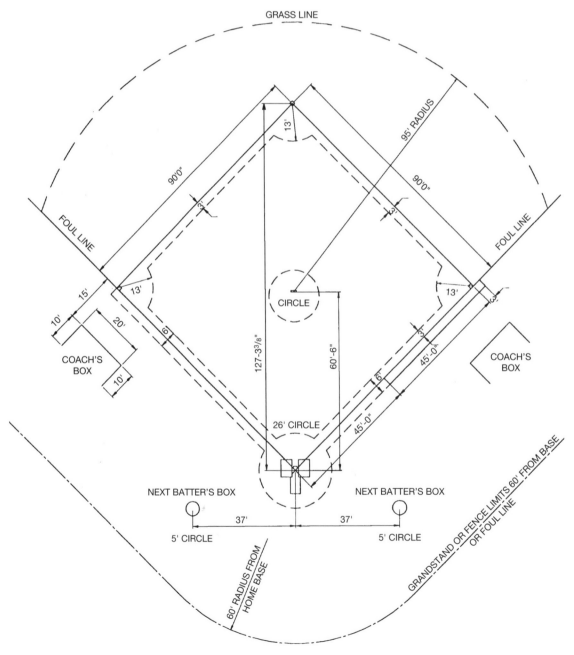

**Playing
Field
Dimensions
(Diagram 2)**

LEGEND

A	1st, 2nd, 3rd BASES
B	BATTER'S BOX
C	CATCHER'S BOX
D	HOME BASE
E	PITCHERS'S PLATE

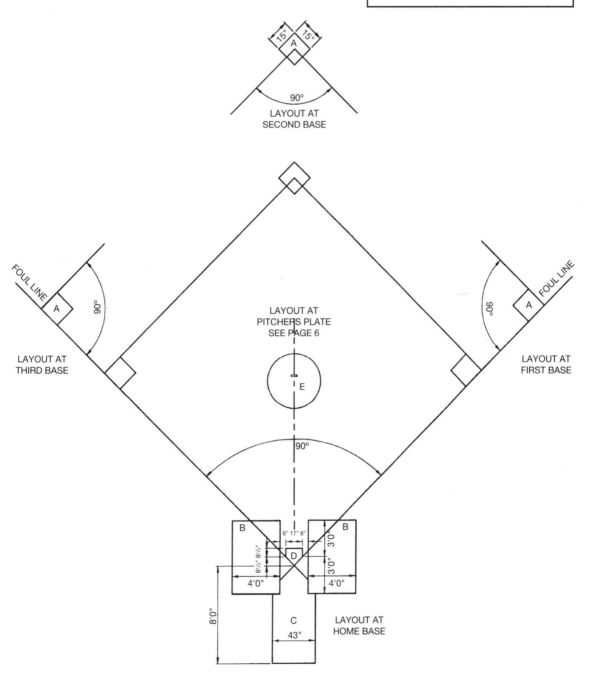

LAYOUT AT
SECOND BASE

LAYOUT AT
PITCHERS PLATE
SEE PAGE 6

FOUL LINE

FOUL LINE

LAYOUT AT
THIRD BASE

LAYOUT AT
FIRST BASE

90°

LAYOUT AT
HOME BASE

5

base is 127 feet, 3 3/8 inches. All measurements from home base shall be taken from the point where the first and third base lines intersect.

The catcher's box, the batters' boxes, the coaches' boxes, the three-foot first base lines and the next batter's boxes shall be laid out as shown in Diagrams 1 and 2. The foul lines and all other playing lines indicated in the diagrams by solid black lines shall be marked with wet, unslaked lime, chalk or other white material.

Club Discretion

The grass lines and dimensions shown on the diagrams are those used in many fields, but they are not mandatory and each club shall determine the size and shape of the grassed and bare areas of its playing field.

NOTE: (a) Any Playing Field constructed by a professional club after June 1, 1958, shall provide a minimum distance of 325 feet from home base to the nearest fence, stand or other obstruction on the right and left field foul lines, and a minimum distance of 400 feet to the center field fence.

(b) No existing playing field shall be remodeled after June 1, 1958, in such manner as to reduce the distance from home base to the foul poles and to the center field fence below the minimum specified in paragraph (a) above.

Pitcher's Mound Dimensions (Diagram 3)

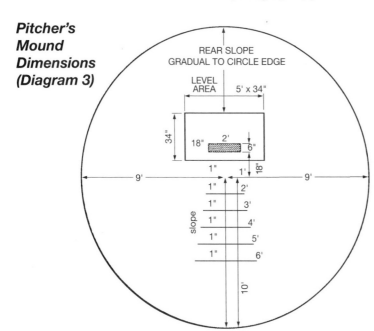

The degree of slope from a point 6" in front of the pitcher's plate to a point 6' toward home plate shall be 1" to 1', and such degree of slope shall be uniform.

Pitching Mound—An 18' diameter circle, center of which is 59' from back of home plate.

Locate front edge of rubber 18" behind center of mound.

Front edge of rubber to back point of home plate, 60'6".

Slope starts 6" from front edge of rubber.

Slope shall be 6" from starting point, 6" in front of rubber to point 6' in front of rubber and slope shall be uniform.

Level area surrounding rubber should be 6" in front of rubber, 18" to each side and 22" to rear of rubber. Total level area 5' x 34".

DIMENSIONS OF FIELD

The dimensions of the American League playing fields shall not be altered or changed by the erection or removal of any barrier or seats between the opening day and the close of the championship season, except with the approval of the President of the league.

WARNING TRACKS

All parks must have warning tracks extending a minimum distance of 10 feet from outfield fences.

FOUL POLES

Clubs shall erect tall foul poles at the fence line with a wire netting at least two feet wide extending along the side of the pole in fair territory above the fence.

CHECKING HEIGHT OF PITCHING MOUNDS

Umpires will check the height of the pitching mounds and bull pens and the slope thereof each spring.

Crew chiefs and the entire crew shall check the mounds in accordance with a schedule issued from the League office and submit a report on their findings.

SUGGESTED LAYOUT OF PITCHING MOUND

If uniformity is to be secured in National League mounds the following dimensions should be followed:

A - Center of mound—An 18' diameter circle,

B - Locate front edge of rubber 18" behind the center of mound,

C - Front edge of rubber to back point of plate 60'6"

D - The degree of slope from a point 6" in front of the pitcher's rubber to a point 6' toward home plate shall be 1" to 1', and such degree of slope shall be uniform,

E - Level area surrounding rubber should be 6" in front of rubber—18" to each side of and 22" to rear of rubber—making this total level area 5'x34".

Home Base Dimensions 1.05 Home base shall be marked by a five-sided slab of whitened rubber. It shall be a 17-inch square with two of the corners removed so that one edge is 17 inches long, two adjacent sides are 8 1/2 inches and the remaining two sides are 12 inches and set at an angle to make a point. It shall be set in the ground with the point at the intersection of the lines extending from home base to first base and to third base; with the 17-inch edge facing the pitcher's plate, and the two 12-inch edges coinciding with the first and third base lines. The top edges of home base shall be beveled and the base shall be fixed in the ground level with the ground surface. (See drawing D in Diagram 2.)

Base Dimensions 1.06 First, second and third bases shall be marked by white canvas bags, securely attached to the ground as indicated in Diagram 2. The first and third base bags shall be entirely within the infield.

The second base bag shall be centered on second base. The bags shall be 15 inches square, not less than three nor more than five inches thick, and filled with soft material.

Pitcher's Plate Dimensions 1.07 The pitcher's plate shall be a rectangular slab of whitened rubber, 24 inches by 6 inches. It shall be set in the ground as shown in Diagrams 1 and 2, so that the distance between the pitcher's plate and home base (the rear point of home plate) shall be 60 feet, 6 inches.

Players' Benches 1.08 The home club shall furnish players' benches, one each for the home and visiting teams. Such benches shall not be less than twenty-five feet from the base lines. They shall be roofed and shall be enclosed at the back and ends.

PHONE FROM FIELD TO PRESS BOX

Each American League park must be equipped with a telephone from the Press Box to some point handy to the field, in order that media representatives may be informed concerning happenings on the field essential in writing their accounts of the game.

Ball Dimensions 1.09 The ball shall be a sphere formed by yarn wound around a small core of cork, rubber or similar material, covered with two stripes of white horsehide or cowhide, tightly stitched together. It shall weigh not less than five nor more than 5 1/4 ounces avoirdupois and measure not less than nine nor more than 9 1/4 inches in circumference.

Bat Dimensions 1.10 (a) The bat shall be a smooth, round stick not more than 2 3/4 inches in diameter at the thickest part and not more than 42 inches in length. The bat shall be one piece of solid wood.

NOTE: No laminated or experimental bats shall be used in a professional game (either championship season or exhibition games) until the manufacturer has secured approval from the Rules Committee of his design and methods of manufacture.

(b) Cupped Bats. An indentation in the end of the bat up to one inch in depth is permitted and may be no wider than two inches and no less than one inch in diameter. The indentation must be curved with no foreign substance added.

Bat Handle (c) The bat handle, for not more than 18 inches from its end, may be covered or treated with any material or substance to improve the grip. Any such material or substance, which extends past the 18 inch limitation, shall cause the bat to be removed from the game.

NOTE: If the umpire discovers that the bat does not conform to (c) above until a time during or after which the bat has been used in play, it shall not be grounds for declaring the batter out, or ejected from the game.

(d) No colored bat may be used in a professional game unless approved by the Rules Committee.

BATS

The cupped bat (Japanese style) is legal.

The Cooper (Canadian) bat is legal.

Umpires should be on the alert for any equipment that has been tampered with, such as bats, balls, gloves, spikes.

LEGAL BAT CRITERIA

BATS MUST PASS THE FOLLOWING CRITERIA TO BE USED IN GAME SITUATIONS

Bat Manufacturers' Names and Trademarks—

1. Manufactures' names, marks and rings are to appear in only one area of the bat.
2. This area is not to exceed 4 inches in length or 2 inches in height, and should start 18 inches from the knob end of the bat.
3. If trademark rings are used as part of the manufacturer's I.D., they are not to exceed 1 inch and are to start 18 inches from the knob end of the bat.

Player Name/Model Number—

Should be placed in a position which will end 2 inches from the top of the barrel. The area reserved is not to exceed 3 inches in length or 2 inches in height which would include one line for the bat model number (no corporate I.D.), a second area for player's name or signature, and a bottom line for the club name.

Club Markings—

Club logos, name or bat emblem may be placed in one of two areas on the bat not to exceed 4 inches in length or 2 inches in height:

1. Centered between the manufacturer's I.D. and the player's name and model number; or
2. In an area on the side of the bat opposite from the manufacturer's marks and player/model number.

PROTECTIVE MATERIAL (This section also applies to Official Rules 1.10-1.16.)

The umpire-in-chief has the authority to permit the use of tape, protective material or equipment, which is not in violation of the rules. He shall prohibit any player from using material or equipment which, in his judgment, is contrary to the intent and spirit of Official Playing Rules 1.10, 1.11, 1.12, 1.13, 1.14, 1.15, and 1.16.

Particular attention is called to the following prohibitions:

1. No colored bats, such as red, blue or green **[see Rule 1.10 (d)]**.

2. **Bats shall not have any pine tar on the barrel of the bat [see Rule 1.10 (c)].**
3. **Cupped bats deeper than one inch in depth [see Rule 1.10 (b)].**
4. Any pitcher starting or entering the game wearing a colored glove must wear the same colored glove for his entire participation in that game.
5. Players on a particular club must wear shoes of the same color. However, some players on the same club may wear striped shoes while others on the same club may wear shoes without stripes.
6. Any players wearing golf gloves underneath their playing gloves may not rub balls for use by the pitchers.
7. The catcher may not substitute a fielder's glove or a first base-man's mitt for his catcher's mitt during the progress of the game or on any individual play.
8. All players in the Major League who played with a National Association club the previous year shall wear ear-flap helmets while at bat. The enforcement of this rule will be in the hands of the team field manager **(see Rule 1.16)**.

The catcher may use a catcher's glove with a vinyl florescent piece attached.

Uniforms 1.11   (a)   (1) All players on a team shall wear uniforms identical in color, trim and style, and all players uniforms shall include minimal six-inch numbers on their backs. (2) Any part of an undershirt exposed to view shall be of a uniform solid color for all players on a team. Any player other than the pitcher may have numbers, letters, insignia attached to the sleeve of the undershirt. (3) No player whose uniform does not conform to that of his teammates shall be permitted to participate in a game.

Home and Away Colors   (b)   A league may provide that (1) each team shall wear a distinctive uniform at all times, or (2) that each team shall have two sets of uniforms, white for home games and a different color for road games.

(c)   (1) Sleeve lengths may vary for individual players, but the sleeves of each individual player shall be approximately the same length. (2) No player shall wear ragged, frayed or slit sleeves.

(d)   No player shall attach to his uniform tape or other material of a different color from his uniform.

(e)   No part of the uniform shall include a pattern that imitates or suggests the shape of a baseball.

(f)   Glass buttons and polished metal shall not be used on a uniform.

(g)　No player shall attach anything to the heel or toe of his shoe other than the ordinary shoe plate or toe plate. Shoes with pointed spikes similar to golf or track shoes shall not be worn.

(h)　No part of the uniform shall include patches or designs relating to commercial advertisements.

Player Names

(i)　A league may provide that the uniforms of its member teams include the names of its players on their backs. Any name other than the last name of the player must be approved by the League President. If adopted, all uniforms for a team must have the names of its players.

PLAYERS' APPEARANCE AND UNIFORMS

The American League recognizes the importance of players appearing on the field at all times in clean uniforms. Extra sets of uniforms are provided by all clubs and club officials should give this matter their personal attention and insist that this regulation be complied with at all times. No player should ever be allowed to start a championship game in a soiled uniform.

Rule 1.11 of the official playing rules outlines provisions covering a player's uniform. Club uniforms should conform to these provisions and clubs should make certain that players wear their uniforms properly.

NUMBERING

All American League players must have numbers on their uniforms. Names on the back of uniforms are optional. When sending advance information for use on official score cards, the club secretary will be expected to give the numbers assigned each player on his team.

WRIST BANDS—JEWELRY

Players shall not wear white wrist bands.

Players will not be allowed to wear distracting jewelry of any kind.

SHOES

Players shall not wear pointed spikes, similar to golf or track shoes.

Excessive or distracting flaps on shoes, particularly those of pitchers, will not be allowed. Players may not call time to change shoes upon becoming a base runner.

GOLF GLOVES

No pitcher shall be allowed to wear a golf glove while pitching; other defensive players may wear a golf glove on their glove hand but they shall not rub the ball with the golf glove on their hand.

Catcher's Mitt　1.12　The catcher may wear a leather mitt not more than thirty-eight inches in circumference, nor more than fifteen and one-half inches from top to bottom. Such limits shall include all lacing and any leather band or facing attached to the outer edge of the mitt. The space between the thumb section and the finger section of the mitt shall not exceed six inches at the top of the mitt and four inches at the base of the thumb crotch. The web shall measure not more than seven inches across the top or more than six inches from its top to the base of the thumb crotch. The web may be either a lacing or lacing through leather tunnels, or a center piece of leather which may be an extension of the palm, connected to the mitt with lacing and constructed so that it will not exceed any of the above mentioned measurements.

OVERSIZED GLOVES

Rules 1.12, 1.13 and 1.14 describing proper glove measurements will be enforced. The key measurements are "J" and "A" lines. The "J" line from the top of the index finger (first finger) to bottom edge cannot measure more than 12 inches. The "A" line, palm width, measured from the inside seam at base of index or first finger to outside edge of little finger of glove cannot be more than 7 3/4 inches. The first baseman's glove cannot be more than 12 inches from top to bottom, and the catcher's glove cannot be more than 15 1/2 inches from top to bottom or more than 38 inches in circumference.

Measurements should be made from the front or receiving side of glove and the measuring tape should be placed in contact with the glove and follow all contours.

The umpire may measure questionable gloves at his discretion or the opposing manager may request a glove be measured. Each manager is limited to two such requests per game. All measurements will be taken by the umpire between innings only. If a glove is illegal, it will be temporarily confiscated. A player refusing to obey the umpire's order may be ejected from the game. Play that has transpired prior to the measurement will be allowed to stand.

First Baseman's Glove 1.13 The first baseman may wear a leather glove or mitt not more than twelve inches long from top to bottom and not more than eight inches wide across the palm, measured from the base of the thumb crotch to the outer edge of the mitt. The space between the thumb section and the finger section of the mitt shall not exceed four inches at the top of the mitt and three and one-half inches at the base of the thumb crotch. The mitt shall be constructed so that this space is permanently fixed and cannot be enlarged, extended, widened, or deepened by the use of any materials or process whatever. The web of the mitt shall measure not more than five inches from its top to the base of the thumb crotch. The web may be either a lacing, lacing through leather tunnels, or a center piece of leather which may be an extension of the palm connected to the mitt with lacing and constructed so that it will not exceed the above mentioned measurements. The webbing shall not be constructed of wound or wrapped lacing or deepened to make a net type of trap. The glove may be of any weight.

Fielders' Gloves	1.14	Each fielder, other than the first baseman or catcher, may use or wear a leather glove. The measurements covering size of glove shall be made by measuring front side or ball receiving side of glove. The tool or measuring tape shall be placed to contact the surface or feature of item being measured and follow all contours in the process. The glove shall not measure more than 12" from the tip of any one of the 4 fingers, through the ball pocket to the bottom edge or heel of glove. The glove shall not measure more than 7 3/4" wide, measured from the inside seam at base of first finger, along base of other fingers, to the outside edge of little finger edge of glove. The space or area between the thumb and first finger, called crotch, may be filled with leather webbing or back stop. The webbing may be constructed of two plies of standard leather to close the crotch area entirely, or it may be constructed of a series of tunnels made of leather, or a series of panels of leather, or of lacing leather thongs. The webbing may not be constructed of wound or wrapped lacing to make a net type of trap. When webbing is made to cover entire crotch area, the webbing can be constructed so as to be flexible. When constructed of a series of sections, they must be joined together. These sections may not be so constructed to allow depression to be developed by curvatures in the section sides. The webbing shall be made to control the size of the crotch opening. The crotch opening shall measure not more than 4 1/2" at the top, not more than 5 3/4" deep, and shall be 3 1/2" wide at its bottom. The opening of crotch shall not be more than 4 1/2" at any point below its top. The webbing shall be secured at each side, and at top and bottom of crotch. The attachment to be made with leather lacing, these connections to be secured. If they stretch or become loose, they shall be adjusted to their proper condition. The glove can be of any weight.

Pitcher's Glove	1.15	(a)	The pitcher's glove shall be uniform in color, including all stitching, lacing and webbing. The pitcher's glove may not be white or gray.
		(b)	No pitcher shall attach to his glove any foreign material of a color different from the glove.

Objectives of the Game

Batting Helmets   1.16   A Professional League shall adopt the following rule pertaining to the use of helmets:

(a)   All players shall use some type of protective helmet while at bat.

(b)   All players in National Association Leagues shall wear a double ear-flap helmet while at bat.

(c)   All players entering the Major Leagues commencing with the 1983 championship season and every succeeding season thereafter must wear a single ear-flap helmet (or at the player's option, a double ear-flap helmet), except those players who were in the Major League during the 1982 season, and who, as recorded in that season, objected to wearing a single ear-flap helmet.

(d)   All catchers shall wear a catcher's protective helmet, while fielding their position.

(e)   All bat/ball boys or girls shall wear a protective helmet while performing their duties.

If the umpire observes any violation of these rules, he shall direct the violation to be corrected. If the violation is not corrected within a reasonable time, in the umpire's judgment, the umpire shall eject the offender from the game, and disciplinary action, as appropriate, will be recommended.

Logos   1.17   Playing equipment including but not limited to the bases, pitcher's plate, baseball, bats, uniforms, catcher's mitts, first baseman's gloves, infielders and outfielders gloves and protective helmets, as detailed in the provisions of this rule, shall not contain any undue commercialization of the product. Designations by the manufacturer on any such equipment must be in good taste as to the size and content of the manufacturer's logo or the brand name of the item. The provisions of this Section 1.17 shall apply to professional leagues only.

NOTE: Manufacturers who plan innovative changes in baseball equipment for professional baseball leagues should submit same to the Official Playing Rules Committee prior to production.

Definitions of Terms

2.00	Definitions of Terms. (All definitions in Rule 2.00 are listed alphabetically.)
ADJUDGED	is a judgment decision by the umpire.
An APPEAL	is the act of a fielder in claiming violation of the rules by the offensive team.
A BALK	is an illegal act by the pitcher with a runner or runners on base, entitling all runners to advance one base.
A BALL	is a pitch which does not enter the strike zone in flight and is not struck at by the batter.

> If the pitch touches the ground and bounces through the strike zone it is a "ball." If such a pitch touches the batter, he shall be awarded first base. If the batter swings at such a pitch after two strikes, the ball cannot be caught, for the purposes of Rule 6.05 (c) and 6.09 (b). If the batter hits such a pitch, the ensuing action shall be the same as if he hit the ball in flight.

A BASE	is one of four points which must be touched by a runner in order to score a run; more usually applied to the canvas bags and the rubber plate which mark the base points.
A BASE COACH	is a team member in uniform who is stationed in the coach's box at first or third base to direct the batter and the runners.
A BASE on BALLS	is an award of first base granted to a batter who, during his time at bat, receives four pitches outside the strike zone.
A BATTER	is an offensive player who takes his position in the batter's box.
BATTER-RUNNER	is a term that identifies the offensive player who has just finished his time at bat until he is put out or until the play on which he became a runner ends.
The BATTER'S BOX	is the area within which the batter shall stand during his time at bat.
The BATTERY	is the pitcher and catcher.
BENCH or DUGOUT	is the seating facilities reserved for players, substitutes and other team members in uniform when they are not actively engaged on the playing field.

Definitions of Terms

A BUNT
is a batted ball not swung at, but intentionally met with the bat and tapped slowly within the infield.

A CALLED GAME
is one in which, for any reason, the umpire-in-chief terminates play.

A CATCH
is the act of a fielder in getting secure possession in his hand or glove of a ball in flight and firmly holding it; providing he does not use his cap, protector, pocket or any other part of his uniform in getting possession. It is not a catch, however, if simultaneously or immediately following his contact with the ball, he collides with a player, or with a wall, or if he falls down, and as a result of such collision or falling, drops the ball. It is not a catch if a fielder touches a fly ball which then hits a member of the offensive team or an umpire and then is caught by another defensive player. If the fielder has made the catch and drops the ball while in the act of making a throw following the catch, the ball shall be adjudged to have been caught. In establishing the validity of the catch, the fielder shall hold the ball long enough to prove that he has complete control of the ball and that his release of the ball is voluntary and intentional.

A catch is legal if the ball is finally held by any fielder, even though juggled, or held by another fielder before it touches the ground. Runners may leave their bases the instant the first fielder touches the ball. A fielder may reach over a fence, railing, rope or other line of demarcation to make a catch. He may jump on top of a railing, or canvas that may be in foul ground. No interference should be allowed when a fielder reaches over a fence, railing, rope or into a stand to catch a ball. He does so at his own risk.

If a fielder, attempting a catch at the edge of the dugout, is "held up" and kept from an apparent fall by a player or players of either team and the catch is made, it shall be allowed.

LEGAL CATCH

The Umpire shall rule whether the ball was or was not caught: (1) If the fielder, after catching the ball, crashes into a stand and drops the ball, it is not a catch. (2) If he collides with another fielder and drops the ball, or if, after he has caught the ball, another fielder collides with him and the ball is dropped, it is not a catch. (3) If the fielder gets his hand or hands on the ball and falls down in the attempt, he must "come up" with the ball to be a catch. A ball will be ruled caught when the momentum of the catch is completed.

These examples do not apply where a fielder has completed a legal catch, and then drops the ball while in the act of drawing back his arm to make a throw.

The fielder cannot jump over any fence, railing or rope marking the limits of the playing field in order to catch the ball. He may (1) reach over such fence, railing or rope to make a catch; (2) fall over the same after completing the catch; or (3) jump on top of a railing or fence marking the boundary of the field or climb onto a fence or on a field canvas and catch the ball, in all of which three cases the catch would be legal, as dictated by the best judgment of the umpire.

The same restrictions apply to a foul ball descending into a stand. A catcher or fielder cannot jump into a stand to catch such a ball, but there is nothing to prevent him from reaching into the stand and making the play.

A fielder or catcher may reach or step into, or go into the dugout with one or both feet to make a catch, and if he holds the ball, the catch shall be allowed. Ball is in play.

If the fielder or catcher, after having made a legal catch, should fall into a stand or among spectators or into the dugout after making a legal catch, or fall while in the dugout after making a legal catch, the ball is dead and runners advance one base without liability to be put out.

In all cases where a fielder or catcher reaches over a fence, railing or rope, he does so at his own risk and no interference should be called. If a fielder, attempting a catch at the edge of the dugout, is "held up" and kept from an apparent fall by a player or players of either team and the catch is made, it shall be allowed.

The CATCHER is the fielder who takes his position back of the home base.

The CATCHER'S BOX is that area within which the catcher shall stand until the pitcher delivers the ball.

The CLUB is a person or group of persons responsible for assembling the team personnel, providing the playing field and required facilities, and representing the team in relations with the league.

A COACH is a team member in uniform appointed by the manager to perform such duties as the manager may designate, such as but not limited to acting as base coach.

A DEAD BALL is a ball out of play because of a legally created temporary suspension of play.

The DEFENSE (or DEFENSIVE) is the team, or any player of the team, in the field.

Definitions of Terms

A DOUBLE-HEADER is two regularly scheduled or rescheduled games, played in immediate succession.

A DOUBLE PLAY is a play by the defense in which two offensive players are put out as a result of continuous action, providing there is no error between putouts.

(a) A force double play is one in which both putouts are force plays.

(b) A reverse force double play is one in which the first out is a force play and the second out is made on a runner for whom the force is removed by reason of the first out. Examples of reverse force plays: runner on first, one out; batter grounds to first baseman, who steps on first base (one out) and throws to second baseman or shortstop for the second out (a tag play). Another example: bases loaded, none out; batter grounds to third baseman, who steps on third base (one out); then throws to catcher for the second out (tag play).

DUGOUT (See definition of BENCH)

A FAIR BALL is a batted ball that settles on fair ground between home and first base, or between home and third base, or that is on or over fair territory when bounding to the outfield past first or third base, or that touches first, second or third base, or that first falls on fair territory on or beyond first base or third base, or that, while on or over fair territory touches the person of an umpire or player, or that, while over fair territory, passes out of the playing field in flight.

A fair fly shall be judged according to the relative position of the ball and the foul line, including the foul pole, and not as to whether the fielder is on fair or foul territory at the time he touches the ball.

If a fly ball lands in the infield between home and first base, or home and third base, and then bounces to foul territory without touching a player or umpire and before passing first or third base, it is a foul ball; or if the ball settles on foul territory or is touched by a player on foul territory, it is a foul ball. If a fly ball lands on or beyond first or third base and then bounces to foul territory, it is a fair hit.

Clubs, increasingly, are erecting tall foul poles at the fence line with a wire netting extending along the side of the pole on fair territory above the fence to enable the umpires more accurately to judge fair and foul balls.

FAIR TERRITORY is that part of the playing field within, and including the first base and third base lines, from home base to the bottom of the playing field fence and perpendicularly upwards. All foul lines are in fair territory.

A FIELDER is any defensive player.

FIELDER'S CHOICE is the act of a fielder who handles a fair grounder and, instead of throwing to first base to put out the batter-runner, throws to another base in an attempt to put out a preceding runner. The term is also used by scorers (a) to account for the advance of the batter-runner who takes one or more extra bases when the fielder who handles his safe hit attempts to put out a preceding runner; (b) to account for the advance of a runner (other than by stolen base or error) while a fielder is attempting to put out another runner; and (c) to account for the advance of a runner made solely because of the defensive team's indifference (undefended steal).

A FLY BALL is a batted ball that goes high in the air in flight.

A FORCE PLAY is a play in which a runner legally loses his right to occupy a base by reason of the batter becoming a runner.

Confusion regarding this play is removed by remembering that frequently the "force" situation is removed during the play. Example: Man on first, one out, ball hit sharply to first baseman who touches the bag and batter-runner is out. The force is removed at that moment and runner advancing to second must be tagged. If there had been a runner on third or second, and either of these runners scored before the tag-out at second, the run counts. Had the first baseman thrown to second and the ball then had been returned to first, the play at second was a force out, making two outs, and the return throw to first ahead of the runner would have made three outs. In that case, no run would score.

Example: Not a force out. One out. Runner on first and third. Batter flies out. Two out. Runner on third tags up and scores. Runner on first tries to retouch before throw from fielder reaches first baseman, but does not get back in time and is out. Three outs. If, in umpire's judgment, the runner from third touched home before the ball was held at first base, the run counts.

Definitions of Terms

A FORFEITED GAME | is a game declared ended by the umpire-in-chief in favor of the offended team by the score of 9 to 0, for violation of the rules.

A FOUL BALL | is a batted ball that settles on foul territory between home and first base, or between home and third base, or that bounds past first or third base on or over foul territory, or that first falls on foul territory beyond first or third base, or that, while on or over foul territory, touches the person of an umpire or player, or any object foreign to the natural ground.

A foul fly shall be judged according to the relative position of the ball and the foul line, including the foul pole, and not as to whether the infielder is on foul or fair territory at the time he touches the ball.

A batted ball not touched by a fielder, which hits the pitcher's rubber and rebounds into foul territory, between home and first, or between home and third base is a foul ball.

FOUL TERRITORY | is that part of the playing field outside the first and third base lines extended to the fence and perpendicularly upwards.

A FOUL TIP | is a batted ball that goes sharp and direct from the bat to the catcher's hands and is legally caught. It is not a foul tip unless caught and any foul tip that is caught is a strike, and the ball is in play. It is not a catch if it is a rebound, unless the ball has first touched the catcher's glove or hand.

A GROUND BALL | is a batted ball that rolls or bounces close to the ground.

The HOME TEAM | is the team on whose grounds the game is played, or if the game is played on neutral grounds, the home team shall be designated by mutual agreement.

ILLEGAL (or ILLEGALLY) | is contrary to these rules.

An ILLEGAL PITCH | is (1) a pitch delivered to the batter when the pitcher does not have his pivot foot in contact with the pitcher's plate; (2) a quick return pitch. An illegal pitch when runners are on base is a balk.

An INFIELDER | is a fielder who occupies a position in the infield.

An INFIELD FLY | is a fair fly ball (not including a line drive nor an attempted bunt) which can be caught by an infielder with ordinary effort, when first and second, or first, second and third bases are occupied, before two are out. The pitcher, catcher and any outfielder who stations himself in the infield on the play shall be considered infielders for the purpose of this rule. When it seems apparent that a batted ball will be an Infield Fly, the umpire shall immediately declare "Infield Fly" for the benefit of the runners. If the ball is near the baselines, the umpire shall declare "Infield Fly, if Fair."

The ball is alive and runners may advance at the risk of the ball being caught, or retouch and advance after the ball is touched, the same as on any fly ball. If the hit becomes a foul ball, it is treated the same as any foul.

If a declared Infield Fly is allowed to fall untouched to the ground, and bounces foul before passing first or third base, it is a foul ball. If a declared Infield Fly falls untouched to the ground outside the baseline, and bounces fair before passing first or third base, it is an Infield Fly.

On the infield fly rule the umpire is to rule whether the ball could ordinarily have been handled by an infielder not by some arbitrary limitation such as the grass, or the base lines. The umpire must rule also that a ball is an infield fly, even if handled by an outfielder, if, in the umpire's judgment, the ball could have been as easily handled by an infielder. The infield fly is in no sense to be considered an appeal play. The umpire's judgment must govern, and the decision should be made immediately.

When an infield fly rule is called, runners may advance at their own risk. If on an infield fly rule, the infielder intentionally drops a fair ball, the ball remains in play despite the provisions of Rule 6.05 (l). The infield fly rule takes precedence.

IN FLIGHT describes a batted, thrown, or pitched ball which has not yet touched the ground or some object other than a fielder.

IN JEOPARDY is a term indicating that the ball is in play and an offensive player may be put out.

An INNING is that portion of a game within which the teams alternate on offense and defense and in which there are three putouts for each team. Each team's time at bat is a half-inning.

INTERFERENCE (a) Offensive interference is an act by the team at bat which interferes with, obstructs, impedes, hinders or confuses any fielder attempting to make a play. If the

Definitions of Terms

umpire declares the batter, batter-runner, or a runner out for interference, all other runners shall return to the last base that was in the judgment of the umpire, legally touched at the time of the interference, unless otherwise provided by these rules.

In the event the batter-runner has not reached first base, all runners shall return to the base last occupied at the time of the pitch.

(b) Defensive interference is an act by a fielder which hinders or prevents a batter from hitting a pitch.

(c) Umpire's interference occurs (1) When an umpire hinders, impedes or prevents a catcher's throw attempting to prevent a stolen base, or (2) When a fair ball touches an umpire on fair territory before passing a fielder.

(d) Spectator interference occurs when a spectator reaches out of the stands, or goes on the playing field, and touches a live ball.

On any interference the ball is dead.

The LEAGUE is a group of clubs whose teams play each other in a pre-arranged schedule under these rules for the league championship.

The LEAGUE PRESIDENT shall enforce the official rules, resolve any disputes involving the rules, and determine any protested games. The league president may fine or suspend any player, coach, manager or umpire for violation of these rules, at his discretion.

LEGAL (or LEGALLY) is in accordance with these rules.

A LIVE BALL is a ball which is in play.

A LINE DRIVE is a batted ball that goes sharp and direct from the bat to a fielder without touching the ground.

The MANAGER is a person appointed by the club to be responsible for the team's actions on the field, and to represent the team in communications with the umpire and the opposing team. A player may be appointed manager.

(a) The club shall designate the manager to the league president or the umpire-in-chief not less than thirty minutes before the scheduled starting time of the game.

(b) The manager may advise the umpire that he has delegated specific duties prescribed by the rules to a player or coach, and any action of such designated representative shall be official. The manager shall always be responsible for his team's conduct, observance of the official rules, and deference to the umpires.

(c) If a manager leaves the field, he shall designate a player or coach as his substitute, and such substitute manager shall have the duties, rights and responsibilities of the manager. If the manager fails or refuses to designate his substitute before leaving, the umpire-in-chief shall designate a team member as substitute manager.

OBSTRUCTION is the act of a fielder who, while not in possession of the ball and not in the act of fielding the ball, impedes the progress of any runner.

If a fielder is about to receive a thrown ball and if the ball is in flight directly toward and near enough to the fielder so he must occupy his position to receive the ball he may be considered "in the act of fielding a ball." It is entirely up to the judgment of the umpire as to whether a fielder is in the act of fielding a ball. After a fielder has made an attempt to field a ball and missed, he can no longer be in the "act of fielding" the ball. For example: an infielder dives at a ground ball and the ball passes him and he continues to lie on the ground and delays the progress of the runner, he very likely has obstructed the runner.

OFFENSE is the team, or any player of the team, at bat.

OFFICIAL SCORER See Rule 10.00.

An OUT is one of the three required retirements of an offensive team during its time at bat.

An OUTFIELDER is a fielder who occupies a position in the outfield, which is the area of the playing field most distant from home base.

OVERSLIDE (or OVERSLIDING) is the act of an offensive player when his slide to a base, other than when advancing from home to first base, is with such momentum that he loses contact with the base.

A PENALTY is the application of these rules following an illegal act.

The PERSON of a player or an umpire is any part of his body, his clothing or his equipment.

Definitions of Terms

A PITCH	is a ball delivered to the batter by the pitcher.
	All other deliveries of the ball by one player to another are thrown balls.
A PITCHER	is the fielder designated to deliver the pitch to the batter.
The PITCHER'S PIVOT FOOT	is that foot which is in contact with the pitcher's plate as he delivers the pitch.
"PLAY"	is the umpire's order to start the game or to resume action following any dead ball.
A QUICK RETURN	pitch is one made with obvious intent to catch a batter off balance. It is an illegal pitch.
REGULATION GAME	See Rules 4.10 and 4.11.
A RETOUCH	is the act of a runner in returning to a base as legally required.
A RUN (or SCORE)	is the score made by an offensive player who advances from batter to runner and touches first, second, third and home bases in that order.
A RUN-DOWN	is the act of the defense in an attempt to put out a runner between bases.
A RUNNER	is an offensive player who is advancing toward, or touching, or returning to any base.
"SAFE"	is a declaration by the umpire that a runner is entitled to the base for which he was trying.
SET POSITION	is one of the two legal pitching positions.
SQUEEZE PLAY	is a term to designate a play when a team, with a runner on third base, attempts to score that runner by means of a bunt.
A STRIKE	is a legal pitch when so called by the umpire, which—

(a) Is struck at by the batter and is missed;

(b) Is not struck at, if any part of the ball passes through any part of the strike zone;

(c) Is fouled by the batter when he has less than two strikes;

(d) Is bunted foul;

(e) Touches the batter as he strikes at it;

(f) Touches the batter in flight in the strike zone; or

(g) Becomes a foul tip.

The STRIKE ZONE   is that area over home plate the upper limit of which is a horizontal line at the midpoint between the top of the shoulders and the top of the uniform pants, and the lower level is a line at the top of the knees. The Strike Zone shall be determined from the batter's stance as the batter is prepared to swing at a pitched ball.

STRIKE ZONE

At the end of the 1987 season the Strike Zone was redefined by the Official Playing Rules Committee. This new definition is in effect for the 1988 season, on a one-year trial basis, with determination for future use to be made at the end of the 1988 season.

"The Strike Zone is that area over home plate the upper limit of which is a horizontal line at the midpoint between the top of the shoulders and the top of the uniform pants, and the lower limit of which is the top of the knees. The strike zone shall be determined from the batter's stance as the batter is prepared to swing at a pitched ball."

The midpoint between the top of the shoulders and the top of the uniform pants can beconsidered the "nipple line".

Umpires as a staff must strive for uniformity and consistency in calling strikes and this requires work and study. The strike zone for the same batter should not vary with umpires. The batter has the right to expect the same call on "strikes" by all umpires. Crew chiefs should confer with crew members on strike calls, if they believe it necessary.

A SUSPENDED GAME   is a called game which is to be completed at a later date.

A TAG   is the action of a fielder in touching a base with his body while holding the ball securely and firmly in his hand or glove; or touching a runner with the ball, or with his hand or glove holding the ball, while holding the ball securely and firmly in his hand or glove.

A THROW   is the act of propelling the ball with the hand and arm to a given objective and is to be distinguished, always, from the pitch.

A TIE GAME   is a regulation game which is called when each team has the same number of runs.

Definitions of Terms

"TIME"   is the announcement by an umpire of a legal interruption of play, during which the ball is dead.

TOUCH   To touch a player or umpire is to touch any part of his body, his clothing or his equipment.

A TRIPLE PLAY   is a play by the defense in which three offensive players are put out as a result of continuous action, providing there is no error between putouts.

A WILD PITCH   is one so high, so low, or so wide of the plate that it cannot be handled with ordinary effort by the catcher.

WIND-UP POSITION   is one of the two legal pitching positions.

Game Preliminaries

3.00   Game Preliminaries.

Before the Game

3.01   Before the game begins the umpire shall—

(a)   Require strict observance of all rules governing implements of play and equipment of players;

(b)   Be sure that all playing lines (heavy lines on Diagrams No. 1 and No. 2) are marked with lime, chalk or other white material easily distinguishable from the ground or grass;

Baseball Supply

(c)   Receive from the home club a supply of regulation baseballs, the number and make to be certified to the home club by the league president. Each ball shall be enclosed in a sealed package bearing the signature of the league president, and the seal shall not be broken until just prior to game time when the umpire shall open each package to inspect the ball and remove its gloss. The umpire shall be the sole judge of the fitness of the balls to be used in the game;

(d)   Be assured by the home club that at least one dozen regulation reserve balls are immediately available for use if required;

(e)   Have in his possession at least two alternate balls and shall require replenishment of such supply of alternate balls as needed throughout the game. Such alternate balls shall be put in play when—

(1)   A ball has been batted out of the playing field or into the spectator area;

(2)   A ball has become discolored or unfit for further use;

(3)   The pitcher requests such alternate ball.

The umpire shall not give an alternate ball to the pitcher until play has ended and the previously used ball is dead. After a thrown or batted ball goes out of the playing field, play shall not be resumed with an alternate ball until the runners have reached the bases to which they are entitled. After a home run is hit out of the playing grounds, the umpire shall not deliver a new ball to the pitcher or the catcher until the batter hitting the home run has crossed the plate.

Game Preliminaries

UMPIRE IN CHARGE OF FIELD BEFORE GAME

One umpire will be at the park and take charge of the field each day one hour and thirty minutes before the advertised time for starting the game. It will be the duty of this official to see that the visiting club is allotted the proper time for batting and fielding practice. The umpire will also prevent players from engaging in bunting in front of the stands. All umpires must be in the dressing room and in uniform fifteen minutes prior to game time, so that they will be ready to take the field and start the game should an emergency arise.

BATTING AND FIELDING PRACTICE

When the condition of the field permits, the home and visiting clubs must take batting and fielding practice, except that either club may be excused from such practice upon notice to the other club at least three hours in advance of the advertised starting time of any game that it does not wish to take batting and/or fielding practice. Whenever possible a club should give notice of such intent the previous day.

The rules of the American League provide that batting and fielding practice will commence ONE HOUR AND TEN MINUTES prior to game time, to be divided as follows:

FORTY minutes batting by the visiting club and TEN minutes fielding practice by home club; then TEN minutes fielding practice by visiting club.

TEN minutes for preparation of the playing field.

Players of the team which has completed its practice should not be permitted to remain on the field, thereby interfering with the practice of the other club and endangering its play-ers. There are occasions when it may be necessary for both teams to be on the field at the same time. If so, stretching exercises should be taken at the fence area, in foul territory, on the teams' side of the field.

BASEBALLS

Clubs will deliver to the umpires' dressing room one hour prior to the advertised time for starting the game five dozen baseballs for a single game and eight dozen for a double-header.

The balls are to be rubbed by the umpires and for a single game five dozen are turned over to the club representative in charge of the balls for his checking and delivery to the field. This same representative will then carry the bag to the playing field and place it in charge of the ball boy or whoever is to handle the balls on the field. The umpire is to take his first consignment of balls from the ball boy on the field.

The club representative will be responsible for returning the ball bag to the umpires' dressing room at the completion of the game. In his presence the remaining balls, if any, will be checked and the slip for the next day's supply of balls prepared. The club representative along with the Umpire In Chief is to sign the slip. The ball bag will then be locked and taken to the club offices by the club representatives.

For double-headers, for the first game five dozen balls will be inspected and placed in the ball bag by the club representative. Three dozen rubbed balls will remain in the umpires' dressing room for the second game. When the club representative returns the ball bag to the umpires' dressing room after completion of the first game, with the umpires he will make a record of the number of balls remaining in the bag and add the three dozen balls which

were left in the umpires' dressing room to make up the supply for the second game. Under this arrangement the only time the umpires will handle the balls is when they soil them.

CHECKING PLAYING AREA BEFORE GAME

Each crew will walk around each park once on its first visit. There have been cases of players complaining about improper padding on the fences and inadequate warning tracks, and in one instance a player has sued the ball club. Please look for these things as well as any unusual things that might create a problem for you.

TORONTO SKYDOME PROCEDURE

The opening or closing of the roof of the Toronto Skydome will be decided by the Toronto Blue Jays up until game time. The closing or the opening of the roof after the game starts will be decided by the Umpire In Chief.

FIELD MARKING AND MOUNDS

Before commencing the game, the umpire should determine that the rules governing marking of the field are strictly complied with. Umpires will pay particular attention to the batter's boxes and the coaches' lines to make certain that they are

legal. When double-headers are played, the umpire will insist that the ground-crew help re-mark the batter's box before the start of the second game.

Umpires should also make a careful inspection of the base bags and see that they are replaced if they in any way are damaged.

Umpires shall be on the alert for pitching mounds that are not regulation height and slope.

Simply, the slope of mounds may be checked as follows:

Obtain a 2x4 and drive a spike a few feet in front of the rubber and place the 2x4 flush to the ground and 6" in front of the rubber, placing the other end on the spike. Put a level at the middle of the board and tap the spike until the level shows even. Take a measure and note the board is flush at the start and distance between the ground and board should increase 1" for every foot for 6'.

CARE OF BASEBALLS

Umpires must fill out the special report on the number of balls used in each game.

Umpires will keep the keys to the ball bag on their persons at all times. This means that key must not be left in uniforms in the dressing rooms overnight.

BEFORE THE GAME

The umpires assigned to work must be at the park at least one hour before the starting time of a championship game or a spring exhibition game. Two umpires of the crew (not the plate umpire that day) shall be in the stands one hour and thirty minutes before game time to observe fraternization.

In the final series between two clubs in a city, the umpire crew chief shall be at the ball park four hours before the start of the game if there is any chance the game might be postponed because of weather conditions. Upon arrival, he shall consult with the home club management and if it appears likely that the game will be postponed he should contact the League President and advise him of

the situation. The crew chief should study the League schedule and be apprised when a series is the final home series between the two clubs, and alert himself that he must contact the club if the weather is threatening.

RUBBING BASEBALLS

Five (5) dozen, or in some cases six (6) dozen, baseballs will be delivered by the home club management to the umpires' dressing room one hour before game time. After the umpires have rubbed them, all of these base-balls shall be delivered to the baseball attendant who will come to the umpires' dressing room. The plate umpire attendant will take the number of balls necessary to start the game.

At the end of the game and before the umpires leave the playing field, the plate umpire will deliver any baseballs in his possession to the baseball attendant. The baseball attendant will take the baseballs to the home club management who will make a report on the baseballs used for the game.

Umpires shall take precaution that all balls are rubbed uniformly.

Umpires are not to take baseballs for their own use, without permission from the club's management.

PUTTING NEW BALL IN PLAY AFTER HOME RUN

After a home run is hit out of the playing grounds, the umpire shall not deliver a new ball to the pitcher or the catcher until the batter hitting the home run crosses the plate.

BASEBALLS

Official Baseballs. The Official National League baseball, adopted by action, shall be used in all championship games.

Delivery and Accounting.

(a) The home club shall deliver to the umpires' dressing room one hour before the scheduled starting time of the game five dozen baseballs for a single game and five dozen baseballs for the second game of a doubleheader.

(b) The umpire-in-chief shall submit a signed written report to the home club at the end of each game showing:

(1) number of usable balls delivered by the club at the start of the game;

(2) number of usable balls delivered by the umpire to the club at the end of the game; and

(3) number of unusable balls delivered by the umpire to the club at the end of the game.

The League shall furnish each club standard forms for this report and the club shall deliver such forms to the umpires before each game.

Altering the Ball 3.02 No player shall intentionally discolor or damage the ball by rubbing it with soil, rosin, paraffin, licorice, sand-paper, emery-paper or other foreign substance.

PENALTY: The umpire shall demand the ball and remove the offender from the game. In case the umpire cannot locate the offender, and if the pitcher delivers such discolored or damaged ball to the batter, the pitcher shall be removed from the game at once and shall be suspended automatically for ten days.

Player   3.03
Substitutions

A player, or players, may be substituted during a game at any time the ball is dead. A substitute player shall bat in the replaced player's position in the team's batting order. A player once removed from a game shall not re-enter that game. If a substitute enters the game in place of a player-manager, the manager may thereafter go to the coaching lines at his discretion. When two or more substitute players of the defensive team enter the game at the same time, the manager shall, immediately before they take their positions as fielders, designate to the umpire-in-chief such players' positions in the team's batting order and the umpire-in-chief shall so notify the official scorer. If this information is not immediately given to the umpire-in-chief, he shall have authority to designate the substitutes' places in the batting order.

A pitcher may change to another position only once during the same inning; e.g. the pitcher will not be allowed to assume a position other than a pitcher more than once in the same inning.

Any player other than a pitcher substituted for an injured player shall be allowed five warm-up throws. (See Rule 8.03 for pitchers.)

ANNOUNCING SUBSTITUTES

When two defensive players enter the game, the umpire shall require the manager to announce the changes simultaneously. If a designated hitter is removed from the game, the substitute designated hitter need not be announced until it becomes his turn to bat.

WARM-UP PITCHES

When a pitcher takes his position at the beginning of each inning, or when he relieves another pitcher he shall be permitted to pitch not to exceed eight preparatory pitches to his catcher during which play shall be suspended. Such preparatory pitches shall not consume more than one minute of time. The pitcher shall not intentionally delay the game by throwing the ball to players other than the catcher, when the batter is in position, except in an attempt to retire a runner. If a sudden emergency causes a pitcher to be summoned into the game without any opportunity to warm up, the Umpire In Chief shall allow him as many pitches as the umpire deems necessary. Any substitute player or players shall be allowed five warm-up throws.

When a pitcher moves to a defensive position and then returns to pitch in the same inning, he will be permitted only five (5) warm-up pitches.

WARM-UPS DURING GAME

A pitcher will not be allowed to return to the bull pen for additional warm-ups once he has entered the game.

Outfielders may take warm-up throws with each other while a relief pitcher takes his warm-up, provided it does not delay the game.

A designated hitter about to enter a game defensively may warm up in the bull pen the preceding inning.

PITCHER CHANGING POSITIONS

A pitcher may change to another position only once during the same inning; e.g., a pitcher will not be allowed to assume a position other than pitcher more than once the same inning.

SUBSTITUTES (This section also applies to Official Rules 3.06 –3.08)

A substitution is completed and the player considered as having entered the game when the manager, or his designated representative, notifies the umpire-in-chief of such substitution. If no such notification is given, or if after notice no announcement is made, the player shall be considered as having entered the game when he takes his position as provided in 3.08(a)-2-3-4 when the umpire calls **"PLAY"** or if a **proper** pitcher is substituted when he delivers any pitch (preparatory or otherwise) or attempts a play, whether he has been announced or not and shall pitch until the batter is out or becomes a base runner, or a runner is retired, as provided in 3.05(b).

If a player's name appears in the original batting order and before he appears at bat, another player takes this player's position on the field or at bat, and no notification is made to the umpire and no announcement thereof is made over the P.A. system, the player shall be considered as entering the game only as a substitute player. This is not a batting out of order situation where the opposing manager could protest later in the game. As provided in Rule 3.08(b) any play or any hit made by such unannounced substitute would be legal.

The umpire should be alert at all times to correct the batting order in case of substitution.

When a manager makes two or more substitutions at the same time he must advise, at the same moment, the umpire-in-chief the names of the substitutes, their defensive positions, and in what place each will hit in the batting order. The manager cannot give notice of one of the substitutions, leave the umpire, come back to the umpire-in-chief and locate the other player in the lineup. In case the manager fails or refuses to make a decision, the umpire-in-chief is authorized to decide the necessary batting order changes and his decision is final. Just as soon as the substitutions are legal, announcements should be made over the P.A. system.

Opposing managers, upon request, are entitled to know where substitutes are placed in the batting order. The umpire shall call the manager's attention to obvious mistakes the manager might make in the batting order when substitutions are made so they may be corrected before play starts. This is not to be confused with 6.07, which restricts the umpire from calling attention to appearance in batter's box of improper batter.

Substitute Runners 3.04   A player whose name is on his team's batting order may not become a substitute runner for another member of his team.

This rule is intended to eliminate the practice of using so-called courtesy runners. No player in the game shall be permitted to act as a courtesy runner for a teammate. No player who has been in the game and has been taken out for a substitute shall return as a courtesy runner. Any player not in the lineup, if used as a runner, shall be considered as a substitute player.

Pitcher 3.05
Substitution

(a) The pitcher named in the batting order handed the umpire-in-chief, as provided in Rules 4.01 (a) and 4.01 (b), shall pitch to the first batter or any substitute batter until such batter is put out or reaches first base, unless the pitcher sustains injury or illness which, in the judgment of the umpire-in-chief, incapacitates him from pitching.

(b) If the pitcher is replaced, the substitute pitcher shall pitch to the batter then at bat, or any substitute batter, until such batter is put out or reaches first base, or until the offensive team is put out, unless the substitute pitcher sustains injury or illness which, in the umpire-in-chief's judgment, incapacitates him for further play as a pitcher.

(c) If an improper substitution is made for the pitcher, the umpire shall direct the proper pitcher to return to the game until the provisions of this rule are fulfilled. If the improper pitcher is permitted to pitch, any play that results is legal. The improper pitcher becomes the proper pitcher as soon as he makes his first pitch to the batter, or as soon as any runner is put out.

> If a manager attempts to remove a pitcher in violation of Rule 3.05 (c) the umpire shall notify the manager of the offending club that it cannot be done. If, by chance, the umpire-in-chief has, through oversight, announced the incoming improper pitcher, he should still correct the situation before the improper pitcher pitches. Once the improper pitcher delivers a pitch he becomes the proper pitcher.

STATUS OF IMPROPER PITCHER

If a manager attempts to remove a pitcher in violation of Rule 3.05(c), the umpire shall notify the manager of the offending club that it cannot be done. If, by chance, the umpire-in-chief has, through oversight, announced the incoming improper pitcher, he should still correct the situation before the improper pitcher pitches. Once the improper pitcher delivers a pitch he becomes the proper pitcher.

Umpire 3.06
Notification

The manager shall immediately notify the umpire-in-chief of any substitution and shall state to the umpire-in-chief the substitute's place in his batting order.

> Players for whom substitutions have been made may remain with their team on the bench or may "warm-up" pitchers. If a manager substitutes another player for himself, he may continue to direct his team from the bench or the coach's box. Umpires should not permit players for whom substitutes have been made, and who

are permitted to remain on the bench, to address any remarks to any opposing player or manager, or to the umpires.

PLAYER REMOVED FROM THE GAME (Substitute)

When a player has been removed from the game by his manager, he will be permitted to remain on the bench during the remainder of the game, if the manager so desires. In consideration of this permission being given, the managers have agreed that such players will conduct themselves properly.

If a playing manager removes himself from the game, he will be permitted to direct his club from the bench during the remainder of that game. However, should he so desire, he can return to the coaching lines at his discretion.

MANAGER NOTIFIES UMPIRE OF SUBSTITUTES

The manager or his coach or captain and not the substitute himself should officially **notify the umpire-in-chief** of substitutions. The manager, coach or captain should tell the umpire-in-chief the **name** of the substitute, rather than have the manager or coach or captain point or make gestures as to who the substitute will be.

Players for whom substitutions have been made may remain on the bench or be "warm-up" catchers. A batter or base runner, officially announced as being in the game, shall not reappear in the line-up even though he was himself substituted for before he actually participated in any play.

Substitution Announcement 3.07

The umpire-in-chief, after having been notified, shall immediately announce, or cause to be announced, each substitution.

Lack of Substitution Announcement 3.08

(a) If no announcement of a substitution is made, the substitute shall be considered as having entered the game when—

(1) If a pitcher, he takes his place on the pitcher's plate;

(2) If a batter, he takes his place in the batter's box;

(3) If a fielder, he reaches the position usually occupied by the fielder he has replaced, and play commences;

(4) If a runner, he takes the place of the runner he has replaced.

(b) Any play made by, or on, any of the above mentioned unannounced substitutes shall be legal.

Fraternization 3.09

Players in uniform shall not address or mingle with spectators, nor sit in the stands before, during, or after a game. No manager, coach or player shall address any spectator before or during a game. Players of opposing teams shall not fraternize at any time while in uniform.

CONDUCT OF PLAYERS DURING PROGRESS OF GAME

During the progress of championship games, all players of the club at bat must be on the bench, except when they have some duty to perform, as coaches, base runner, batsman or succeeding batsman. Players of the side at bat will not be permitted to fraternize with players in the "bull pen" either of their own or of the visiting club, but must come to their own bench even if, in their judgment, they are not likely to be called upon to bat in the inning. Base-runners retired before reaching first base, or put out on the bases, must return to the bench until the inning is ended.

Only pitchers and catchers and players serving as catchers should be permitted to stay in the bull pen during the game. Players assigned to the bull pen should not recline on the bench or occupy seats in the stands.

A substitute player who will enter the game at the end of the half inning, or a designated hitter who will enter the game as a defensive player, will be permitted to warm up in the bull pen.

Players who are participating in the game will not be allowed to lie down or sit on the bases when time is called for the purpose of making a substitution.

Players shall not converse with spectators or sign autographs from the start of infield practice until the conclusion of the game.

Visitors will not be allowed on the players' bench or on the field at any time.

Smoking in uniform in view of spectators is prohibited and offenders will be penalized.

Currently players on the Disabled List are allowed to sit on the bench in uniform. Opposing managers no longer need to give permission for this to occur. This is a courtesy and the disabled player while on the bench will not be permitted to:

1. Shout at or harass the umpires or members of the opposing team.

2. Go on the field or to participate in any arguments or confrontations in the field. Failure to adhere to the above conditions will result in immediate ejection from the game and subsequent fining.

FRATERNIZATION, PEPPER GAMES

Players, managers and coaches are not permitted to engage in conversation with opposing players. This is not only an American League Regulation, but is part of the Official Playing Rules (3.09). Umpires are instructed to report any violation of this rule and players so reported may be disciplined.

Players, managers and coaches must not intentionally throw balls into the stands. Umpires are instructed to report any violation of this rule and players so reported may be disciplined. Players should be careful in engaging in "pepper" games, not to bat balls toward the stands.

Game Preliminaries

FRATERNIZATION

The non-fraternization rule must be observed. Fraternization shall be called:

(a) When players prolong standing by the batting cage when opponents are hitting. No opposing player, manager or coach shall sit, stand or loiter around the batting cage during batting practice time allotted to the opposing club.

(b) When a player walks across the field and stands alongside the coach or player fungoing to the outfield and talks to him for several minutes.

(c) When players go out of their way and hold long conversations, possibly more than several minutes.

Umpires observing infractions shall tell players to break up fraternization immediately and if players do not do so, umpire shall then report by telegram the infraction to the League President. Fine for infraction shall be $50.00 for each offense. Umpires shall observe until both clubs have completed batting practice and one of the clubs has actually started its infield workout on the diamond.

The Non-Fraternizing rule is directed to players and managers fraternizing with opposing players while in uniform on the field. It is not directed to players conversing with fans before the game starts. A player's relationship with fans should be a matter of the player's judgment and his club's regulations. If such relationship with fans detracts from the player's practice work, the matter should be dealt with by the manager. No one in uniform should do any autographing **during the progress of the game** and players and **umpires must avoid conversation with fans during the game.**

PEPPER GAMES

There shall be no batting or bunting toward the grandstand after the gates are officially opened for spectators. So called "pepper games" should be held at a place and in a manner where the ball is not likely to be batted, bunted or fouled into the stands.

If players do not stop pepper games when so warned, advise the League President by wire of the offense.

During the period when either team is taking pre-game batting or fielding practice, the opposing team players shall not run in the outfield.

The umpire-in-chief shall inspect the batter's and catcher's boxes to see that they are in conformity with the rules. Base umpires should examine the bases to see that they are properly attached and in good order.

The second-base umpire shall place an official rosin bag behind the pitcher's mound and then return it to the umpire's room after the game. Umpires shall carry two rosin bags with them at all times. Improvised rosin bags furnished by the home club are acceptable, if, in the umpire's judgment, they generally conform to regulations.

DEPORTMENT OF PLAYING PERSONNEL ON FIELD

Fraternizing with Opponents. Managers, players and coaches shall not fraternize with members of the opposing team when on the field or in uniform. Two umpires assigned to each championship game shall be in the stands one hour before the scheduled starting time of the game to report any violation of this rule.

Relations with Fans. Managers, players and coaches on the field in uniform shall not conduct lengthy conversations with patrons. While a game is in progress, no player shall converse with patrons or sign any autographs.

Caution in Practice.

(a) Managers, players and coaches engaging in "pepper" games shall not bat the ball towards the stands or any spectator areas.

(b) Managers, players and coaches shall not toss or throw baseballs into the stands or towards a patron.

Game Postponement 3.10

(a) The manager of the home team shall be the sole judge as to whether a game shall be started because of unsuitable weather conditions or the unfit condition of the playing field, except for the second game of a doubleheader. EXCEPTION: Any league may permanently authorize its president to suspend the application of this rule as to that league during the closing weeks of its championship season in order to assure that the championship is decided each year on its merits. When the postponement of, and possible failure to play, a game in the final series of a championship season between any two teams might affect the final standing of any club in the league, the president, on appeal from any league club, may assume the authority granted the home team manager by this rule.

(b) The umpire-in-chief of the first game shall be the sole judge as to whether the second game of a doubleheader shall not be started because of unsuitable weather conditions or the unfit condition of the playing field.

(c) The umpire-in-chief shall be the sole judge as to whether and when play shall be suspended during a game because of unsuitable weather conditions or the unfit condition of the playing field; as to whether and when the play shall be resumed after such suspension; and as to whether and when a game shall be terminated after such suspension. He shall not call the game until at least thirty minutes after he has suspended play. He may continue the suspension as long as he believes there is any chance to resume play.

The umpire-in-chief shall at all times try to complete a game. His authority to resume play following one or more suspensions of as much as thirty minutes each shall be absolute and he shall terminate a game only when there appears to be no possibility of completing it.

Game Preliminaries

RIGHT TO POSTPONE

The management of the home team shall be the sole judge as to whether a game shall not be started because of unsuitable weather conditions or the unfit condition of the playing field, except for the second game of a double-header.

EXCEPTION: The League President is authorized to suspend the application of the "right to postpone" if the final standings can be affected by the postponement of, and possible failure to play a game between two clubs in their FINAL series of the championship season. As league representatives the umpires are instructed to review the schedule, contact the home club early in the day, be at the park early, and cooperate with the home club management.

Final decision shall be the responsibility of the Umpire In Chief only during the final series of the year between two teams.

WEATHER

After time has been called because of weather conditions. Official Playing Rule 5.10 authorizes the umpire to terminate the game after a wait of thirty minutes, but if, in his judgment, there is any chance to resume play, he may continue such suspension as long as his judgment warrants. There is no idea, however, of using the lights to indefinitely delay calling a day game halted by weather conditions. The Umpire In Chief shall be the sole judge in determining the length of suspension and fitness of the playing field, once time has been called.

Umpires should not confine themselves to the thirty-minute period if the weather is clearing, and if in their judgment the grounds can be placed in condition to warrant continuation of play. When the weather is threatening, previous to the starting of a game, umpires should arrange with the ground keeper to be prepared with materials and canvas to cover the field in case of emergency.

After calling time, on account of temporary darkness due to the approach of a storm of rain, umpires must remain near benches to take advantage of any relief from the above conditions, to resume play at the earliest possible moment.

When two games are advertised for one admission, the first game must be played to a finish before the second game can be started. Umpires should not automatically call off the 2nd game of a double-header.

IN CASE OF RAIN

Umpire crew chiefs should contact the home club upon arrival at the park on days when rain or rain showers are likely and request the latest weather report. The names of the club representatives to telephone or speak to for weather conditions will be bulletined to the umpires annually.

In addition to contacting the club, the umpire crew chief should contact the local weather bureau for a report.

Modern weather technology has greatly improved the prediction of rain in local areas and umpires should know fairly accurately at game time what the weather conditions are likely to be for the next two or three hours. All members of the crew should have the full report on the weather when the crew goes out on the field to start the game.

When the umpires call "time" to suspend the game for rain, the umpire-in-chief and crew chief shall remain on one of the club's benches to observe rain conditions and see that the ground crew is performing its function properly.

Official Playing Rules require that umpires wait 30 minutes before postponing a game. **However, National League umpires are instructed to wait at least one hour and fifteen minutes before calling a game.** If there is a second delay, umpires must wait at least 45 minutes before calling the game. For third and subsequent delays, umpires must wait at least 30 minutes before calling the game. Modern machinery has been employed very effectively in making artificial surfaces playable after a heavy rain.

Umpires should reach the conclusion when postponing a game that bad weather conditions are likely to continue, or that the field is too wet and dangerous to the players to continue the game. This decision shall be made on the field and not in the dressing room.

The umpire-in-chief, with the approval of the crew chief, shall be the sole judge in determining the length of suspension once "time" has been called.

The umpire-in-chief shall call in home club management when it is decided to terminate play, so that the management can alert the stadium staff that the game is called.

The following National League Rule 4.1(d) was adopted in 1981:

A game that has become a legal game stopped because of weather conditions after 12:45 a.m. shall be called immediately and become a suspended game. A game that has NOT become a legal game stopped because of weather conditions after 12:45 a.m. shall be called immediately and become a postponed game. Provided, however, that the present rules on rain delays will apply in the last game of the season between two clubs.

> NOTE: This rule applies only to games that are actually delayed or halted by weather conditions at 12:45 a.m. or thereafter. If the

weather condition has abated and the ground crew is getting the field into playing condition, the game shall be continued.

Rescheduling Postponed or Tied Games.

If a day game is postponed, and the home club desires to play it off that night, it may do so with approval of the visiting club. The home club shall notify the League and the umpires immediately.

Notice of Schedule Changes.

(a) The club on whose grounds the game is to be played is responsible for giving notice of any schedule changes to the League.

(b) Whenever the playoff of a postponed or tied game is set for a date in the same series, the visiting club, the umpires and the League shall be notified before 8:00 p.m. on the date of the postponed or tied game. In case of postponed or tied night games, such notice shall be given before 1:30 a.m. of the day of the postponed or tied game.

Right to Postpone.

(a) The home club shall have the right to determine whether a game shall not be started because of unsuitable weather conditions or the unfit condition of the playing field. Once a game has started, the umpire-in-chief shall have sole right to determine whether it shall be terminated because of bad weather or playing conditions. Under the provisions of the Official Playing Rules, the umpire-in-chief shall have sole and unquestioned authority to determine whether and when play shall be halted during a game; whether and when play shall be resumed, and whether and when a game shall be terminated because of bad weather or unfit playing conditions.

(b) EXCEPTION: The President may assume the authority vested in the

home club by Rule 3.4(a) during the final series of any season on the home grounds of either club, when the result of a possible postponement of a game during that series might affect the final standing of any club in the championship race.

The President may assume the authority granted by Rule 3.4(b) at any time prior to the scheduled starting time of any game in such final season series by notification to the home club. Such notification may be given in person, by mail, or by telegraph, electronic mail or telephone. In such notification, the President may delegate the authority vested in him by Rule 3.4(b) to the umpire-in-chief or to any other officer or employee of the League.

Playing Field Fitness   3.11

Between games of a doubleheader, or whenever a game is suspended because of the unfitness of the playing field, the umpire-in-chief shall have control of ground-keepers and assistants for the purpose of making the playing field fit for play.

PENALTY: For violation, the umpire-in-chief may forfeit the game to the visiting team.

DRAGGING INFIELD

During the progress of the game, the infield must not be dragged until the completion of the fifth inning. The Umpire in Chief has the authority to forbid the dragging of the infield if, in his judgment, the completion of the game may be in jeopardy by the action.

DRAGGING INFIELD

Between the end of the fifth inning and the start of the sixth inning of each League game, the home club's ground crew shall smooth the skinned part of the infield by dragging it. When conditions justify, dragging the infield during the game may be suspended with the approval of the umpires.

It is the responsibility of the manager of the home club to have the ground crew ready to drag the infield at the proper time, and the responsibility of the first base and/or third base umpire to see that the crew works promptly with no delay in the game. If the infield is not dragged at the proper time, the umpire-in-chief shall make a report to the League office, advising why the infield was not dragged. Play shall not be delayed for failure of the home club to drag the infield.

Miscellaneous

Dragging Infield. Dragging the infield may be suspended on windy days with the approval of the umpires.

Calling "Time"   3.12   When the umpire suspends play he shall call "Time." At the umpire's call of "Play," the suspension is lifted and play resumes. Between the call of "Time" and the call of "Play" the ball is dead.

Ground Rules   3.13   The manager of the home team shall present to the umpire-in-chief and the opposing manager any ground rules he thinks necessary covering the overflow of spectators upon the playing field, batted or thrown balls into such overflow, or any other contingencies. If these rules are acceptable to the opposing manager they shall be legal. If these rules are unacceptable to the opposing manager, the umpire-in-chief shall make and enforce any special ground rules he thinks are made necessary by ground conditions, which shall not conflict with the official playing rules.

GROUND RULES

Special Ground Rules for each park are printed on the reverse side of the batting order cards. In the event of a change in the ground rules they must be agreed upon by the Umpire In Chief. The League President should be notified of a conflict with the Playing Rules.

GROUND RULES

Special ground rules in a park shall not be in conflict with the Official Playing Rules. The special ground rules for each park have been printed on the reverse side of the home club batting order cards.

When there are special ground rules not on the batting order cards, the umpire-in-chief shall have such rules announced to the fans.

If any ground rule is in conflict with the playing rules, the crew chief shall so advise the League President.

Clearing Field   3.14   Members of the offensive team shall carry all gloves and other equipment off the field and to the dugout while their team is at bat. No equipment shall be left lying on the field, either in fair or foul territory.

Individuals Allowed on Field   3.15   No person shall be allowed on the playing field during a game except players and coaches in uniform, managers, news photographers authorized by the home team, umpires, officers of the law in uniform and watchmen or other employees of the home club. In case of unintentional interference with play by any person herein authorized to be on the playing field (except members of the offensive team participating in the game, or a coach in the coach's box, or an umpire) the ball is alive and in play. If the interference is intentional, the ball shall be dead at the moment of the interference and the umpire shall impose such penalties as in his opinion will nullify the act of interference.

NOTE: See Rule 7.11 for individuals excepted above, also see Rule 7.08 (b).

The question of intentional or unintentional interference shall be decided on the basis of the person's action. For example: a bat boy, ball attendant, policeman, etc., who tries to avoid being touched by a thrown or batted ball but still is touched by the ball would be involved in unintentional interference. If, however, he kicks the ball or picks it up or pushes it, that is considered intentional interference, regardless of what his thought may have been.

PLAY: Batter hits ball to shortstop, who fields ball but throws wild past first baseman. The offensive coach at first base, to avoid being hit by the ball, falls to the ground and the first baseman on his way to retrieve the wild thrown ball, runs into the coach; the batter-runner finally ends up on third base. The question is asked whether the umpire should call interference on the part of the coach. This would be up to the judgment of the umpire and if the umpire felt that the coach did all he could to avoid interfering with the play, no interference need be called. If it appeared to the umpire that the coach was obviously just making it appear he was trying not to interfere, the umpire should rule interference.

PHOTOGRAPHERS

The American League will furnish clubs with a supply of official identification cards for the use of recognized photographers. Clubs will issue these cards to persons who are known to them as entitled to same. No photographer will be permitted on the playing field, during the progress of a championship game, unless he can show the umpire one of these official cards.

MASCOTS

Club mascots will not be permitted on the field once the game has started except when the infield is being dragged in the 5th inning or if there is a rain delay.

Mascots must never become involved with the umpires, unless there is a special reason. In such a case, permission must be obtained from the umpire crew chief prior to the game.

UNINTENTIONAL VS. INTENTIONAL INTERFERENCE

Any act by a person authorized to be on the field under Rule 3.15 in which he **voluntarily** touches a ball in play is to be considered "intentional" interference and the ball is dead when touched and such penalty imposed as will nullify the interference elsewhere. A ball which in the umpire's judgment "accidentally" touches any person authorized to be on the field under Rule 3.15 should be considered "unintentional" and the ball alive and in play.

The question of intentional or unintentional interference shall be decided on the basis of the person's **action.** For example: a bat boy, ball attendant, police, etc. who tries to avoid being

touched by a thrown or batted ball but still is touched by the ball would be involved in **unintentional** interference. If however, he kicks the ball or picks it up or pushes it, that is considered **intentional** interference regardless of what his thought may have been.

In assessing the penalties, umpires should decide what in their judgment would reasonably have taken place if the intentional interference did not occur.

PLAY—Batter hits ball to shortstop, who fields ball but throws wild past first baseman. The offensive coach at *first base to avoid being hit by the ball falls to the ground and the first baseman on the way to retrieve the wild thrown ball, runs into the coach; the batter-runner finally ends up on third base. The question is asked whether the umpire should call interference on the part of the coach. This would be up to the judgment of the umpire and if the umpire felt that the coach did all he could to avoid interfering with the play, no interference need be called. If it appeared to the umpire that the coach was obviously just making it appear he was trying not to interfere, the umpire should rule interference.*

Spectator 3.16
Interference

When there is spectator interference with any thrown or batted ball, the ball shall be dead at the moment of interference and the umpire shall impose such penalties as in his opinion will nullify the act of interference.

APPROVED RULING: If spectator interference clearly prevents a fielder from catching a fly ball, the umpire shall declare the batter out.

There is a difference between a ball which has been thrown or batted into the stands, touching a spectator thereby being out of play even though it rebounds onto the field and a spectator going onto the field or reaching over, under or through a barrier and touching a ball in play or touching or otherwise interfering with a player. In the latter case it is clearly intentional and shall be dealt with as intentional interference as in Rule 3.15. Batter and runners shall be placed where in the umpire's judgment they would have been had the interference not occurred.

No interference shall be allowed when a fielder reaches over a fence, railing, rope or into a stand to catch a ball. He does so at his own risk. However, should a spectator reach out on the playing field side of such fence, railing or rope, and plainly prevent the fielder from catching the ball, then the batsman should be called out for the spectator's interference.

Example: Runner on third base, one out and a batter hits a fly ball deep to the outfield (fair or foul). Spectator clearly interferes with the outfielder attempting to catch the fly ball. Umpire calls the batter out for spectator interference. Ball is dead at the time of the

Game Preliminaries

call. Umpire decides that because of the distance the ball was hit, the runner on third base would have scored after the catch if the fielder had caught the ball which was interfered with, therefore, the runner is permitted to score. This might not be the case if such fly ball was interfered with a short distance from home plate.

LEGAL CATCH-SPECTATOR INTERFERENCE

The fielder is confined to the limits of the playing field; however he may reach over any fence, railing, or any other line of demarcation to make a catch.

He may jump on top of a railing, marking the boundary of the field, or on any canvas that may be on foul ground.

No interference should be allowed where the fielder or catcher reaches over a fence, railing, rope or into a stand to catch a ball. He does so at his own risk.

SPECTATOR INTERFERENCE

When a spectator interferes with a ball in play, whether a batted ball or a thrown ball, the umpire shall impose such penalty or penalties as in his judgment will nullify the act of the interference. This gives the umpire the right to declare a batter out if, in his judgment, a spectator clearly prevents a player from catching a fly ball and gives him the right to place the batter and the runners at the bases where, in his judgment, they would have reached had the interference not occurred. There is a difference between a ball which has been thrown or batted into the stands touching a spectator thereby being out of play even though it rebounds onto the field, and a spectator going onto the field or reaching over, under or through a barrier and touching a ball in play or touching or otherwise interfering with a player. In the latter case it is clearly intentional and shall be **dealt with as intentional interference** and as "intentional" interference is covered in Rule 3.15. Batters and runners shall be placed where in the umpire's judgment they would have been had the interference not occurred.

No interference shall be allowed when a fielder reaches over a fence railing, rope or into a stand to catch a ball. **He does so at his own risk.** However, should a spectator reach out on the playing field side of such fence, railing or rope, and plainly prevent the fielder from catching the ball, then the batsman should be called out fo the spectator's interference.

When there is intentional interference with a ball in play, either by a spectator or by a person permitted on the playing field (as covered in Rule 3.15), the ball is dead the instant the interference occurs. The umpire who calls the interference (any umpire may call it) should consult with other umpires to determine what reasonably might have happened had the interference not occurred.

The spectator interference rule states specifically the umpire shall impose such penalty or penalties as in his judgment will nullify the act of the interference and the ball is dead the instant the interference occurs.

For example: Runner on third base, one out and a batter hits a fly ball deep to the outfield (fair or foul). Spectator clearly interferes with the

outfielder attempting to catch the fly ball. Umpire calls the batter out for spectator interference. Ball is dead at the time of the call. Umpire decides that because of the distance the ball was hit, the runner on third base would have scored after the catch if the fielder had caught the ball which was interfered with, therefore the runner is permitted to score. This might not be the case if such a fly ball was interfered with only a short distance from home plate.

It is possible to have "spectator interference" on a ball pitched to the batter. **If a wild pitch does not go into the stands** but remains in play and is interfered with by a spectator, the **"Spectator Interference"** penalty shall apply.

The very nature of the game requires different consideration of what may at first seem the same play, and the umpires should consider all factors in determining penalties for spectator interference.

Team Benches   3.17

Players and substitutes of both teams shall confine themselves to their team's benches unless actually participating in the play or preparing to enter the game, or coaching at first or third base. No one except players, substitutes, managers, coaches, trainers and bat boys shall occupy a bench during a game.

PENALTY: For violation the umpire may, after warning, remove the offender from the field.

Players on the disabled list are permitted to participate in pre-game activity and sit on the bench during a game but may not take part in any activity during the game such as warming up a pitcher, bench-jockeying, etc. Disabled players are not allowed to enter the playing surface at any time or for any purpose during the game.

THE SUCCEEDING BATSMAN

Clubs designate with a circle the spot for the succeeding batsman. He must occupy and kneel in the spot indicated.

When a manager contemplates using a pinch-hitter, the next batter in the batting order must occupy the spot indicated for the on-deck batter.

No other player of the side at bat will be permitted on the field except the batsman, base runners and coaches.

The bat boy must not be permitted to occupy the circle with the batsman, but should be kept on or near

his respective bench whenever he has no duty to perform on the playing field. All bat/ball boys or girls shall ware a protective helmet while performing their duties.

Catchers are not to wear their shin guards while in the "on deck" circle. All catchers shall wear a catcher's protective helmet while fielding their position.

CLUBHOUSE AND BENCH

(a) No persons shall be admitted to the team clubhouse or permitted to enter or visit the bench except accredited photographers and

accredited representatives of the press, radio and television. Such authorized visitors shall not be permitted in the dugout during a game, nor shall they enter the clubhouse except at times authorized by the manager.

(b) No one except (a) the manager, (b) the coaches, players and substitutes in uniform, (c) bat boys in uniform, (d) trainers and equipment or property men, may occupy the bench during the progress of a game.

(c) No children shall be permitted on the playing field after the gates are opened except that a boy who has been selected as an honorary bat boy for a specific period may occupy the bench in uniform and assist the regular bat boy during the period form which he was selected. Children who are participating in any pre-game program or ceremony approved by the club may be on the field during such program or ceremony.

(d) No pay telephones are to be allowed in or near the clubhouse. All calls must be made through the office switchboard.

CLUBHOUSE AND BENCH

(a) No persons shall be admitted to the team clubhouse or permitted to enter or visit the bench except accredited photographers and accredited representatives of the press, radio and television. Such authorized visitors shall not be permitted in the dugout during a game, nor shall they enter the clubhouse except at times authorized by the manager.

(b) No one except (a) the manager, (b) coaches, players and substitutes in uniform, (c) one bat boy in uniform and (d) one trainer and one equipment or property man may occupy the bench or bull pen during the progress of a game.

(c) No children shall be permitted on the playing field after the gates are opened, except that a boy who has been selected as an honorary bat boy for a specific period may occupy the bench in uniform and assist the regular bat boy during the period for which he was selected. Children who are participating in any pre-game program or ceremony approved by the club may be on the field during such program or ceremony.

(d) No pay telephones are to be allowed in or near the clubhouse. All calls must be made through the office switchboard.

Rule 8 to Be Posted. The League shall furnish each club with printed copies of Rule 8, and the clubs shall keep a copy posted in the umpires' rooms, in the home and visitors' clubhouses, and in the home and visitors' benches.

Police Protection   3.18   The home team shall provide police protection sufficient to preserve order. If a person, or persons, enter the playing field during a game and interfere in any way with the play, the visiting team may refuse to play until the field is cleared.

PENALTY: If the field is not cleared in a reasonable length of time, which shall in no case be less than fifteen minutes after the visiting team's refusal to play, the umpire may forfeit the game to the visiting team.

CROWD CONTROL

If fans enter the playing field in numbers or are otherwise interfering with the orderly procedure of the game by throwing objects, halt the game and remove both teams from the playing field.

After a reasonable time, if order is restored, recommence the game, giving both pitchers as much time as needed to warm up.

If order is not restored or if, in your judgment, the situation has gotten completely out of control, forfeit the game to the visiting club.

Starting and Ending
a Game

4.00   Starting and Ending a Game.

Pre-Game Activities   4.01   Unless the home club shall have given previous notice that the game has been postponed or will be delayed in starting, the umpire, or umpires, shall enter the playing field five minutes before the hour set for the game to begin and proceed directly to home base where they shall be met by the managers of the opposing teams.

In sequence—

(a)   First, the home manager shall give his batting order to the umpire-in-chief, in duplicate.

(b)   Next, the visiting manager shall give his batting order to the umpire-in-chief, in duplicate.

(c)   The umpire-in-chief shall make certain that the original and copies of the respective batting orders are identical, and then tender a copy of each batting order to the opposing manager. The copy retained by the umpire shall be the official batting order. The tender of the batting order by the umpire shall establish the batting orders. Thereafter, no substitutions shall be made by either manager, except as provided in the rules.

Umpires Take Charge   (d)   As soon as the home team's batting order is handed to the umpire-in-chief the umpires are in charge of the playing field and from that moment they shall have sole authority to determine when a game shall be called, suspended or resumed on account of weather or the condition of the playing field.

Obvious errors in the batting order, which are noticed by the umpire-in-chief before he calls "Play" for the start of the game, should be called to the attention of the manager or captain of the team in error, so the correction can be made before the game starts. For example, if a manager has inadvertently listed only eight men in the batting order, or has listed two players with the same last name but without an identifying initial and the errors are noticed by the umpire before he calls "play," he shall cause such error or errors to be corrected before he calls "play" to start the game. Teams should not be "trapped" later by some mistake that obviously was inadvertent and which can be corrected before the game starts.

Starting and Ending a Game

STARTING TIMES

The regular starting time of a game, as per the approved American League schedule, shall not be changed without League approval. The regular starting time may be delayed for reasons of weather. If delayed for other causes for more than 30 minutes, the consent of the visiting club or the League is required.

Mangers should have their pitchers warmed up and in the dugout at the scheduled start for the game.

OFFICIAL BATTING ORDER

Each manager will be prepared to announce his probable batting order to the press, etc., at least 30 minutes before the advertised starting time of a game.

Under the Playing Rules from the moment the Umpire In Chief receives the batting order from the manager of the home team or his uniformed representative until termination of the game, he shall enforce all of the rules.

Each manager will furnish the Umpire In Chief at the home plate the original and three copies of his official batting order (on cards furnished by the American League). Five minutes before the advertised time for starting the game, first, the home manager (or his uniformed representative) shall give his signed batting order to the Umpire In Chief, in quadruplicate. Next, the visiting manager (or his uni-

formed representative) shall give his signed batting order to the Umpire In Chief, in quadruplicate. The Umpire In Chief shall immediately send a copy of both batting orders to the official scorer in the Press Box.

The official batting orders must show the positions to be played, as well as the names of the players who will start the game. After the game starts, if two or more substitutions are made at the same time by the club in the field, the manager or his representative must notify the Umpire In Chief where each man will bat and this information must be announced to the Press Box at once. In the event of failure on the part of the manager to designate where the substitute will bat, the Umpire In Chief will have such authority.

OFFICIAL BATTING ORDER

The official lineup should be listed at the left side of the page. The other eligible players can be listed in the right column. the listing of the names in the right eligible column is a courtesy, and is not to be considered official. In other words, the listing of an inappropriate name or the omission of one or more names incurs no penalty. The final responsibility of knowing the eligible players on the opposing team rests with each manager. The lineup slips should be made out in triplicate—one for each manager and one for the Umpire In Chief.

STARTING A GAME

Unless the home club shall have given previous notice that the game has been postponed or will be delayed in starting, the umpire, or umpires, shall enter the playing field five minutes before the hour set for the game to begin and **proceed directly to home base** where they shall be met by the managers of the opposing teams.

AT THE PLATE BEFORE THE GAME

All umpires assigned to work a game should walk together as a team of four to the plate five minutes before the start of the game. In some parks, where the National Anthem is played after the players take their positions on the field, five minutes may not be sufficient. The crew chief should fix the time for arriving at the plate early

enough to permit ground rules discussion to be completed so that the game starts (umpire calls "Play") within a few seconds of the official starting time.

All managers, coaches, trainers, players and umpires are directed, during the playing of the National Anthems, to stand at attention, feet together, head steady, facing the flag with cap in right hand placed over the heart and left arm extended downward along the left pants leg.

STARTING TIMES OF GAMES

All games will start promptly at the "official starting time" fixed by the club and there shall be no change either earlier or later unless directed by an official of the home club (not the manager of either club, P.A. announcer, network representative or any employee of the club.) Some clubs start games at 5 minutes past the hour or half hour and umpires shall know the precise starting time in each National League city.

If the home club wishes to delay the start of the game because of a large number of fans arriving at the park late, the plate umpire should accommodate the delay, but advise the visiting club manager of the revised starting time.

The umpire crew chief shall be responsible for calling the road secretary each time he arrives in the city where he is scheduled to work, giving the secretary his local address in case the club would want to reach him, at the same time determining the starting times of all games in the series. If there is a change in the schedule because of a postponement, changing a single game to a double-header or playing a night game instead of a day game, or any other change that would affect the starting time of the game, the crew chief shall so advise his team.

BATTING ORDER CARDS

The **home club manager, coach, or captain** must first deliver his batting order, in bound triplicate form as furnished by the League, to the umpire-in-chief. As soon as this batting order is delivered, the umpires are the sole judge of whether or not weather and ground conditions are such that the game shall be played. The visiting club manager or representative does not have the right to examine the home club's batting order until he has given the plate umpire his batting order.

Then, the visiting club manager, coach, or captain shall deliver his batting order, in bound triplicate form as furnished by the League, to the umpire-in-chief. The umpire shall then examine both batting order cards for correctness, and if and when they are correct, hand each manager a copy of his own batting order and a copy of the opposing team's batting order. The umpire shall retain the original of each team's batting order, and these shall be considered official. If either manager, coach or captain takes out a player after receiving his copy of the batting order, the player so removed cannot thereafter appear in the game.

Batting orders must be signed by the manager and abbreviations of names will not be accepted by the umpires. Batting orders must not contain corrections when presented at the start of the game.

Each manager shall write the names of his entire eligible team on the face of his batting order card in addition to furnishing the starting lineup.

STARTING TIME AND TIME LIMITS

Starting Time.

(a) Subject to the scheduling provisions of the Basic Agreement, the home club shall have the right to fix the starting time of all games.

Starting and Ending a Game

(b) Each club shall advise the President on or before April 1 each year of the hour at which it proposes to start games scheduled in its park, listing the proposed starting times for weekday games, night games, weekday doubleheaders, twilight-night doubleheaders, Sunday and holiday single games and Sunday and holiday doubleheaders; and shall advise the President of any changes in these starting times during the season.

(c) No club shall be permitted to change by more than thirty minutes the usual starting time of a game without the consent of the visiting club and the approval of the President.

Miscellaneous

Batting Order Cards. The League shall supply each club with official batting order cards, which shall be used by the managers in giving their batting orders to the umpire-in-chief. The cards furnished each club shall have that club's standard ground rules printed on the back of the cards. Each club shall advise the League office immediately of any changes in its ground rules.

Starting the Game 4.02 The players of the home team shall take their defensive positions, the first batter of the visiting team shall take his position in the batter's box, the umpire shall call "Play" and the game shall start.

Starting Positions 4.03 When the ball is put in play at the start of, or during a game, all fielders other than the catcher shall be on fair territory.

(a) The catcher shall station himself directly back of the plate. He may leave his position at any time to catch a pitch or make a play except that when the batter is being given an intentional base on balls, the catcher must stand with both feet within the lines of the catcher's box until the ball leaves the pitcher's hand.

PENALTY: Balk.

(b) The pitcher, while in the act of delivering the ball to the batter, shall take his legal position;

(c) Except the pitcher and the catcher, any fielder may station himself anywhere in fair territory;

(d) Except the batter, or a runner attempting to score, no offensive player shall cross the catcher's lines when the ball is in play.

CATCHER'S BOX

When the situation is such that, in the plate umpire's judgment, the batter might be walked intentionally, he shall require the catcher to keep both feet within the lines of the catcher's box until the ball leaves the pitcher's hand. Managers and catchers must realize that the umpires will not always be correct in deciding when an intentional walk is being attempt-

ed, but the umpire will exercise his best judgment in the matter and his judgment will not be questioned. The catcher may leave his catching box when, in the umpire's judgment, the pitcher is not giving an intentional walk to the batter. If an intentional walk is not being given, he could leave his catching box before the pitcher pitches the ball (as on a pitch-out to catch a runner).

Batting Order   4.04   The batting order shall be followed throughout the game unless a player is substituted for another. In that case the substitute shall take the place of the replaced player in the batting order.

Base Coaches   4.05

(a) The offensive team shall station two base coaches on the field during its term at bat, one near first base and one near third base.

(b) Base coaches shall be limited to two in number and shall (1) be in team uniform, and (2) remain within the coach's box at all times.

PENALTY: The offending base coach shall be removed from the game, and shall leave the playing field.

It has been common practice for many years for some coaches to put one foot outside the coach's box or stand astride or otherwise be slightly outside the coaching box lines. The coach shall not be considered out of the box unless the opposing manager complains, and then, the umpire shall strictly enforce the rule and require all coaches (on both teams) to remain in the coach's box at all times.

It is also common practice for a coach who has a play at his base to leave the coach's box to signal the player to slide, advance or return to a base. This may be allowed if the coach does not interfere with the play in any manner.

Coach's
Box
(Diagram 4)

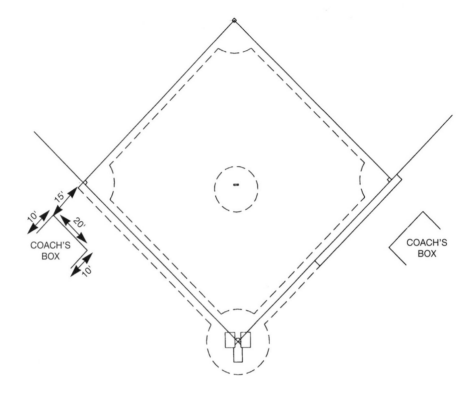

COACH'S BOX

Rules require coaches to remain in the coach's box at all times. It has been common practice for many years, however, for some coaches to put one foot outside the coach's box or stand astride or otherwise be slightly outside the coaching box lines. The coach shall not be considered out of the box unless the opposing manager complains, and then, the umpire shall strictly enforce the rule and require all coaches (on both teams) to remain in the coach's box at all times.

It is also common practice for a coach who has a play at his base to leave the coach's box to signal the player to slide, advance or return to a base. This may be allowed if the coach does not interfere with the play in any manner. The coach cannot run down the third base line to confuse the defensive team, nor can he physically assist a base runner, or otherwise interfere with play, without penalty.

Failure of a team to place two coaches on the field should be reported to the League President. Such action should not delay the game.

Team
Conduct

4.06   (a)   No manager, player, substitute, coach, trainer or bat boy shall at any time, whether from the bench, the coach's box or on the playing field, or elsewhere—

     (1)   Incite, or try to incite, by word or sign a demonstration by spectators;

(2) Use language which will in any manner refer to or reflect upon opposing players, an umpire, or any spectator;

(3) Call "Time," or employ any other word or phrase or commit any act while the ball is alive and in play for the obvious purpose of trying to make the pitcher commit a balk.

(4) Make intentional contact with the umpire in any manner.

(b) No fielder shall take a position in the batter's line of vision, and with deliberate unsportsmanlike intent, act in a manner to distract the batter.

PENALTY: The offender shall be removed from the game and shall leave the playing field, and, if a balk is made, it shall be nullified.

Ejections 4.07 When a manager, player, coach or trainer is ejected from a game, he shall leave the field immediately and take no further part in that game. He shall remain in the club house or change to street clothes and either leave the park or take a seat in the grandstand well removed from the vicinity of his team's bench or bullpen.

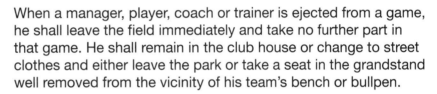

If a manager, coach or player is under suspension he may not be in the dugout or press box during the course of a game.

EJECTIONS AND SUSPENSIONS

When a player, coach or manager is put out of the game or removed from the bench by an umpire, he must leave the field immediately. Managers or coaches who have been removed from the game must not stand in the runway between clubhouse and dugout or sit in the stands in the vicinity of the club's bench. If a manager is under suspension he must leave the stadium during the course of a game.

EJECTED MEN MUST LEAVE FIELD

"Field" in this rule means playing field, bench and bull pen.

National League Rule 5.1 provides:

"(a) When a manager, player, coach or trainer is put out of a game by an umpire, he shall leave the field immediately.

"(b) If he is ejected in the first game of a doubleheader, a manager, player, coach or trainer shall be eligible for the second game, but after being put out of the first game, he shall go immediately to his clubhouse and remain there until his team takes the field for the second game.

"(c) If he is ejected from a single game, or from the second game of a doubleheader, a manager, player, coach or trainer shall remain in the clubhouse until the

game is ended or change to street clothes and either leave the park or take a seat in the grandstand well removed from the vicinity of his club's bench and the club's bull pen. **Violation of this section shall subject the offender to further penalties".**

Umpires shall report such infractions to the League office. Violators will be subject to fine or suspension.

EFFECT OF SUSPENSION

National League Rule 5.2 provides:

"A manager, coach, player or trainer who has been suspended by the President may take part in his team's activities prior to the start of the game. During the term of his suspension, he shall leave the field before the game starts, change to street clothes, and either leave the park or take a seat in the grandstand well removed from the vicinity of his club's bench and his club's bull pen. (He should not occupy the press box, or radio or TV announcers' booth during a championship game.)

"A manager who has been suspended shall take no part in directing his team during a game, either directly or indirectly."

Violation of this League Rule shall subject the offending manager to further penalties at the discretion of the President, including an extension of the period of suspension.

Bench Conduct

4.08

When the occupants of a player's bench show violent disapproval of an umpire's decision, the umpire shall first give warning that such disapproval shall cease. If such action continues—

PENALTY: The umpire shall order the offenders from the bench to the club house. If he is unable to detect the offender, or offenders, he may clear the bench of all substitute players. The manager of the offending team shall have the privilege of recalling to the playing field only those players needed for substitution in the game.

THROWING EQUIPMENT

Players throwing equipment in disgust over an umpire's call may be reported to the President in lieu of ejection of the player so notified. Normal fine is $100.00. (This does not mean that a player cannot be ejected if his actions warrant it.)

PROHIBITIONS

1) Throwing Equipment - Players throwing their equipment (glove, cap, bat or ball) in disgust over an umpire's call will be fined $100.00. The player shall be so advised by the umpire when such an incident occurs. A call shall be made to the League President advising that the player has been notified of the $100.00 fine.

2) Players shall not throw baseballs into the stands, or among spectators, and such action shall be reported. Umpires shall not throw baseballs to spectators in the stands.

3) A pitcher may wear a jacket when he is a base-runner but he may not wear a jacket when he is a batter. No other person will be permitted to wear a jacket when he is a

base-runner, a batter, a defensive player, or a coach on the base-lines.

4) Shoes with pointed spikes similar to golf or track shoes shall not be worn. Excessive and distracting flaps on shoes, particularly those on pitchers, will not be permitted.

5) Players may not wear white wrist-bands, either while at bat or on the field. Wristbands of the team's colors are allowed.

6) Players may not sit in photographers stands adjacent to dugouts, but must remain in the dugout.

7) Players shall not take bats into the open bull pen areas which increases the chance of interference with a ball in play.

8) A player on the Disabled List may be in uniform on the bench or in the bull pen during the playing of a game. However, he may not enter the playing field at any time or "jockey" opposing players or umpires while he is on the Disabled List.

9) Players, especially pitchers, will not be allowed to wear distracting jewelry of any kind.

In a protested game or a controversy over an interpretation of a playing rule or a ground rule, which will be decided by the League President, the umpire should not prejudge the action the League President will take, and in these cases it would be better for the umpire to state that he prefers not to comment, but the umpire can certainly explain what actually happened on the field.

In situations where a manager, coach or player is ejected from a game, all the umpire need do is tell the media that the man was ejected for something he said, or for some gestures he used, or for violating the rule against manager or coach leaving the bench to protest the call of a strike or a ball, etc.

Umpires are required to use judgment in answering various questions which the press, radio and TV representatives ask them. They want further facts so they can write a more informative story for the fans. There is no restriction on the umpire commenting to the extent of relating the actual facts of the decision. In fact, such cooperation helps to get the matter properly before the fans through the media.

The crew chief, or the crew chief and the umpire involved in the play, if he wishes to express himself on the decision, shall do the explaining to the media and this is better done outside the dressing room. Give the facts—do not prejudge the President's action, and be courteous.

During the process of a game umpires are not to give information to anyone as to why a player, coach or manager was ejected from the game, or why he ruled on a certain play as he did.

There is no objection to umpires appearing for TV or radio interviews regarding a controversial play, or a matter which would help to promote baseball. However, umpires should not appear on TV or radio during the process of a game.

How a Team Scores

4.09   HOW A TEAM SCORES.

(a)   One run shall be scored each time a runner legally advances to and touches first, second, third and home base before three men are put out to end the inning. EXCEPTION: A run is not scored if the runner advances to home base during a play in which the third out is made (1) by the batter-runner before he touches first base; (2) by any runner being forced out; or (3) by a preceding runner who is declared out because he failed to touch one of the bases.

(b) When the winning run is scored in the last half-inning of a regulation game, or in the last half of an extra inning, as the result of a base on balls, hit batter or any other play with the bases full which forces the runner on third to advance, the umpire shall not declare the game ended until the runner forced to advance from third has touched home base and the batter-runner has touched first base.

An exception will be if fans rush onto the field and physically prevent the runner from touching home plate or the batter from touching first base. In such cases, the umpires shall award the runner the base because of the obstruction by the fans.

PENALTY: If the runner on third refuses to advance to and touch home base in a reasonable time, the umpire shall disallow the run, call out the offending player and order the game resumed. If, with two out, the batter-runner refuses to advance to and touch first base, the umpire shall disallow the run, call out the offending player, and order the game resumed. If, before two are out, the batter-runner refuses to advance to and touch first base, the run shall count, but the offending player shall be called out.

Approved Ruling: No run shall score during a play in which the third out is made by the batter-runner before he touches first base. Example: One out, Jones on second, Smith on first. The batter, Brown, hits safely. Jones scores. Smith is out on the throw to the plate. Two outs. But Brown missed first base. The ball is thrown to first, an appeal is made, and Brown is out. Three outs. Since Jones crossed the plate during a play in which the third out was made by the batter-runner before he touched first base, Jones' run does not count.

Approved Ruling: Following runners are not affected by an act of a preceding runner unless two are out.

Example: One out, Jones on second, Smith on first, and batter, Brown, hits home run inside the park. Jones fails to touch third on his way to the plate. Smith and Brown score. The defense holds the ball on third, appeals to umpire, and Jones is out. Smith's and Brown's runs count.

Approved Ruling: Two out, Jones on second, Smith on first and batter, Brown, hits home run inside the park. All three runs cross the plate. But Jones missed third base, and on appeal is declared out. Three outs. Smith's and Brown's runs are voided. No score on the play.

Approved Ruling: One out, Jones on third, Smith on second. Batter Brown flies out to center. Two out. Jones scores after catch and Smith scores on bad throw to plate. But Jones, on appeal, is adjudged to have left third before the catch and is out. Three outs. No runs.

Approved Ruling: Two out, bases full, batter hits home run over fence. Batter, on appeal, is declared out for missing first base. Three outs. No run counts.

Here is a general statement that covers:

When a runner misses a base and a fielder holds the ball on a missed base, or on the base originally occupied by the runner if a fly ball is caught, and appeals for the umpire's decision, the runner is out when the umpire sustains the appeal; all runners may score if possible, except that with two out the runner is out at the moment he misses the bag, if an appeal is sustained as applied to the following runners.

Approved Ruling: One out, Jones on third, Smith on first, and Brown flies out to right field. Two outs. Jones tags up and scores after the catch. Smith attempted to return to first but the right fielder's throw beat him to the base. Three outs. But Jones scored before the throw to catch Smith reached first base, hence Jones' run counts. It was not a force play.

FAN INTERFERING ON GAME-WINNING HOME RUN

This rule shall be treated just as it is written. An exception will be if fans rush onto the field and physically prevent the runner from touching home plate or the batter from touching first base. In such cases, the umpire shall award the runner the base because of the obstruction by the fans.

Regulation Game 4.10   (a)   A regulation game consists of nine innings, unless extended because of a tie score, or shortened (1) because the home team needs none of its half of the ninth inning or only a fraction of it, or (2) because the umpire calls the game. EXCEPTION: National Association leagues may adopt a rule providing that one or both games of a doubleheader shall be seven innings in length. In such games, any of these rules applying to the ninth inning shall apply to the seventh inning.

(b) If the score is tied after nine completed innings play shall continue until (1) the visiting team has scored more total runs than the home team at the end of a completed inning, or (2) the home team scores the winning run in an uncompleted inning.

Called Game

(c) If a game is called, it is a regulation game:

(1) If five innings have been completed;

(2) If the home team has scored more runs in four or four and a fraction half-innings than the visiting team has scored in five completed half-innings;

(3) If the home team scores one or more runs in its half of the fifth inning to tie the score.

(d) If each team has the same number of runs when the game ends, the umpire shall declare it a "Tie Game."

(e) If a game is called before it has become a regulation game, the umpire shall declare it "No Game."

(f) Rain checks will not be honored for any regulation or suspended game which has progressed to or beyond a point of play described in 4.10(c).

Scoring in a Regulation Game

4.11 The score of a regulation game is the total number of runs scored by each team at the moment the game ends.

(a) The game ends when the visiting team completes its half of the ninth inning if the home team is ahead.

(b) The game ends when the ninth inning is completed, if the visiting team is ahead.

(c) If the home team scores the winning run in its half of the ninth inning (or its half of an extra inning after a tie), the game ends immediately when the winning run is scored. EXCEPTION: If the last batter in a game hits a home run out of the playing field, the batter-runner and all runners on base are permitted to score, in accordance with the base-running rules, and the game ends when the batter-runner touches home plate.

APPROVED RULING: The batter hits a home run out of the playing field to win the game in the last half of the ninth or an extra inning, but is called out for passing a preceding runner. The game ends immediately when the winning run is scored.

Called Game Becomes Suspended Game

(d) A called game ends at the moment the umpire terminates play. EXCEPTION: If the game is called while an inning is in progress and before it is completed, the game becomes a SUSPENDED game in each of the following situations:

(1) The visiting team has scored one or more runs to tie the score and the home team has not scored;

(2) The visiting team has scored one or more runs to take the lead and the home team has not tied the score or retaken the lead.

National Association Leagues may also adopt the following rules for suspended games in addition to 4.11 (d) (1) & (2) above. (If adopted by a National Association League, Rule 4.10 (c) (d) & (e) would not apply to their games.):

(3) The game has not become a regulation game (4 1/2 innings with the home team ahead, or 5 innings with the visiting club ahead or tied).

(4) Any regulation game tied at the point play is stopped because of weather, curfew or other reason.

(5) If a game is suspended before it becomes a regulation game, and is continued prior to another regularly scheduled game, the regularly scheduled game will be limited to seven innings.

(6) If a game is suspended after it is a regulation game, and is continued prior to another regularly scheduled game, the regularly scheduled game will be a nine inning game.

EXCEPTION: The above sections (3), (4), (5) & (6) will not apply to the last scheduled game between the two teams during the championship season, or League Playoffs.

Any suspended game not completed prior to the last scheduled game between the two teams during the championship season, will become a called game.

Suspended Games 4.12 SUSPENDED GAMES.

(a) A league shall adopt the following rules providing for completion at a future date of games terminated for any of the following reasons:

(1) A curfew imposed by law;

(2) A time limit permissible under league rules;

(3) Light failure or malfunction of a mechanical field device under control of the home club. (Mechanical field device shall include automatic tarpaulin or water removal equipment).

(4) Darkness, when a law prevents the lights from being turned on.

(5) Weather, if the game is called while an inning is in progress and before it is completed, and one of the following situations prevails:

    (i) The visiting team has scored one or more runs to tie the score, and the home team has not scored.

    (ii) The visiting team has scored one or more runs to take the lead, and the home team has not tied the score or retaken the lead.

(b) Such games shall be known as suspended games. No game called because of a curfew, weather, or a time limit shall be a suspended game unless it has progressed far enough to have been a regulation game under the provisions of Rule 4.10. A game called under the provisions of 4.12(a), (3) or (4) shall be a suspended game at any time after it starts.

NOTE: Weather and similar conditions 4.12 (a) (1 through 5)— shall take precedence in determining whether a called game shall be a suspended game. A game can only be considered a suspended game if stopped for any of the five (5) reasons specified in Section (a). Any regulation game called due to weather with the score tied (unless situation outlined in 4.12 (a) (5) (i) prevails) is a tie game and must be replayed in its entirety.

Resuming Suspended Games

(c) A suspended game shall be resumed and completed as follows:

(1) Immediately preceding the next scheduled single game between the two clubs on the same grounds; or

(2) Immediately preceding the next scheduled doubleheader between the two clubs on the same grounds, if no single game remains on the schedule; or

(3)   If suspended on the last scheduled date between the two clubs in that city, transferred and played on the grounds of the opposing club, if possible;

   (i)   Immediately preceding the next scheduled single game, or

   (ii)   Immediately preceding the next scheduled double-header, if no single game remains on the schedule.

(4)   If a suspended game has not been resumed and completed on the last date scheduled for the two clubs, it shall be a called game.

Exact Point of Suspension

(d)   A suspended game shall be resumed at the exact point of suspension of the original game. The completion of a suspended game is a continuation of the original game. The lineup and batting order of both teams shall be exactly the same as the lineup and batting order at the moment of suspension, subject to the rules governing substitution. Any player may be replaced by a player who had not been in the game prior to the suspension. No player removed before the suspension may be returned to the lineup.

A player who was not with the club when the game was suspended may be used as a substitute, even if he has taken the place of a player no longer with the club who would not have been eligible because he had been removed from the lineup before the game was suspended.

If immediately prior to the call of a suspended game, a substitute pitcher has been announced but has not retired the side or pitched until the batter becomes a baserunner, such pitcher, when the suspended game is later resumed may, but is not required to start the resumed portion of the game. However, if he does not start he will be considered as having been substituted for and may not be used in that game.

(e)   Rain checks will not be honored for any regulation or suspended game which has progressed to or beyond a point of play described in 4.10 (c).

Starting and Ending a Game

CURFEWS

American League games shall be subject to a curfew which provides that no inning shall start after 1:00 a.m., local time.

In making a decision as to when to invoke a curfew, the umpire shall rule that an inning or half-inning stars immediately after the third out in the preceding inning is made.

If a game is delayed by inclement weather and as a result reaches the time of curfew during or after the delay and inning in progress will be completed if possible.

Curfews shall be waived for the final series of the season in each of the two parks of two contesting teams.

SUSPENDED GAMES

National League Rule 4.1 has adopted the provisions of the Official Playing Rules.

While curfew and time limits for calling a game are unlikely, umpires are still advised that if "Time" is called because of weather and a curfew or time limit is reached before play can be resumed, the game will be considered as having been terminated because of **weather** and shall not be a suspended game, but shall be treated as any other game terminated because of weather.

If a game is temporarily halted because of weather when there is a curfew or time limit in effect and the umpires decide 15 or more minutes before the curfew or time limit that play can be resumed, **the weather factor will then be removed.** Actual play will start as soon as possible, but if not actually started before the curfew or time limit is reached, the game shall then be terminated because of the **curfew** or **time limit** and shall be a suspended game. For example: "Time" is called because of rain at 6:00 p.m. with a 7:00 p.m. curfew. By 6:40 p.m. the rain has stopped and the umpires examine the field and direct the ground crew to take the cover off and the teams to get ready to play. **That removes the weather factor** and if there is no more rain before the curfew, play shall start as

soon as possible if only for 3 or 4 minutes, but if there is delay so actual play is not started by 7:00 p.m. the game will be called **because of the curfew** and shall be a suspended game. If in the case rain did not stop until 6:50 p.m., then the umpires will consider that there is not sufficient time to get ready to play and shall terminate the game because of weather and it shall not be a suspended game. If the umpire calls a further halt to the game after he has told the ground crew to take the cover off and the teams are ready for play, and there is less than 15 minutes **at this time** before the curfew hour, the game shall be called because of weather.

Any legal game called due to weather with the score tied is a tie game and must be replayed in its entirety.

BATTING ORDER WHEN SUSPENDED GAME RENEWED

National League Rule 4.2(c) provides "The lineup and batting order of both teams in the playoff of a suspended game shall be exactly the same as the lineup and batting order (except the pitcher) at the time the game was called, except that substitutions may be made for players no longer with the club or physically incapacitated. No player removed for a substitute in the original game shall be eligible to return to the lineup in the playoff. The playoff of a suspended game is a continuation of the original game."

If, in a suspended game, a substitute pitcher has been announced but has not retired the side or pitched until the batter becomes a base runner, when the game is resumed, such a pitcher **may,** but is not **required to,** start the resumed portion of the game. If he does not start when the game is resumed, he will be considered as having been substituted for and may not be used in that game.

BATTING ORDER CARDS OF SUSPENDED GAME

When a regulation game becomes a suspended game, the umpire-in-chief of the game which is suspended shall retain the batting order cards of the two clubs if the suspended game is to be played in the same series. When the suspended game is resumed, the umpire-in-chief shall be the same umpire who worked behind the plate when the game was suspended. He shall take his copy of the batting order to the plate when the suspended game is resumed, and ask each manager to give him his copy of the batting orders and be certain that the names of all players substituted for in the lineup shall be written on each manager's batting order card. Should a manager wish to make eligible substitutes, he shall so notify the umpire at this time. The umpire shall then advise the managers of the official lineups under which the game will resume, including giving the names of the first batter to bat for the defensive team. The game should not start unless the proper players are in the lineup. (It must be remembered that the manager has the right at the time play is resumed to substitute players in the lineup that have not participated in the previously played suspended game.) The umpires do not have the responsibility of checking players inserted into the lineup after the suspended game is in progress. Once the suspended game is resumed, the manager is responsible for seeing that he does not insert players into the lineup who are not eligible to participate in the resumed suspended game. If there is any dispute as to the lineup and batting order, the official scorer shall be consulted.

In the event the suspended game is not continued in the same series, the umpire-in-chief shall send to the League office the batting order cards of both clubs with the score of the game at the time of suspension, number of outs, names of runners and what base each was on, name of proper batter and ball and strike count on him, and also the name of the proper first batter for the defensive team.

SUSPENDED GAMES

Definition. A suspended game is a game which has become a regulation game according to the Official Playing Rules and terminated by a curfew fixed by law or by a time limit. If a game is terminated by light failure at any time either before or after it becomes a legal game it is a suspended game:

(a) If, after nine innings have been completed, a game is terminated by a curfew fixed by law, or a time limit with the score tied at the end of a completed, inning, it shall be a suspended game.

(b) If a curfew law sets a specific time for calling a game, play shall continue until that time; but not beyond the curfew limit.

(c) A game stopped because of darkness, rain or other unfavorable weather conditions shall not be a suspended game. Legal games called because of darkness in parks where there are no lights to continue play in darkness shall be a "suspended game"; provided, however, that the final game of a series in a park where there are no lights which is called because of darkness and which is a legal game shall be an official game rather than a "suspended game"

when such series is the last meeting between the two clubs involved for that season.

(d) A game that has become a legal game stopped because of weather conditions after 12:45 a.m. shall be called immediately and become a suspended game. A game that has NOT become a legal game stopped because of weather conditions after 12:45 a.m. shall be called immediately and become a postponed game. Provided, however, that this Rule 4.1(d) shall not be applicable in the last game of the season between two clubs.

Completing Suspended Games.

(a) A suspended game shall be resumed and completed as follows:

(1) immediately preceding the next scheduled single game between the two clubs on the same grounds; or

(2) immediately preceding the next scheduled doubleheader between the two clubs on the same grounds, if no single game remains on the schedule; or

(3) if suspended on the last scheduled date between the two clubs in that city, transferred and played on the grounds of the opposing club, if possible:

(i) immediately preceding the next scheduled single game; or

(ii) immediately preceding the next scheduled doubleheader, if no single game remains on the schedule.

(b) The playoff shall begin at the exact point of suspension of the original game.

(c) The lineup and batting order of both teams in the playoff shall be exactly the same as the lineup and batting order (except the pitcher) at the time the game was called except that substitutions may be made for players no

longer with the club or physically incapacitated. No player removed for a substitute in the original game shall be eligible to return to the lineup in the playoff. The playoff of a suspended game is a continuation of the original game.

STARTING TIMES AND TIME LIMITS

Time Limits.

(a) The home club and the visiting club, by mutual agreement, may set a time limit on a game with approval of the League President. Such time limit shall be a specific time after which no inning may be started. Any inning started before such time limit shall be completed. If nine innings are not completed, such game shall be a suspended game.

(b) If either the home club or the visiting club believes a time limit necessary in order that its team may reach its next scheduled stop not less than three hours before the starting time of its next scheduled League game, and the two clubs cannot agree upon a time limit, the President, on appeal from either club, shall have the authority to set a time limit.

(c) The fact that a time limit has been set, and what time it is, shall be announced to the public before the start of the game.

Authority to Set Time Limits. The home club shall advise the umpire-in-chief if a time limit has been set on a game. Only authorized representatives of the two clubs shall be empowered to set a time limit. No manager shall set or agree to a time limit, nor shall an umpire suggest or set a time limit.

Finishing Games. Every game shall be played to its conclusion under the Official Playing Rules unless it becomes necessary to call it because of local curfew law, or a time limit approved by the President.

Double-
headers

4.13   RULES GOVERNING DOUBLEHEADERS.

(a)   (1) Only two championship games shall be played on one date. Completion of a suspended game shall not violate this rule.
(2) If two games are scheduled to be played for one admission on one date, the first game shall be the regularly scheduled game for that date.

(b)   After the start of the first game of a doubleheader, that game shall be completed before the second game of the double-header shall begin.

(c)   The second game of a doubleheader shall start twenty minutes after the first game is completed, unless a longer interval (not to exceed thirty minutes) is declared by the umpire-in-chief and announced to the opposing managers at the end of the first game. EXCEPTION: If the league president has approved a request of the home club for a longer interval between games for some special event, the umpire-in-chief shall declare such longer interval and announce it to the opposing managers. The umpire-in-chief of the first game shall be the timekeeper controlling the interval between games.

Second
Game

(d)   The umpire shall start the second game of a doubleheader, if at all possible, and play shall continue as long as ground conditions, local time restrictions, or weather permit.

(e)   When a regularly scheduled doubleheader is delayed in starting for any cause, any game that is started is the first game of the doubleheader.

(f)   When a rescheduled game is part of a doubleheader the rescheduled game shall be the second game, and the first game shall be the regularly scheduled game for that date.

FIRST GAME CALLED FOR RAIN	PLAYER EJECTED FROM FIRST GAME OF DOUBLE-HEADER
If a double-header is scheduled and the first game is started and afterwards called off on account of rain, the second game is also called off. After the first game of a double-header has been started, it must be completed before another game may be played.	When a manager, player or coach has been put out of the game or removed from the bench by the umpire during the first game of a double-header (when two games are being played for one admission), he may participate in the second game unless prohibited from participation in the second game on orders from the League Office.

Starting and Ending a Game

TIME BETWEEN GAMES OF DOUBLE-HEADER

Whenever two games are scheduled to be played, the second game must be started promptly thirty minutes after the first game has been completed. Managers failing to have their clubs on the field ready to start the second game thirty minutes after the completion of the first game will be subject to a fine.

EXCEPTION: When a twi-night game is scheduled as a makeup game before an originally scheduled night game, a club may wait longer than 30 minutes between games in order to conform to the starting time of the originally scheduled night game.

Advance approval must be obtained from the League Office if more time is desired between games of a particular double-header.

DOUBLEHEADERS

Under all conditions the first game of a doubleheader must be completed before the second game may be started.

When "Play" is suspended because of rain early in the first game of a doubleheader, umpires must wait as long as one hour and fifteen minutes before calling off the game, because—if the first game is postponed the second game must be postponed also.

The umpire-in-chief of the first game is the timekeeper and sole judge as to whether or not the second game is to start. The home manager or captain has no jurisdiction in determining this. Under the National League Rules, **the second game shall be started within 30 minutes after completion of the first game unless a shorter intermission of 20 minutes is ordered by the umpire-in-chief.** At the conclusion of the first game, the umpire-in-chief shall advise both managers of the exact starting time of the second game.

Playing Field Lights   4.14   The umpire-in-chief shall order the playing field lights turned on whenever in his opinion darkness makes further play in daylight hazardous.

TURNING ON THE LIGHTS

In order that every game may be completed if at all possible on the grounds on which it is scheduled, any day game during the championship season must be finished under the lights.

If it becomes necessary to turn on the lights to complete a day game, they shall be turned on at the direction of the umpire-in-chief. The umpire-in-chief only has that authority. Umpires are instructed that when darkness appears imminent, lights should be turned on at the **start** of an inning **but**

the lights maybe turned on at any point in the ball game, regardless of what the situation may be. Umpires should keep in mind that lighting systems in modern parks take as long as five minutes to warm up and be fully aglow. If possible, let home club know an inning in advance that lights will be turned on. Umpires should not order lights turned on if playing conditions are satisfactory without them.

Lights may be turned on to complete games started in daylight on Sunday or any other day.

Umpires are the sole judges as to when lights are to be turned on and off during a game and sole judges whether fights are required to start a game.

Finishing Day Games Under Lights. If it becomes too dark to continue play during any day game (including any Sunday game) the lights shall be turned on and the game shall be played to a conclusion. If darkness threatens to prevent. the start of the second game of any daytime double-header (including a Sunday double-header) the lights shall be turned on and the game played to a conclusion. The plate umpire shall have authority to determine when light conditions make it advisable to turn the lights on or off, and he may order the lights turned on or off any time during any day game.

Light Failure. In the event of a failure of lights while a ball is in flight or a play is in progress, the umpire shall immediately call "Time".

When play is resumed, either when the lights are turned on again or at a later date in a continued suspended game, each runner shall return to the last base he had touched at the moment the umpire called "Time". Should the batter be compelled to return to the batter's box, he shall assume the count of balls and strikes, if any, that prevailed at the moment the umpire called "Time".

Curfew. The only curfew in effect on night games, or late Sunday after-noon games, is that imposed by law of the place where the game is played.

Forfeited Game— General 4.15 A game may be forfeited to the opposing team when a team—

(a) Fails to appear upon the field, or being upon the field, refuses to start play within five minutes after the umpire has called "Play" at the appointed hour for beginning the game, unless such delayed appearance is, in the umpire's judgment, unavoidable;

(b) Employs tactics palpably designed to delay or shorten the game;

(c) Refuses to continue play during a game unless the game has been suspended or terminated by the umpire;

(d) Fails to resume play, after a suspension, within one minute after the umpire has called "Play;"

(e) After warning by the umpire, willfully and persistently violates any rules of the game;

(f) Fails to obey within a reasonable time the umpire's order for removal of a player from the game;

(g) Fails to appear for the second game of a doubleheader within twenty minutes after the close of the first game unless the umpire-in-chief of the first game shall have extended the time of the intermission.

Starting and Ending a Game

FORFEITS (This section also applies to Official Rules 4.16–4.18.)

A member shall be entitled to forfeited games—to count in its series as games won—by a score of nine runs to none—in case where the umpire of any championship game shall award the game to such member on account of the violation by contesting club of the League Constitution, or of any playing rule. In the event of said forfeiture being caused by the withdrawal of the players during the progress of a game or by failure of a member of the League to report with its team at the time fixed for the game, unless official notice has been received from the home member that the game cannot be played; then such forfeiting member shall incur a penalty of one thousand dollars ($1,000.00), which sum shall be payable to the Treasurer of the League within 10 days thereafter for the use and benefit of non-offending member, but said fine may be remitted or modified upon appeal to and hearing by the President of the League provided, that notice of such appeal be given to the President of the League by mail or telegraph within such period of ten days.

STALLING

Any manager or player who, in the judgment of the umpire, is guilty of conduct intended to stall or delay; or to hurry completion of a game by failing to put forth his best effort offensively, shall be subject to fine of not less than $100.00 or more than $250.00 or suspension, as the case may warrant, in the judgment of the League President.

FORFEITED AND PROTESTED GAMES

Forfeited Games.

(a) Under certain circumstances specified in the Official Playing Rules, the umpire-in-chief may declare a championship game forfeited to one club, by a score of 9-0. Such forfeited games shall count in the championship standings just as a game played to a legal decision.

(b) The President shall investigate such forfeiture, and impose such fines and penalties on the offending club and its manager as he deems necessary. If the President, after such investigation, shall find the forfeiture not justified by the Official Playing Rules, he may set it aside and order the game replayed in whole or in part.

(c) If a member fails to present its team at the time and place it is scheduled to play any championship game because of the lack of any agreement with the home club regarding television broadcasting rights, the President shall declare the game forfeited to the home club.

(1) The lack of such agreement shall not be considered a "condition beyond the control of a club or its officers" as specified in Section 3.8(f) of the Constitution, and the offending club shall also be subject to such further penalties as may be imposed under the provisions of Section 3.9.

Forfeited Game 4.16 A game shall be forfeited to the visiting team if, after it has been suspended, the order of the umpire to groundskeepers respecting preparation of the field for resumption of play are not complied with.

Forfeited Game 4.17 A game shall be forfeited to the opposing team when a team is unable or refuses to place nine players on the field.

Report of Forfeit 4.18 If the umpire declares a game forfeited he shall transmit a written report to the league president within twenty-four hours thereafter, but failure of such transmittal shall not effect the forfeiture.

FORFEITED GAME

The umpire-in-chief and the crew chief shall telephone the League President when any game is declared forfeited and follow such telephone report immediately with a detailed written report. Crew chiefs only have authority to forfeit a game. **Announcements shall be made over the P.A. system that the game has been forfeited.**

Protesting Games 4.19 PROTESTING GAMES. Each league shall adopt rules governing procedure for protesting a game, when a manager claims that an umpire's decision is in violation of these rules. No protest shall ever be permitted on judgment decisions by the umpire. In all protested games, the decision of the League President shall be final.

Even if it is held that the protested decision violated the rules, no replay of the game will be ordered unless in the opinion of the League President the violation adversely affected the protesting team's chances of winning the game.

Whenever a manager protests a game because of alleged misapplication of the rules the protest will not be recognized unless the umpires are notified at the time the play under protest occurs and before the next pitch is made or a runner is retired. A protest arising on a game-ending play may be filed until 12 noon the following day with the League Office.

PROTEST PROCEDURE

Notice that the game is being played under protest must be filed with the Umpire In Chief by the manager immediately at the time of the disputed decision and before the next pitched ball to a batsman. Public announcement should be made over the public address system. Written report setting forth all of the facts of the protest must be sent to the League President within twentyfour (24) hours of the date of the protest by both the umpire and the protesting club.

No consideration, however, will be given to a protest unless notice is

(Protest Procedure cont.)

served on the Umpire In Chief as provided above.

The press box should be made aware of all substitutions, unusual plays or protests that occur during a game, and it is the responsibility of the umpires to advise the press box. Protests and the grounds for protest should be announced. An umpiring crew, before announcing a protest, may engage in a thorough discussion before making their decision.

PROTESTED GAME

Whenever a manager protests a game because of alleged misapplication of the rules, the protest will not be recognized unless the umpires are notified at the time the play under protest occurs and **before the next pitch is made or a runner is retired.** Detailed reports of the protest must be filed by the protesting club within twenty-four hours of the time the game was completed. Umpires must call the League office immediately that the manager has protested the game and give his reasons for doing so. Umpires must also report to the League office in writing immediately pertinent facts of the protested game. Whenever a game is played under protest, the umpire-in-chief shall direct the P.A. attendant to announce to the fans that the game is protested and give the reason for the protest. Batting order cards in possession of the umpire-in-chief shall be mailed to the office with umpire's report of protest, unless the League President advises otherwise.

If a manager officially protests a game, the crew chief shall confer with his crew and discuss the play or situation on which the protest is lodged. It must be determined by the crew that the umpire making the call has the proper understanding of the Official Playing Rules or the ground rules. If the manager has not indicated his reason for the protest, the crew chief shall ask him on what grounds, or rule, he is making his protest. If the crew chief believes the manager has misapplied the rule on which he bases his protest, he should so advise him.

The League office wants the umpires to fully explore the justification for any protested game before announcement is made over the public address system that the game is being played under protest.

As per playing rule change made in December 1978, even if it is held that the protested decision violated the rules, no replay of the game will be ordered unless in the opinion of the League President the violation adversely affected the protesting team's chances of winning the game.

Protested Games. A manager may protest the result of a game if he claims an umpire has violated or condoned the violation of the Official Playing Rules. No protest shall be made or considered which is based on a charge of incorrect judgment by an umpire.

Notice of Protest.

(a) The manager shall give notice to the umpire-in-chief that the game is being played under protest. Such notice shall be given immediately at the time of the disputed decision and before the next pitch is made or a runner is retired. The umpire-in-chief shall immediately cause an announcement of the protest to be made over the public address system.

(b) The protesting manager shall file a written report with the President,

(Protested Game cont.)

setting out all the facts of the protest, within 24 hours after the protested game has been completed. Failure to file such report shall cancel the protest.

(c) The umpire-in-chief and the umpire involved in the disputed decision also shall file written reports with the President, setting forth all the facts of the protest, within 24 hours after the protested game has been completed.

(d) After considering the written reports of the protesting manager and the umpires, and any additional information or evidence he may deem necessary, the President shall determine whether the protest shall be allowed. Such determination shall be made within five days after the date the President receives the written protest, and shall not be subject to any appeal.

Putting the Ball
in Play

Umpire Calls "Play"	5.00	Putting the Ball in Play. Live Ball.
	5.01	At the time set for beginning the game the umpire shall call "Play."

Ball in Play 5.02 After the umpire calls "Play" the ball is alive and in play and remains alive and in play until for legal cause, or at the umpire's call of "Time" suspending play, the ball becomes dead. While the ball is dead no player may be put out, no bases may be run and no runs may be scored, except that runners may advance one or more bases as the result of acts which occurred while the ball was alive (such as, but not limited to a balk, an overthrow, interference, or a home run or other fair ball hit out of the playing field).

Should a ball come partially apart in a game, it is in play until the play is completed.

Delivery to Batter 5.03 The pitcher shall deliver the pitch to the batter who may elect to strike the ball, or who may not offer at it, as he chooses.

Offense's Objective 5.04 The offensive team's objective is to have its batter become a runner, and its runners advance.

Defense's Objective 5.05 The defensive team's objective is to prevent offensive players from becoming runners, and to prevent their advance around the bases.

Scoring a Run 5.06 When a batter becomes a runner and touches all bases legally he shall score one run for his team.

A run legally scored cannot be nullified by subsequent action of the runner, such as but not limited to an effort to return to third base in the belief that he had left the base before a caught fly ball.

Changing Sides 5.07 When three offensive players are legally put out, that team takes the field and the opposing team becomes the offensive team.

Thrown Ball Hits Coach or Umpire 5.08 If a thrown ball accidently touches a base coach, or a pitched or thrown ball touches an umpire, the ball is alive and in play. However, if the coach interferes with a thrown ball, the runner is out.

Putting the Ball in Play

PITCH STRIKING UMPIRE (This section also applies to Official Rule 5.09.)

If a foul tip hits the umpire and is caught by a fielder on the rebound, the ball is "dead" and the batsman cannot be called out. The same shall apply where such foul tip lodges in the umpire's mask or other paraphernalia.

If a third strike (not a foul tip) passes the catcher and hits an umpire, the ball is in play. If such ball re-bounds and is caught by a fielder before it touches the ground, the batsman is not out on such a catch; but the ball remains in play and the batsman may be retired at first base, or touched with the ball for the out.

If a pitched ball passes the catcher and lodges in the umpire's mask or paraphernalia, the ball is "dead". Each base runner is entitled to advance one base. If this happens on the third strike of fourth ball, then the batter is entitled to first base and all runners advance one base.

Advancing Runners 5.09 The ball becomes dead and runners advance one base, or return to their bases, without liability to be put out, when—

(a) A pitched ball touches a batter, or his clothing, while in his legal batting position; runners, if forced, advance;

(b) The plate umpire interferes with the catcher's throw; runners may not advance.

NOTE: The interference shall be disregarded if the catcher's throw retires the runner.

(c) A balk is committed; runners advance; (See Penalty 8.05).

(d) A ball is illegally batted; runners return;

(e) A foul ball is not caught; runners return. The umpire shall not put the ball in play until all runners have retouched their bases;

(f) A fair ball touches a runner or an umpire on fair territory before it touches an infielder including the pitcher, or touches an umpire before it has passed an infielder other than the pitcher;

If a fair ball touches an umpire working in the infield after it has bounded past, or over, the pitcher, it is a dead ball. If a batted ball is deflected by a fielder in fair territory and hits a runner or an umpire while still in flight and then caught by an infielder it shall not be a catch, but the ball shall remain in play.

If a fair ball goes through, or by, an infielder, and touches a runner immediately back of him, or touches a runner after being deflected by an infielder, the ball is in play and the umpire shall not declare the runner out. In making such decision the umpire must be convinced that the ball passed through, or by, the infielder and that no other infielder had the chance to make a play on the ball; runners advance, if forced;

Ball Lodged in Mask

(g) A pitched ball lodges in the umpire's or catcher's mask or paraphernalia, and remains out of play, runners advance one base;

If a foul tip hits the umpire and is caught by a fielder on the rebound, the ball is "dead" and the batsman cannot be called out. The same shall apply where such foul tip lodges in the umpire's mask or other paraphernalia.

If a third strike (not a foul tip) passes the catcher and hits an umpire, the ball is in play. If such ball rebounds and is caught by a fielder before it touches the ground, the batsman is not out on such a catch, but the ball remains in play and the batsman may be retired at first base, or touched with the ball for the out.

If a pitched ball lodges in the umpire's or catcher's mask or paraphernalia, and remains out of play, on the third strike or fourth ball, then the batter is entitled to first base and all runners advance one base. If the count on the batter is less than three balls, runners advance one base.

(h) Any legal pitch touches a runner trying to score; runners advance.

BATTED BALL STRIKING THE RUNNER (This section also applies to Official Rules 6.08d, 6.09c, 7.04b and 7.08f.)

The following was discussed at length and there was a difference of opinion on how these situations should be handled.

Despite the differences of opinion, it was agreed that the thinking proposed would simplify the situations for the umpires and that the following would be adhered to and that managers, etc., will be so notified.

RE: Rules 5.09f, 6.08d, 6.09c, 7.04b and 7.08f: A FAIR BATTED BALL

STRIKING A RUNNER BEFORE OR AFTER IT HAS BEEN TOUCHED BY AN INFIELDER (INCLUDING THE PITCHER), OR STRIKING A RUNNER BEFORE OR AFTER PASSING AN INFIELDER (EXCLUDING THE PITCHER).

GENERAL STATEMENTS:

When considering a fair batted ball striking a runner or umpire before or after being **touched** by an infielder, the pitcher is included. However, when considering a fair batted ball striking a runner or umpire before or after **passing** by an infielder without being touched by him, the pitcher is excluded.

Putting the Ball in Play

The factors determining whether the ball becomes dead or remains alive when striking a runner or an umpire are the same for each (runner and umpire). The penalties following a dead ball ruling, however, are different when the ball strikes a runner as compared to when the ball strikes an umpire:

If the ball is ruled dead after it strikes a runner, the runner is declared out, the batter-runner is awarded 1st base, and other runners advance only if forced. No run can score when the ball is ruled dead for striking a runner.

If the ball is ruled dead after it strikes an umpire, no one is declared out, the batter-runner is awarded 1st base, and other runners advance only if forced. It is possible to score a run when the ball is ruled dead for striking an umpire, if the play began with the bases loaded.

The concept of the runner being in jeopardy after the ball goes past an infielder and strikes him in a situation where another infielder still has a chance to make a play on the ball applies **ONLY** when the ball **PASSES** the first infielder without being touched or deflected by him. This concept does **NOT APPLY** if the ball is touched and deflected by the 1st infielder, even though another infielder has a chance to make a play on the ball.

The reasoning for the above concept is that a runner cannot be expected to avoid a deflected ball while he is running and should not, therefore, be in jeopardy of being called out for being struck by such a deflected ball. Of course, a runner may still be guilty of intentional interference even after an infielder deflects that ball if he (the runner) deliberately deflects it or allows it to strike him when he could have reasonably avoided it. The fact that the ball has been

deflected by an infielder should not be taken as license for a runner to intentionally interfere. (See rules 7.09 g and h).

A. PLAYS INVOLVING A FAIR BATTED BALL STRIKING A RUNNER BEFORE OR AFTER PASSING AN INFIELDER (EXCLUDING THE PITCHER). (NOTE: THE CONCEPT OF ANOTHER INFIELDER HAVING A CHANCE TO MAKE A PLAY ON THE BALL DOES APPLY TO THESE PLAYS):

1. The runner on 1st is stealing on the next pitch. The batter hits a ground ball toward the 2nd baseman, which strikes R-1 before it reaches the 2nd baseman. Is R-1 out? **ANSWER:** Yes R-1 is out and the batter-runner is awarded 1st base.

2. Runners on 1st and 3rd, no outs. Infield is playing in. R-1 is running on the pitch, which the batter hits on the ground toward the 2nd baseman. The ball goes through the 2nd baseman without being touched by him, strikes R-1 and skips into right field. (Assume no other infielder had a chance.) Is R-1 out? **ANSWER:** No. The ball remains alive and in play. R-1 was struck by the ball after it had passed by an infielder other than the pitcher, and no other infielder had a chance.

3. Runner on 2nd base, one out. The batter hits a ball on the ground toward the hole. The 3rd baseman charges in on the grass to try to cut it off, as the shortstop breaks deep toward the hole as R-2 advances. The ball gets past the 3rd baseman without being touched by him and strikes R-2 in the base path. (Assume the shortstop had a play on the ball.) Is R-2 out? **ANSWER:** Yes. R-2 is out

and the batter-runner is awarded 1st base. The ball passed by, but was not touched by, an infielder other than the pitcher before striking R-2. However, another fielder behind R-2 was deprived of an opportunity to field the ball.

B. PLAYS INVOLVING A FAIR BATTED BALL STRIKING A RUNNER BEFORE OR AFTER BEING TOUCHED AND DEFLECTED BY AN INFIELDER (INCLUDING THE PITCHER). (NOTE: THE CONCEPT OF ANOTHER INFIELDER HAVING A CHANCE TO MAKE A PLAY ON THE BALL DOES NOT APPLY TO THESE PLAYS):

1. Runner on 2nd, one out. The batter hits a ground ball toward the hole. The 3rd baseman charges in on the grass to cut it off and the shortstop breaks deep toward the hole, as R-2 advances. The ball is deflected by the 3rd baseman in the direction of the shortstop. The shortstop would have had a play on the ball, but the ball struck R-2, resulting in no play being possible. Is R-2 out? **ANSWER:** No. The ball is alive and in play (assuming no intentional interference by R-2). The fact that the shortstop would have been able to have a play on the ball had it not struck R-2 is disregarded because the ball was deflected by the first infielder.

2. Runner on 1st base, one out, R-1 is running on the next pitch. The batter hits a ground ball back toward the pitcher. The pitcher deflects the ball in the direction of the 2nd baseman, who definitely has a chance to make a play on it. However, the ball strikes R-1 before it reaches the 2nd baseman. Is R-1 out? **ANSWER:** No. The ball remains alive and in

play (assuming no intentional interference by R-1).

3. Runner on 1st base, one out. R-1 is running on the next pitch. The batter hits a ground ball back toward the pitcher. The pitcher deflects the ball in the direction of the 2nd baseman, who definitely has a chance to make a play on it. However, the ball strikes R-1 before it reaches the 2nd baseman. As a result of striking R-1, the ball caroms into the shortstop's glove and the shortstop throws out the batter-runner at 1st base, while R-1 goes into 2nd. Is R-1 out? **ANSWER:** No. The ball remains alive and in play (assuming no intentional interference by R-1). The batter-runner is out and R-1 is allowed to remain at 2nd base.

4. Bases loaded, no outs. The infield is playing in. The batter hits a sharp ground ball, which the 3rd baseman deflects in the direction of the shortstop. R-2, seeing that the shortstop definitely will have good chance of making a play on the ball, allows it to strike him. The ball caroms into left field and all runners take off. Is R-2 out? **ANSWER:** Yes. R-2 is guilty of intentionally interfering with a batted ball to break up a possible double play. R-2 is out and so is the batter-runner. R-1 and R-3 return to 1st and 3rd bases respectively. Once the ball was deflected by the 3rd baseman, the fact that the shortstop had a play on it was irrelevant to the basic rules we have been considering. however, R-2 was guilty of violating Rule 7.09g regarding a runner intentionally interfering with a batted ball for the purpose of preventing a double play.

RETOUCH BASES AFTER FOUL BALL

After a foul ball, runners must return and retouch the base they legally held when the ball was pitched. The umpire shall not put the ball into "Play" until the runners have retouched their bases. Deliberate prolonged refusal of a runner to retouch a base is cause for ejection.

BATTED BALL HITTING UMPIRE

A batted ball whether in flight or a ground ball which hits an umpire after going through, or by, an infielder (not the pitcher) or which is deflected by a fielder, including the pitcher, shall be in play and all subsequent plays ruled the same as if the ball had not touched the umpire. However, if a batted ball is deflected by a fielder in fair territory and hits a runner or an umpire while still in flight, if then caught by an infielder it shall not be a catch, but the ball shall remain in play.

Calling "Time"

5.10   The ball becomes dead when an umpire calls "Time." The umpire-in-chief shall call "Time"—

(a)   When in his judgment weather, darkness or similar conditions make immediate further play impossible;

(b)   When light failure makes it difficult or impossible for the umpires to follow the play;

NOTE: A league may adopt its own regulations governing games interrupted by light failure.

(c)   When an accident incapacitates a player or an umpire;

(1)   If an accident to a runner is such as to prevent him from proceeding to a base to which he is entitled, as on a home run hit out of the playing field, or an award of one or more bases, a substitute runner shall be permitted to complete the play.

(d)   When a manager requests "Time" for a substitution, or for a conference with one of his players.

(e)   When the umpire wishes to examine the ball, to consult with either manager, or for any similar cause.

(f)   When a fielder, after catching a fly ball, falls into a bench or stand, or falls across ropes into a crowd when spectators are on the field. As pertains to runners, the provisions of 7.04 (c) shall prevail.

Fielder Steps into Bench

If a fielder after making a catch steps into a bench, but does not fall, the ball is in play and runners may advance at their own peril.

(g)   When an umpire orders a player or any other person removed from the playing field.

(h)   Except in the cases stated in paragraphs (b) and (c) (1) of this rule, no umpire shall call "Time" while a play is in progress.

TEMPORARY FAILURE OF LIGHTS

In the event of a temporary failure of lights while a ball is in flight or a play in progress, the umpire will immediately call "Time". When the lights are turned on again and play is resumed, the batsman and all runners shall return to the last base touched by them at the time of suspension. If the batter has not reached first base at the time of suspension, he shall return to the batter's box and assume the same count of balls and strikes he had at the time of suspension.

In the event of inability to complete a double play because of failure of lights, a decision will be rendered only on that part of the play completed before time was called for light failure.

Resuming Play   5.11   After the ball is dead, play shall be resumed when the pitcher takes his place on the pitcher's plate with a new ball or the same ball in his possession and the plate umpire calls "Play." The plate umpire shall call "Play" as soon as the pitcher takes his place on his plate with the ball in his possession.

The Batter

6.00   The Batter.

Batting Order 6.01 (a) Each player of the offensive team shall bat in the order that his name appears in his team's batting order.

(b) The first batter in each inning after the first inning shall be the player whose name follows that of the last player who legally completed his time at bat in the preceding inning.

Batter's Box 6.02 (a) The batter shall take his position in the batter's box promptly when it is his time at bat.

(b) The batter shall not leave his position in the batter's box after the pitcher comes to Set Position, or starts his windup.

PENALTY: If the pitcher pitches, the umpire shall call "Ball" or "Strike," as the case may be.

The batter leaves the batter's box at the risk of having a strike delivered and called, unless he requests the umpire to call "Time." The batter is not at liberty to step in and out of the batter's box at will.

Once a batter has taken his position in the batter's box, he shall not be permitted to step out of the batter's box in order to use the resin or the pine tar rag, unless there is a delay in the game action or, in the judgment of the umpires, weather conditions warrant an exception.

Umpires will not call "Time" at the request of the batter or any member of his team **once the pitcher has started his windup or has come to a set position** even though the batter claims "dust in his eyes," "steamed glasses," "didn't get the sign" or for any other cause.

Umpires may grant a hitter's request for "Time" once he is in the batter's box, but the umpire should eliminate hitters walking out of the batter's box without reason. If umpires are not lenient, batters will understand that they are in the batter's box and they must remain there until the ball is pitched.

If pitcher delays once the batter is in his box and the umpire feels that the delay is not justified he may allow the batter to step out of the box momentarily.

If after the pitcher starts his windup or comes to a "set position" with a runner on, he does not go through with his pitch because the batter has stepped out of the box, it shall not be called a balk.

Both the pitcher and batter have violated a rule and the umpire shall call time and both the batter and pitcher start over from "scratch."

(c) If the batter refuses to take his position in the batter's box during his time at bat, the umpire shall order the pitcher to pitch, and shall call "Strike" on each such pitch. The batter may take his proper position after any such pitch, and the regular ball and strike count shall continue, but if he does not take his proper position before three strikes are called, he shall be declared out.

THIRD STRIKE

If under this rule a third strike is called and the catcher misses the ball, it shall be treated as any other third strike not caught by the catcher.

Batter's Box (Diagram 5)

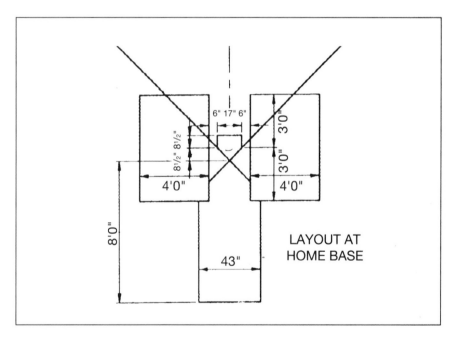

6" 17" 6"

8 1/2" 8 1/2"

3'0"

3'0"

4'0"

4'0"

8'0"

43"

LAYOUT AT HOME BASE

Legal Batting Position

6.03 The batter's legal position shall be with both feet within the batter's box.

APPROVED RULING: The lines defining the box are within the batter's box.

BATTER TO STAND LEGALLY
IN BOX

Umpires are directed to keep the batter within the box when he bats, particularly not to allow a hitter to stand so close to the plate that he is out of the batter's box. No part of the batter's foot is to be closer than 6 inches from the side of home plate.

Legal Time at Bat 6.04   A batter has legally completed his time at bat when he is put out or becomes a runner.

Batter is Out 6.05   A batter is out when—

(a)   His fair or foul fly ball (other than a foul tip) is legally caught by a fielder;

(b)   A third strike is legally caught by the catcher;

"Legally caught" means in the catcher's glove before the ball touches the ground. It is not legal if the ball lodges in his clothing or paraphernalia; or if it touches the umpire and is caught by the catcher on the rebound.

If a foul-tip first strikes the catcher's glove and then goes on through and is caught by both hands against his body or protector, before the ball touches the ground, it is a strike, and if third strike, batter is out. If smothered against his body or protector, it is a catch provided the ball struck the catcher's glove or hand first.

(c)   A third strike is not caught by the catcher when first base is occupied before two are out;

(d)   He bunts foul on third strike;

(e)   An Infield Fly is declared;

(f)   He attempts to hit a third strike and the ball touches him;

(g)   His fair ball touches him before touching a fielder;

Bat Hits Ball Twice   (h)   After hitting or bunting a fair ball, his bat hits the ball a second time in fair territory. The ball is dead and no runners may advance. If the batter-runner drops his bat and the ball rolls against the bat in fair territory and, in the umpire's judgment, there was no intention to interfere with the course of the ball, the ball is alive and in play;

If a bat breaks and part of it is in fair territory and is hit by a batted ball or part of it hits a runner or fielder, play shall continue and

The Batter

no interference called. If batted ball hits part of broken bat in foul territory, it is a foul ball.

If a whole bat is thrown into fair territory and interferes with a defensive player attempting to make a play, interference shall be called, whether intentional or not.

In cases where the batting helmet is accidently hit with a batted or thrown ball, the ball remains in play the same as if it has not hit the helmet.

If a batted ball strikes a batting helmet or any other object foreign to the natural ground while on foul territory, it is a foul ball and the ball is dead.

If, in the umpire's judgment, there is intent on the part of a baserunner to interfere with a batted or thrown ball by dropping the helmet or throwing it at the ball, then the runner would be out, the ball dead and runners would return to last base legally touched.

Deflecting Foul Ball

(i)   After hitting or bunting a foul ball, he intentionally deflects the course of the ball in any manner while running to first base. The ball is dead and no runners may advance;

(j)   After a third strike or after he hits a fair ball, he or first base is tagged before he touches first base;

Three-Foot Line

(k)   In running the last half of the distance from home base to first base, while the ball is being fielded to first base, he runs outside (to the right of) the three-foot line, or inside (to the left of) the foul line, and in the umpire's judgment in so doing interferes with the fielder taking the throw at first base; except that he may run outside (to the right of) the three-foot line or inside (to the left of) the foul line to avoid a fielder attempting to field a batted ball;

(l)   An infielder intentionally drops a fair fly ball or line drive, with first, first and second, first and third, or first, second and third base occupied before two are out. The ball is dead and runner or runners shall return to their original base or bases;

APPROVED RULING: In this situation, the batter is not out if the infielder permits the ball to drop untouched to the ground, except when the Infield Fly rule applies.

(m)   A preceding runner shall, in the umpire's judgment, intentionally interfere with a fielder who is attempting to catch a thrown ball or to throw a ball in an attempt to complete any play:

> The objective of this rule is to penalize the offensive team for deliberate, unwarranted, unsportsmanlike action by the runner in leaving the baseline for the obvious purpose of crashing the pivot man on a double play, rather than trying to reach the base. Obviously this is an umpire's judgment play.

Stealing Home

(n) With two out, a runner on third base, and two strikes on the batter, the runner attempts to steal home base on a legal pitch and the ball touches the runner in the batter's strike zone. The umpire shall call "Strike Three," the batter is out and the run shall not count; before two are out, the umpire shall call "Strike Three," the ball is dead, and the run counts.

INTERFERENCE BY OFFENSIVE PLAYER (This also applies to Official Rules 6.06 and 7.08.)

If the umpire declares the batsman or base runner out for interference, all other base runners shall return to the last base that was, in the judgment of the umpire, legally touched at the time of the interference.

If there is a run-down in progress between third and home and the succeeding base runner has advanced and is standing on third base when the player engaged in the run-down is declared out for interference, the base runner standing on third will be sent back to second.

If a part of a broken bat goes into the infield, there will be no interference. If a whole bat is thrown into fair territory and interferes with a defensive player attempting to make a play, interference shall be called, whether intentional or not.

When the batsman strikes at a ball and the momentum of his swing forces his bat into an arc so that contact is made with the ball or the catcher before or after the ball is securely held by the catcher, the umpire shall rule as follows: If, on the third strike, the batsman is declared out, if, on the first or second strike, call a strike only. In no event may bases be run as the result of a batsman's interference.

If, in the judgment of the umpire, the catcher has possession of the ball and is in the act of throwing, or preparing the throw, and the batter illegally interferes [*exception—batter's normal backswing*] with the catcher, the batter shall be declared out regardless of the count. If any interference does occur, but the catcher is able to retire any runner with his first throw, the play shall stand.

In case of a batter-runner and catcher making contact while the catcher is attempting to field the ball, there generally is no violation and nothing should be called. This cannot be interpreted to mean, however, that flagrant contact by either party would not call for either an interference call or an obstruction call. Either one should be called only if the violation is flagrant in nature. A fielder has "right of way" to make the play, but an unavoidable collision cannot be construed as a violation on the part of either the runner or the catcher.

The Batter

BALL STRIKING HELMET

If a helmet comes off unintentionally, and if a batted ball hits the helmet, it shall be considered in play and the ball shall be ruled fair or foul according to its position when it is touched by a defensive player or comes to rest.

The same will hold if a thrown ball should hit a helmet, e.g., helmet comes off unintentionally while the runner is attempting to steal and the ball hits helmet—the ball will be in play—or, as infielder attempts to field ground ball, a runner's hat comes off and hits ball, the ball is in play. A ball hitting a loose helmet is in play.

PITCH STRIKING UMPIRE

If a foul tip hits the umpire and is caught by a fielder on the re-bound, the ball is "dead" and the batsman cannot be called out. The same shall apply where such foul tip lodges in the umpire's mask or other paraphernalia.

If a third strike (not a foul tip) passes the catcher and hits an umpire, the ball is in play. If such ball re-bounds and is caught by a fielder before it touches the ground, the batsman is not out on such a catch; but the ball remains in play and the batsman may be retired at first base, or touched with the ball for the out.

If a pitched ball passes the catcher and lodges in the umpire's mask or paraphernalia, the ball is "dead". Each base runner is entitled to advance one base. If this happens on the third strike or fourth ball, then the batter is entitled to first base and all runners advance one base.

FOUL TIPS

If a foul-tip hits an umpire, and on the rebound is caught on a fly by a fielder, the ball is "dead" and batsman cannot be called out. Same where such foul-tip lodges in umpire's mask or other paraphernalia.

If a third strike (not a foul-tip) passes the catcher and hits the umpire, the ball is in play. If such ball rebounds and is caught by a fielder before touching the ground, the batsman is not out on such a catch; but the ball remains in play the same as if it touched the ground and the batsman may be retired at first, or touched with the ball for the out

If on the third strike (not a foul-tip) the ball passes the catcher and lodges in the umpire's mask or paraphernalia, the ball is "dead" but the batsman will be entitled to first and other runners on bases will be entitled to advance one base [Rule 5.09(g)].

If a foul-tip **first strikes the catcher's glove** and then goes on through and is caught by both hands against his body or protector, before the ball touches the ground, it is a strike, and if third strike, batter is out. If smothered against his body or protector, it is a catch provided the ball struck the catcher's **glove or hand first.**

INFIELD FLY

On the infield fly rule the umpire is to rule whether the ball could ordinarily have been handled by an infielder—not by some arbitrary limitation such as the grass, or the base lines. The umpire must rule also that a ball is an infield fly, even if handled by an outfielder, if, in the umpire's judgment, the ball could have been as easily handled by an infielder. The infield fly must be judged a fair ball and not called until it is determined to be a fair ball, and shall be called decisively by the umpire nearest the play—and other umpires are

instructed to follow the call immediately so that any man on the field, with normal alertness, shall know immediately that an infield fly has been called. The infield fly is in no sense to be considered an appeal play. The umpire's judgment must govern, and the decision should be made immediately.

When an infield fly rule is called, runners may advance at their own risk. If, however, on an infield fly rule call, the infielder intentionally drops a fair ball [as provided in Rule 6.05(l)] runners may advance at their own risk. The infield fly rule prevails.

BROKEN BAT HITTING BALL OR PLAYER

BALL HITTING HELMET

If a bat breaks and part of it is in fair territory and is hit by a batted ball or part of it hits a runner or fielder, play shall continue and no interference called. If a batted ball hits part of broken bat in foul territory, it is a foul ball.

In cases where the batting helmet is accidentally hit with a batted or thrown ball, the ball remains in play the same as if it has not hit the helmet.

If a batted ball strikes a batting helmet or any other object foreign to the natural ground while on foul territory, it is a foul ball and the ball is dead.

If, in the umpire's judgment, there is intent on the part of a baserunner to interfere with a batted or thrown ball by dropping the helmet or throwing it at the ball, then the runner would be out, the ball dead and no runners advance.

MUST BE DROPPED THIRD STRIKE

Is to be interpreted after a **dropped** third strike or after he hits a fair ball, he or first base is tagged before he touches first base.

The batter-runner shall be called out under Rule 6.05(j) if he missed first base or he is tagged before he returns to touch the missed base. **This is not an appeal play.**

BALL DROPPED INTENTIONALLY

When a fielder deliberately drops a fair ball on a line drive to set up a double play situation, runners may safely return to the bases they occupied at the time of the pitch. Same application shall be made if an outfielder has come so close to the infield to set up a double play situation if he intentionally drops the ball.

Runners cannot advance under this rule. Umpires shall immediately call "Time", when, in their judgment, the ball is intentionally dropped.

Batter's Illegal Action

6.06 A batter is out for illegal action when—

(a) He hits a ball with one or both feet on the ground entirely outside the batter's box.

If a batter hits a ball fair or foul while out of the batter's box, he shall be called out. Umpires should pay particular attention to the position of the batter's feet if he attempts to hit the ball while he is being intentionally passed. A batter cannot jump or step out of the batter's box and hit the ball.

Switching Batter's Boxes

(b) He steps from one batter's box to the other while the pitcher is in position ready to pitch;

(c)   He interferes with the catcher's fielding or throwing by stepping out of the batter's box or making any other movement that hinders the catcher's play at home base. EXCEPTION: Batter is not out if any runner attempting to advance is put out, or if runner trying to score is called out for batter's interference.

If the batter interferes with the catcher, the plate umpire shall call "interference." The batter is out and the ball dead. No player may advance on such interference (offensive interference) and all runners must return to the last base that was, in the judgment of the umpire, legally touched at the time of the interference.

If, however, the catcher makes a play and the runner attempting to advance is put out, it is to be assumed there was no actual interference and that runner is out—not the batter. Any other runners on the base at the time may advance as the ruling is that there is no actual interference if a runner is retired. In that case play proceeds just as if no violation had been called.

If a batter strikes at a ball and misses and swings so hard he carries the bat all the way around and, in the umpire's judgment, unintentionally hits the catcher or the ball in back of him on the backswing before the catcher has securely held the ball, it shall be called a strike only (not interference). The ball will be dead, however, and no runner shall advance on the play.

(d)   He uses or attempts to use a bat that, in the umpire's judgment, has been altered or tampered with in such a way to improve the distance factor or cause an unusual reaction on the baseball. This includes, bats that are filled, flat-surfaced, nailed, hollowed, grooved or covered with a substance such as paraffin, wax, etc.

No advancement on the bases will be allowed and any out or outs made during a play shall stand. In addition to being called out, the player shall be ejected from the game and may be subject to additional penalties as determined by his League President.

ILLEGAL BATS (Doctored)

Official playing rule 6.06(d) prohibits the use of "doctored" bats. The use of pine tar in itself shall not be considered doctoring the bat. The 18 inch rule pertaining to the use of pine tar still applies, but violation of the 18 inch rule will not be cause for ejection or suspension.

The bat will be shipped to the League Office for examination. The player and possibly the manager and

club will be punished in an appropriate way if the bat has been altered.

If a manager suspects an opposing player of using or attempting to use a corked or improperly treated or altered bat, the manager may request the umpire crew chief to inspect and impound the bat. If the umpire's visual inspection reveals no irregularities, the bat will be further examined either in the city where the game is played or at the League Office. Each manager is limited to making this request one time per game. The request must be made either prior to or after the batter has batted. The actual process of batting will not be interrupted. Not withstanding the manager's right to one challenge per game, the umpires may at any time during the game or before or after a game inspect and/or impound a bat or bats for testing. If during a game, such action by the umpire would be in addition to the challenge rights of a manager.

Should it be discovered by direct, immediate observation by an umpire during play that a player is using or attempting to use an illegal bat, the provisions of Rule 6.06(d) fully apply and will result in the ejection of the player and in the nullification of any game action immediately attributable to the use of that bat.

Should it be found that an illegal bat was used in the game, the player using an illegal bat, his manager and perhaps his club will all be liable to severe discipline, including fines and suspension as the League President may determine.

If it is not determined until after the completion of a game that an illegal bat was used, discipline will be imposed as noted above but the result of the game will not be altered.

Bat Colors-

Authorized colors are:

1. Natural finish
2. Brown wood stain define
3. Black
4. Half stain (Walker finish)

DEFINITION OF "Attempts to use" AN ILLEGAL BAT

Any player entering the batter's box with an illegal bat, whether it is his or another player's, will be considered attempting to use that particular piece of equipment once he enters the batter's box.

BALL HIT WHILE BATTER OUT OF BOX

Should be interpreted that if a batter hits a ball **fair** or **foul** while out of the batter's box, he shall be called out. Umpires should pay particular attention to the position of the batter's feet if he attempts to hit the ball while he is being intentionally passed. A batter cannot jump or step out of the batters box and hit the ball.

BATTER INTERFERES WITH CATCHER

If the batter interferes with the catcher, the plate umpire shall call "interference". The batter is out and the ball dead. No player may advance on such interference (offensive interference) and all runners must return to the last base that was, in the judgment of the umpire, legally touched at the time of the interference. Exception: Batter is not out if any runner attempting to advance is put out, or if runner trying to score is called out for batter's interference.

If, however, the catcher makes a play and a runner attempting to advance is put out, it is to be assumed there was no actual interference and that runner is out—not

the batter. Any other runners on the base at the time may advance as the ruling is that there is no actual interference if a runner is retired. In that case play proceeds just as if no violation has been called.

FILLED-DOCTORED BATS

Umpires shall request players coming to the plate or at home plate, in the batter's box, to replace an illegal bat with a legal bat. Umpires, however, are not entirely responsible for the use of an illegal bat. The final responsibility rests with the player and any fair hit, or any batted ball which advances a runner, will be declared an illegally batted ball.

Any bat declared illegal under this rule shall be forwarded by the umpires to the League office.

Batting Out of Turn

6.07   BATTING OUT OF TURN.

(a)   A batter shall be called out, on appeal, when he fails to bat in his proper turn, and another batter completes a time at bat in his place.

(1)   The proper batter may take his place in the batter's box at any time before the improper batter becomes a runner or is put out, and any balls and strikes shall be counted in the proper batter's time at bat.

(b)   When an improper batter becomes a runner or is put out, and the defensive team appeals to the umpire before the first pitch to the next batter of either team, or before any play or attempted play, the umpire shall (1) declare the proper batter out; and (2) nullify any advance or score made because of a ball batted by the improper batter or because of the improper batter's advance to first base on a hit, an error, a base on balls, a hit batter or otherwise.

NOTE: If a runner advances, while the improper batter is at bat, on a stolen base, balk, wild pitch or passed ball, such advance is legal.

Improper Batter Becomes Proper

(c)   When an improper batter becomes a runner or is put out, and a pitch is made to the next batter of either team before an appeal is made, the improper batter thereby becomes the proper batter, and the results of his time at bat become legal.

(d)   (1) When the proper batter is called out because he has failed to bat in turn, the next batter shall be the batter whose name follows that of the proper batter thus called out; (2) When an improper batter becomes a proper batter because no appeal is made before the next pitch, the next batter shall be the batter whose name follows that of such legalized improper batter. The instant an improper batter's actions are legalized, the batting order picks up with the name following that of the legalized improper batter.

Umpire to Remain Silent

The umpire shall not direct the attention of any person to the presence in the batter's box of an improper batter. This rule is designed to require constant vigilance by the players and managers of both teams.

There are two fundamentals to keep in mind: When a player bats out of turn, the proper batter is the player called out. If an improper batter bats and reaches base or is out and no appeal is made before a pitch to the next batter, or before any play or attempted play, that improper batter is considered to have batted in proper turn and establishes the order that is to follow.

APPROVED RULING:

To illustrate various situations arising from batting out of turn, assume a first-inning batting order as follows: Abel-Baker-Charles-Daniel-Edward-Frank-George-Hooker-Irwin.

PLAY (1). Baker bats. With the count 2 balls and 1 strike, (a) the offensive team discovers the error or (b) the defensive team appeals. RULING: In either case, Abel replaces Baker, with the count on him 2 balls and 1 strike.

PLAY (2). Baker bats and doubles. The defensive team appeals (a) immediately or (b) after a pitch to Charles. RULING: (a) Abel is called out and Baker is the proper batter; (b) Baker stays on second and Charles is the proper batter.

PLAY (3). Abel walks. Baker walks. Charles forces Baker. Edward bats in Daniel's turn. While Edward is at bat, Abel scores and Charles goes to second on a wild pitch. Edward grounds out, sending Charles to third. The defensive team appeals (a) immediately or (b) after a pitch to Daniel. RULING: (a) Abel's run counts and Charles is entitled to second base since these advances were not made because of the improper batter batting a ball or advancing to first base. Charles must return to second base because his advance to third resulted from the improper batter batting a ball. Daniel is called out, and Edward is the

105

proper batter; (b) Abel's run counts and Charles stays on third. The proper batter is Frank.

PLAY (4). With the bases full and two out. Hooker bats in Frank's turn, and triples, scoring three runs. The defensive team appeals (a) immediately, or (b) after a pitch to George. RULING: (a) Frank is called out and no runs score. George is the proper batter to lead off the second inning; (b) Hooker stays on third and three runs score. Irwin is the proper batter.

PLAY (5). After Play (4) (b) above, George continues at bat. (a) Hooker is picked off third base for the third out, or (b) George flies out, and no appeal is made. Who is the proper lead off batter in the second inning? RULING: (a) Irwin. He became the proper batter as soon as the first pitch to George legalized Hooker's triple; (b) Hooker. When no appeal was made, the first pitch to the lead off batter of the opposing team legalized George's time at bat.

PLAY (6). Daniel walks and Abel comes to bat. Daniel was an improper batter, and if an appeal is made before the first pitch to Abel, Abel is out, Daniel is removed from base, and Baker is the proper batter. There is no appeal, and a pitch is made to Abel. Daniel's walk is now legalized, and Edward thereby becomes the proper batter. Edward can replace Abel at any time before Abel is put out or becomes a runner. He does not do so. Abel flies out, and Baker comes to bat. Abel was an improper batter, and if an appeal is made before the first pitch to Baker, Edward is out, and the proper batter is Frank. There is no appeal, and a pitch is made to Baker. Abel's out is now legalized, and the proper batter is Baker. Baker walks. Charles is the proper batter. Charles flies out. Now Daniel is the proper batter, but he is on second base. Who is the proper batter? RULING: The proper batter is Edward. When the proper batter is on base, he is passed over, and the following batter becomes the proper batter.

Becoming Runner Without Liability 6.08 The batter becomes a runner and is entitled to first base without liability to be put out (provided he advances to and touches first base) when—

(a) Four "balls" have been called by the umpire;

A batter who is entitled to first base because of a base on balls must go to first base and touch the base before other base runners are forced to advance. This applies when bases are full and applies when a substitute runner is put into the game.

If, in advancing, the base runner thinks there is a play and he slides past the base before or after touching it he may be put out by the fielder tagging him. If he fails to touch the base to which he is entitled and attempts to advance beyond that base he may be put out by tagging him or the base he missed.

(b) He is touched by a pitched ball which he is not attempting to hit unless (1) The ball is in the strike zone when it touches the batter, or (2) The batter makes no attempt to avoid being touched by the ball;

If the ball is in the strike zone when it touches the batter, it shall be called a strike, whether or not the batter tries to avoid the ball. If the ball is outside the strike zone when it touches the batter, it shall be called a ball if he makes no attempt to avoid being touched.

APPROVED RULING: When the batter is touched by a pitched ball which does not entitle him to first base, the ball is dead and no runner may advance.

(c)   The catcher or any fielder interferes with him. If a play follows the interference, the manager of the offense may advise the plate umpire that he elects to decline the interference penalty and accept the play. Such election shall be made immediately at the end of the play. However, if the batter reaches first base on a hit, an error, a base on balls, a hit batsman, or otherwise, and all other runners advance at least one base, the play proceeds without reference to the interference.

If catcher's interference is called with a play in progress the umpire will allow the play to continue because the manager may elect to take the play. If the batter-runner missed first base, or a runner misses his next base, he shall be considered as having reached the base, as stated in Note of Rule 7.04 (d).

Examples of plays the manager might elect to take:

1.   Runner on third, one out, batter hits fly ball to the outfield on which the runner scores but catcher's interference was called. The offensive manager may elect to take the run and have batter called out or have runner remain at third and batter awarded first base.

2.   Runner on second base. Catcher interferes with batter as he bunts ball fairly sending runner to third base. The manager may rather have runner on third base with an out on the play than have runners on second and first.

In situations where the manager wants the "interference" penalty to apply, the following interpretation shall be made of 6.08 (c):

If the catcher (or any fielder) interferes with the batter, the batter is awarded first base. If, on such interference a runner is trying to score by a steal or squeeze from third base, the ball is dead and the runner on third scores and batter is awarded first base.

If the catcher interferes with the batter with no runners trying to score from third on a squeeze or steal, then the ball is dead, batter is awarded first base and runners who are forced to advance, do advance. Runners not attempting to steal or not forced to advance remain on the base they occupied at the time of the interference.

If the catcher interferes with the batter before the pitcher delivers the ball, it shall not be considered interference on the batter under Rule 6.08 (c). In such cases, the umpire shall call "Time" and the pitcher and batter start over from "scratch."

(d) A fair ball touches an umpire or a runner on fair territory before touching a fielder.

If a fair ball touches an umpire after having passed a fielder other than the pitcher, or having touched a fielder, including the pitcher, the ball is in play.

BATTER-RUNNER MUST TOUCH BASES

The rule states that after four balls the batter is entitled to first base without liability to be put out. However, a base runner is required to touch all bases in order.

Accordingly, a batter who is entitled to first base because of a base on balls must go to first base and touch the base before other base runners are forced to advance. This applies when bases are full and applies when a substitute runner is put into the game.

Rule 6.08 entitles the batter (who becomes a base runner because of four balls being called) to first base without liability to be put out provided he **advances and touches first base.** The same applies to a base runner who is forced to advance because of a base on balls to the batter. If, in so advancing, the baserunner thinks there is a play and he slides past the base **before** or after touching it he may be put out by the fielder **tagging him.** If he fails to touch the base to which he is entitled and attempts to advance **beyond** that base he may be put out by tagging him **or the base** he missed [as provided under the Note to Rule 7.04(d)].

BATTER HIT IN STRIKE ZONE

If batter is hit by a pitched ball in the strike zone, it shall be called a "strike", and if it is the third strike the batter is out, the ball is dead, and no runners may advance.

INTERFERENCE BY CATCHER

If catcher's interference is called with a play in progress the umpire will allow the play to continue because the manager may elect to take the play, unless the batter reaches first base and all runners advance one base, in which event the manager has no option to take the interference penalty.

The umpire should indicate catcher's interference by pointing to first base so that both clubs know that catcher's interference has been called.

The manager should make his election of the play or take the interference penalty by advising home plate umpire immediately following the play, and once made, cannot be changed.

If the runner-batter missed first base, or a runner misses his next base, he shall be considered as having reached the base, as stated in Note of Rule 7.04(d).

Examples of plays the manager might elect to take:

1. *Runner on third, one out, batter hits fly ball to the outfield on which the runner scores but catcher's interference was called. The offensive manager may elect to take the run and have batter called out or have runner remain at third and batter awarded first base.*

2. *Runner on second base. Catcher interferes with batter as he bunts ball fairly sending runner to third base. The manager may rather have runner on third base with an*

The Batter

out on the play than have runners on second and first.

In situations where the manager wants the "interference" penalty to apply, the following interpretation shall be made of 6.08(c):

If the **catcher** (or any fielder) **interferes with the batter,** the batter is awarded first base. If, on such interference a runner is trying to score by a steal or squeeze from third base, the ball is dead and the runner on third scores and batter is awarded first base. If the catcher interferes with the batter with no runners trying to score from third on a squeeze or steal, then the ball is dead, batter is awarded first base and runners who are forced to advance, do advance. Runners not attempting to steal or not forced to advance remain on the base they occupied at the time of the interference.

If the catcher interferes with the batter before the **pitcher delivers the ball,** *it shall not be considered interference on the batter under Rule 6.08(c). In such cases, the umpire shall call "Time" and the pitcher and batter start over from "scratch".*

Becoming Runner With Liability

6.09   The batter becomes a runner when—

(a)   He hits a fair ball;

(b)   The third strike called by the umpire is not caught, providing (1) first base is unoccupied, or (2) first base is occupied with two out;

> When a batter becomes a base runner on a third strike not caught by the catcher and starts for the dugout, or his position, and then realizes his situation and attempts then to reach first base, he is not out unless he or first base is tagged before he reaches first base. If, however, he actually reaches the dugout or dugout steps, he may not then attempt to go to first base and shall be out.

(c)   A fair ball, after having passed a fielder other than the pitcher, or after having been touched by a fielder, including the pitcher, shall touch an umpire or runner on fair territory;

(d)   A fair ball passes over a fence or into the stands at a distance from home base of 250 feet or more. Such hit entitles the batter to a home run when he shall have touched all bases legally. A fair fly ball that passes out of the playing field at a point less than 250 feet from home base shall entitle the batter to advance to second base only;

(e)   A fair ball, after touching the ground, bounds into the stands, or passes through, over or under a fence, or through or under a scoreboard, or through or under shrubbery, or vines on the fence, in which case the batter and the runners shall be entitled to advance two bases;

**Ball Lands
in Shrubbery**

(f) Any fair ball which, either before or after touching the ground, passes through or under a fence, or through or under a scoreboard, or through any opening in the fence or scoreboard, or through or under shrubbery, or vines on the fence, or which sticks in a fence or scoreboard, in which case the batter and the runners shall be entitled to two bases;

(g) Any bounding fair ball is deflected by the fielder into the stands, or over or under a fence on fair or foul territory, in which case the batter and all runners shall be entitled to advance two bases;

(h) Any fair fly ball is deflected by the fielder into the stands, or over the fence into foul territory, in which case the batter shall be entitled to advance to second base; but if deflected into the stands or over the fence in fair territory, the batter shall be entitled to a home run. However, should such a fair fly be deflected at a point less than 250 feet from home plate, the batter shall be entitled to two bases only.

**Designated
Hitter**
6.10 Any League may elect to use the Designated Hitter Rule.

(a) In the event of inter-league competition between clubs of Leagues using the Designated Hitter Rule and clubs of Leagues not using the Designated Hitter Rule, the rule will be used as follows:

1. In World Series or exhibition games, the rule will be used or not used as is the practice of the home team.

2. In All-Star games, the rule will only be used if both teams and both Leagues so agree.

(b) The Rule provides as follows:

A hitter may be designated to bat for the starting pitcher and all subsequent pitchers in any game without otherwise affecting the status of the pitcher(s) in the game. A Designated Hitter for the pitcher must be selected prior to the game and must be included in the lineup cards presented to the Umpire in Chief.

The designated hitter named in the starting lineup must come to bat at least one time, unless the opposing club changes pitchers.

It is not mandatory that a club designate a hitter for the pitcher, but failure to do so prior to the game precludes the use of a Designated Hitter for that game.

The Batter

Pinch hitters for a Designated Hitter may be used. Any substitute hitter for a Designated Hitter becomes the Designated Hitter. A replaced Designated Hitter shall not re-enter the game in any capacity.

The Designated Hitter may be used defensively, continuing to bat in the same position in the batting order, but the pitcher must then bat in the place of the substituted defensive player, unless more than one substitution is made, and the manager then must designate their spots in the batting order.

A runner may be substituted for the Designated Hitter and the runner assumes the role of Designated Hitter. A Designated Hitter may not pinch run.

A Designated Hitter is "locked" into the batting order. No multiple substitutions may be made that will alter the batting rotation of the Designated Hitter.

Once the game pitcher is switched from the mound to a defensive position this move shall terminate the Designated Hitter role for the remainder of the game.

Designated Hitter Terminated

Once a pinch hitter bats for any player in the batting order and then enters the game to pitch, this move shall terminate the Designated Hitter role for the remainder of the game.

Once the game pitcher bats for the Designated Hitter this move shall terminate the Designated Hitter role for the remainder of the game. (The game pitcher may only pinch-hit for the Designated Hitter).

Once a Designated Hitter assumes a defensive position this move shall terminate the Designated Hitter role for the remainder of the game. A substitute for the Designated Hitter need not be announced until it is the Designated Hitter's turn to bat.

THE DESIGNATED HITTER
The designated hitter may not sit in the bull pen.

The Runner

7.00   The Runner.

Title to a Base   7.01   A runner acquires the right to an unoccupied base when he touches it before he is out. He is then entitled to it until he is put out, or forced to vacate it for another runner legally entitled to that base. If a runner legally acquires title to a base, and the pitcher assumes his pitching position, the runner may not return to a previously occupied base.

Touching Bases in Order   7.02   In advancing, a runner shall touch first, second, third and home base in order. If forced to return, he shall retouch all bases in reverse order, unless the ball is dead under any provision of Rule 5.09. In such cases, the runner may go directly to his original base.

RUNNER MUST TOUCH MISSED BASE When a runner is returning to a missed base, he must retouch all intervening bases in reverse order	before he may again advance from the missed base.

One Runner per Base   7.03   Two runners may not occupy a base, but if, while the ball is alive, two runners are touching a base, the following runner shall be out when tagged. The preceding runner is entitled to the base.

Baserunner Advancement Without Liability   7.04   Each runner, other than the batter, may without liability to be put out, advance one base when:

(a)   There is a balk;

(b)   The batter's advance without liability to be put out forces the runner to vacate his base, or when the batter hits a fair ball that touches another runner or the umpire before such ball has been touched by, or has passed a fielder, if the runner is forced to advance;

A runner forced to advance without liability to be put out may advance past the base to which he is entitled only at his peril. If such a runner, forced to advance, is put out for the third out before a preceding runner, also forced to advance, touches home plate, the run shall score.

Play. Two out, bases full, batter walks but runner from second is overzealous and runs past third base toward home and is tagged out on a throw by the catcher. Even though two are out, the run would score on the theory that the run was forced home by the base on balls and that all the runners needed to do was proceed and touch the next base.

(c) A fielder, after catching a fly ball, falls into a bench or stand, or falls across ropes into a crowd when spectators are on the field;

A fielder or catcher may reach or step into, or go into the dugout with one or both feet to make a catch, and if he holds the ball, the catch shall be allowed. Ball is in play.

If the fielder or catcher, after having made a legal catch, should fall into a stand or among spectators or into the dugout after making a legal catch, or fall while in the dugout after making a legal catch, the ball is dead and runners advance one base without liability to be put out.

(d) While he is attempting to steal a base, the batter is interfered with by the catcher or any other fielder.

NOTE: When a runner is entitled to a base without liability to be put out, while the ball is in play, or under any rule in which the ball is in play after the runner reaches the base to which he is entitled, and the runner fails to touch the base to which he is entitled before attempting to advance to the next base, the runner shall forfeit his exemption from liability to be put out, and he may be put out by tagging the base or by tagging the runner before he returns to the missed base.

FIELDER FALLING INTO DUGOUT OR STANDS

If a fielder catches a fly ball in the dugout, the ball remains in play and the base-runner or runners advance at their own peril. If a fielder after catching a fly ball falls down in the dugout, or falls into a dugout, bench or stand at any point, the base-runner or runners shall be entitled to advance one base and the ball shall be dead.

RUNNER FORCED TO COUNT AS SCORED

PLAY—Two out, bases full, batter walks, but runner from second is over zealous and runs past third base toward home and is tagged out on a throw by the catcher. Even though two are out, the run would score on the theory that the run was forced home by the base on balls and that all the runners needed to do was proceed and touch the next base.

All Runners Advance Without Liability 7.05   Each runner including the batter-runner may, without liability to be put out, advance:

(a)   To home base, scoring a run, if a fair ball goes out of the playing field in flight and he touched all bases legally; or if a fair ball which, in the umpire's judgment, would have gone out of the playing field in flight, is deflected by the act of a fielder in throwing his glove, cap, or any article of his apparel;

(b)   Three bases, if a fielder deliberately touches a fair ball with his cap, mask or any part of his uniform detached from its proper place on his person. The ball is in play and the batter may advance to home base at his peril;

(c)   Three bases, if a fielder deliberately throws his glove at and touches a fair ball. The ball is in play and the batter may advance to home base at his peril;

(d)   Two bases, if a fielder deliberately touches a thrown ball with his cap, mask or any part of his uniform detached from its proper place on his person. The ball is in play;

(e)   Two bases, if a fielder deliberately throws his glove at and touches a thrown ball. The ball is in play;

In applying (b-c-d-e) the umpire must rule that the thrown glove or detached cap or mask has touched the ball. There is no penalty if the ball is not touched.

Under (c-e) this penalty shall not be invoked against a fielder whose glove is carried off his hand by the force of a batted or thrown ball, or when his glove flies off his hand as he makes an obvious effort to make a legitimate catch.

(f)   Two bases, if a fair ball bounces or is deflected into the stands outside the first or third base foul lines; or if it goes through or under a field fence, or through or under a scoreboard, or through or under shrubbery or vines on the fence; or if it sticks in such fence, scoreboard, shrubbery or vines;

(g)   Two bases when, with no spectators on the playing field, a thrown ball goes into the stands, or into a bench (whether or not the ball rebounds into the field), or over or under or through a field fence, or on a slanting part of the screen above the backstop, or remains in the meshes of a wire screen protecting spectators. The ball is dead. When such wild throw is the first play by an infielder, the umpire, in awarding such bases, shall be governed by the position of the runners at the time the ball was pitched; in all other cases the umpire shall be governed by the position of the runners at the time the wild throw was made;

APPROVED RULING: If all runners, including the batter-runner, have advanced at least one base when an infielder makes a wild throw on the first play after the pitch, the award shall be governed by the position of the runners when the wild throw was made.

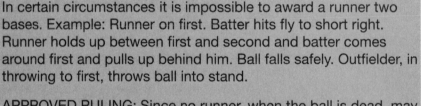

In certain circumstances it is impossible to award a runner two bases. Example: Runner on first. Batter hits fly to short right. Runner holds up between first and second and batter comes around first and pulls up behind him. Ball falls safely. Outfielder, in throwing to first, throws ball into stand.

APPROVED RULING: Since no runner, when the ball is dead, may advance beyond the base to which he is entitled, the runner originally on first base goes to third base and the batter is held at second base.

The term "when the wild throw was made" means when the throw actually left the player's hand and not when the thrown ball hit the ground, passes a receiving fielder or goes out of play into the stands.

The position of the batter-runner at the time the wild throw left the thrower's hand is the key in deciding the award of bases.

If the batter-runner has not reached first base, the award is two bases at the time the pitch was made for all runners. The decision as to whether the batter-runner has reached first base before the throw is a judgment call.

If an unusual play arises where a first throw by an infielder goes into stands or dugout but the batter did not become a runner (such as catcher throwing ball into stands in attempt to get runner from third trying to score on passed ball or wild pitch) award of two bases shall be from the position of the runners at the time of the throw. (For the purpose of Rule 7.05 (g) a catcher is considered an infielder.)

PLAY. Runner on first base, batter hits a ball to the shortstop, who throws to second base too late to get runner at second, and second baseman throws toward first base after batter has crossed first base. Ruling Runner at second scores. (On this play, only if batter-runner is past first base when throw is made is he awarded third base.)

Wild Throw by Pitcher

(h)   One base, if a ball, pitched to the batter, or thrown by the pitcher from his position on the pitcher's plate to a base to catch a runner, goes into a stand or a bench, or over or through a field fence or backstop. The ball is dead;

APPROVED RULING: When a wild pitch or passed ball goes through or by the catcher, or deflects off the catcher, and goes directly into the dugout, stands, above the break, or any area where the ball is dead, the awarding of bases shall be one base. One base shall also be awarded if the pitcher while in contact with the rubber, throws to a base, and the throw goes directly into the stands or into any area where the ball is dead.

If, however, the pitched or thrown ball goes through or by the catcher or through the fielder, and remains on the playing field, and is subsequently kicked or deflected into the dugout, stands or other area where the ball is dead, the awarding of bases shall be two bases from position of runners at the time of the pitch or throw.

Ball Lodged in Umpire's Equipment

(i)   One base, if the batter becomes a runner on Ball Four or Strike Three, when the pitch passes the catcher and lodges in the umpire's mask or paraphernalia.

If the batter becomes a runner on a wild pitch which entitles the runners to advance one base, the batter-runner shall be entitled to first base only.

The fact a runner is awarded a base or bases without liability to be put out does not relieve him of the responsibility to touch the base he is awarded and all intervening bases. For example: batter hits a ground ball which an infielder throws into the stands but the batter-runner missed first base. He may be called out on appeal for missing first base after the ball is put in play even though he was "awarded" second base.

If a runner is forced to return to a base after a catch, he must retouch his original base even though, because of some ground rule or other rule, he is awarded additional bases. He may retouch while the ball is dead and the award is then made from his original base.

PLAY OR ATTEMPTED PLAY

A play or attempted play (Rule 7.05(g)-7.10) shall be interpreted as a legitimate effort by a defensive player who has possession of the ball to actually retire a runner. This may include an actual attempt to tag a runner, a fielder running toward a base with the ball in an attempt to force or tag a runner or actually throwing to another defensive player in an attempt to retire a runner. A fake or a feint to throw shall not be deemed a play or an attempted play. (The fact that the runner is not out is not relevant.)

Examples:

A play or attempted play:

1. Runners on 1st and 2nd, ground ball to the shortstop who makes a swipe at the runner from 2nd but misses and then throws beyond 1st base into the stands. The swipe by the shortstop is an attempted play, thus the throw to first is not the first play by an infielder (even though it is the first throw), and proper award of bases would be from the time of the throw.

2. Runner on 1st and ground ball to 2nd baseman who flips ball to short to get runner from 1st but who is safe. Shortstop throws beyond 1st into the stands. The flip by the 2nd baseman to the shortstop is an attempted play, even though unsuccessful. The throw to 1st is not the first play by an infielder and thus runner should be placed from the time of the throw. Runner who was on 1st would score and batter-runner would be placed at second.

Not a play or attempted play:

1. A fake or feint to a base but not actually throwing, even though the fielder draws his arm back to feint a throw.

2. A pitcher feinting a throw toward a base to hold or check a runner's progress in order to complete an appeal play at another base.

3. Runner on 1st, ground ball to the shortstop, who starts to flip the ball to the 2nd baseman but doesn't and throws the ball beyond 1st and out of play. The feint to the 2nd baseman is not considered a play or attempted play and award of bases is from the time of the pitch.

4. Runners on 1st and 3rd, runner on 1st stealing as ground ball is hit to shortstop. The shortstop feints a throw home but does not throw—instead throws to 1st and into the stands, during this the runner from 1st has rounded 2nd base.

The feint by the shortstop toward home is not considered a play or attempted play; thus his throw beyond 1st is the first play by an infielder and awards should be made from the time of the pitch.

PLAYER TOUCHING A PITCHED BALL WITH DETACHED EQUIPMENT

Official Baseball Rule 7.05(d)(e) states that a player touching a thrown ball with detached equipment entitles the runner to two (2) bases and mentions nothing of touching a pitched ball. Any player touching a pitched ball with detached equipment (such as a catcher's mask, etc.) Will entitle all runners to advance one base without liability to be put out. The ball is in play.

The fact a runner is awarded a base or bases without liability to be put out does not relieve him of the responsibility to touch the base he is awarded and all intervening bases. For example: batter hits a ground ball which an infielder throws into the stands but the batter-runner missed first base. He may be called out on appeal for missing first base after the ball is put in play even though he was "awarded" second base.

If a runner is forced to return to a base after a catch, he must retouch his original base even though, because of some ground rule or other rule, he is awarded additional bases. He may retouch while the ball is dead and the award is then made from his original base.

AWARDING BASES ON WILD THROWS

APPROVED RULING of this rule provides when the first throw is by an infielder **after runners and batter have advanced one base, then runners are awarded two bases from their position when the throw was made.** This can happen on a high fly an infielder goes back to catch but drops the ball during which time batter and runners have clearly advanced one base, then in an attempt to put out the batter-runner after he has passed first base, he throws the ball into the stands. While it is the first throw by an infielder, the **runners, including batter-runner, has advanced one base** before the throw and accordingly are awarded two bases from the base they last touched when the throw was made. Before awarding two bases from the base last touched by the runners the umpire must judge that **all the runners have definitely advanced to the next base before the throw was made.**

In any play where the wild throw is **not** the first throw by an infielder or the throw is made by an outfielder, the runner or runners shall be governed by the position of the runners when the wild throw was made.

The term "when the wild throw was made" means when the throw actually left the player's hand and not when the thrown ball hit the ground, passes a receiving fielder or goes out of play into the stands.

The position of the batter-runner at the time the wild throw left the thrower's hand is the key in deciding the award of bases. **If the batter-runner has not reached first base, the award is two bases at the time the pitch was made for all runners.** The decision as to whether the batter-runner has reached first base before the throw is a judgment call.

If an unusual play arises where a first throw by an infielder goes into the stands or dugout but the batter did **not** become a runner (such as catcher throwing ball into stands in attempt to get runner from third trying to score on a passed ball or wild pitch) award of two bases shall be from the position of the runners at the time of the throw. (For the purpose of Rule 7.05(g) a catcher is considered an infielder.)

*PLAY—Runner on first base, batter hits a ball to the shortstop, who throws to second base too late to get runner at second, and second baseman throws toward first base **after** batter has crossed first base. Ruling-Runner at second scores. (On this play, only if batter-runner is past first base when throw is made is he awarded third base.)*

Calling these plays requires alertness by **all** umpires to visualize the position of runners when the throw was made. This is strictly a judgment play.

The Runner

Obstruction 7.06   When obstruction occurs, the umpire shall call or signal "Obstruction."

Play on Obstructed Runner

(a) If a play is being made on the obstructed runner, or if the batter-runner is obstructed before he touches first base, the ball is dead and all runners shall advance, without liability to be put out, to the bases they would have reached, in the umpire's judgment, if there had been no obstruction. The obstructed runner shall be awarded at least one base beyond the base he had last legally touched before the obstruction. Any preceding runners, forced to advance by the award of bases as the penalty for obstruction, shall advance without liability to be put out.

> When a play is being made on an obstructed runner, the umpire shall signal obstruction in the same manner that he calls "Time," with both hands overhead. The ball is immediately dead when this signal is given; however, should a thrown ball be in flight before the obstruction is called by the umpire, the runners are to be awarded such bases on wild throws as they would have been awarded had not obstruction occurred. On a play where a runner was trapped between second and third and obstructed by the third baseman going into third base while the throw is in flight from the shortstop, if such throw goes into the dugout the obstructed runner is to be awarded home base. Any other runners on base in this situation would also be awarded two bases from the base they last legally touched before obstruction was called.

No Play on Obstructed Runner

(b) If no play is being made on the obstructed runner, the play shall proceed until no further action is possible. The umpire shall then call "Time" and impose such penalties, if any, as in his judgment will nullify the act of obstruction.

> Under 7.06(b) when the ball is not dead on obstruction and an obstructed runner advances beyond the base which, in the umpire's judgment, he would have been awarded because of being obstructed, he does so at his own peril and may be tagged out. This is a judgment call.
>
> NOTE: The catcher, without the ball in his possession, has no right to block the pathway of the runner attempting to score. The base line belongs to the runner and the catcher should be there only when he is fielding a ball or when he already has the ball in his hand.

OBSTRUCTION

Obstruction is the act of a fielder who, while not in possession of the ball and not in the act of fielding the ball, impedes the progress of any runner. When obstruction occurs, the umpire shall call or signal "obstruction".

If a fielder is about to receive a thrown ball and if the ball is in flight directly toward and **near** enough to the fielder so he must occupy his position to receive the ball he may be considered "in the act of fielding a ball". It is entirely up to the judgment of the umpire as to whether a fielder is in the act of fielding a ball. After a fielder has made an attempt to field a ball and missed it, he can no longer be in the "act of fielding" that ball. For example: an infielder dives at a ground ball and the ball passes him and he continues to lie on the ground and delays the progress of the runner, he very likely has obstructed the runner.

In all cases of obstruction the umpire calling the play should have the benefit of the advice of his associates. The umpire watching the obstruction will have difficulty in determining position of other players and runners. It is recommended that when "Time" is called on obstruction if there is any doubt in the minds of the umpires about where the runner or runners shall be located, the umpires shall confer.

PLAY MADE ON OBSTRUCTED RUNNER

Provides for penalty when obstruction occurs **when a play is being made on the obstructed runner, or if the batter-runner is obstructed before he touches first base.** This would include all run-down plays in the infield, and any play where the outfielder makes a direct throw to a base in an attempt to throw out a runner or batter-runner. It would not include a play where a throw is directed toward a runner other than the obstructed runner.

When a play is being made on an obstructed runner the umpire shall signal obstruction in the same manner that he calls "Time", with both hands overhead. **The ball is immediately dead when this signal is given;** however, should a thrown ball be in flight before the obstruction is called by the umpire, the runners are to be awarded such bases on wild throws as they would have been awarded had no obstruction occurred. On a play where a runner was trapped between second and third and obstructed by the third baseman going into third base while the throw is in flight from the shortstop, if such throw goes into the dugout the obstructed runner is to be awarded two bases from the base he last legally touched before obstruction was called. Under 7.06(a) umpires have the responsibility of determining whether a throw is made **before** or **after** obstruction is called. If the umpire judges a throw was made **after** obstruction is called, the obstructed runner will be awarded only one base from the base he last touched when obstruction is called.

RUNNER OBSTRUCTED GOING TO FIRST BASE

Takes care of all obstruction on the batter-runner going to first base. **In those instances, batter-runner is awarded first base and any runner or runners forced to advance, advance.** When a catcher and batter-runner going to first base have contact when the catcher is fielding the ball, there is generally no violation and nothing should be called. "Obstruction" by a fielder attempting to field a ball should be called only in very flagrant and violent cases because the rules give him the right of way, but of course such "right of

way" is not a license to, for example, intentionally trip a runner even though fielding the ball. If the catcher is fielding the ball and the first baseman or pitcher obstructs a runner going to first base, "obstruction" shall be called and the base runner awarded first base.

PLAY NOT BEING MADE ON OBSTRUCTED RUNNER

The Obstruction Rule takes care of play situations where obstruction occurs but **where no play is being made on the obstructed runner.** In these situations, any play which is developing continues until there is no further action, after which "Time" shall be called and the umpire shall impose penalties.

PLAY - Runner on second base and batter singles to right field, runner on second is on his way home and past third base when the batter is obstructed after rounding first base, the ball is thrown wild over the catcher's head and goes into the stands. Ruling: Runner scores and runner obstructed is awarded third base. The reason for this ruling is

that the ball remains in play when a play is not being made on the obstructed runner, and since the wild throw went into the stands, the obstructed runner is to be awarded two bases from where he was at the time the throw was made.

Under 7.06(b) when the ball is not dead on obstruction and an obstructed runner advances beyond the base which, in the umpire's judgment, he would have been awarded because of being obstructed, he does so at his own peril and maybe tagged out. This is a judgment call.

Under 7.06(b) umpires shall verbally (loudly and clearly) call obstruction and at the same moment point laterally at the obstructed runner. The overhead "hands up" signal should not be used under 7.06(b) as employed under 7.06(a) because ball is not yet "dead".

CATCHER NOT TO BLOCK PLATE

Umpires should watch attempts by the catcher to block the plate or hold a runner when the catcher is not in the act of fielding the ball. This is obstruction.

Interference 7.07 With Batter

If, with a runner on third base and trying to score by means of a squeeze play or a steal, the catcher or any other fielder steps on, or in front of home base without possession of the ball, or touches the batter or his bat, the pitcher shall be charged with a balk, the batter shall be awarded first base on the interference and the ball is dead.

Runner is Out 7.08

Any runner is out when—

(a) (1) He runs more than three feet away from a direct line between bases to avoid being tagged unless his action is to avoid interference with a fielder fielding a batted ball; or (2) after touching first base, he leaves the baseline, obviously abandoning his effort to touch the next base;

Any runner after reaching first base who leaves the baseline heading for his dugout or his position believing that there is no further play, may be declared out if the umpire judges the act of the runner to be considered abandoning his efforts to run the bases. Even though an out is called, the ball remains in play in regard to any other runner.

This rule also covers the following and similar plays: Less than two out, score tied last of ninth inning, runner on first, batter hits a ball out of park for winning run, the runner on first passes second and thinking the home run automatically wins the game, cuts across diamond toward his bench as batter-runner circles bases. In this case, the base runner would be called out "for abandoning his effort to touch the next base" and batter-runner permitted to continue around bases to make his home run valid. If there are two out, home run would not count (see Rule 7.12). This is not an appeal play.

PLAY. Runner believing he is called out on a tag at first or third base starts for the dugout and progresses a reasonable distance still indicating by his actions that he is out, shall be declared out for abandoning the bases.

In the above two plays the runners are considered actually abandoning their base paths and are treated differently than the batter who struck out as described. APPROVED RULING OF 7.08 (a).

APPROVED RULING: When a batter becomes a runner on third strike not caught, and starts for his bench or position, he may advance to first base at any time before he enters the bench. To put him out, the defense must tag him or first base before he touches first base.

(b) He intentionally interferes with a thrown ball; or hinders a fielder attempting to make a play on a batted ball;

A runner who is adjudged to have hindered a fielder who is attempting to make a play on a batted ball is out whether it was intentional or not.

If, however, the runner has contact with a legally occupied base when he hinders the fielder, he shall not be called out unless, in the umpire's judgment, such hindrance, whether it occurs on fair or foul territory, is intentional. If the umpire declares the hindrance intentional, the following penalty shall apply: With less than two out, the umpire shall declare both the runner and batter out. With two out, the umpire shall declare the batter out.

If, in a run-down between third base and home plate, the succeeding runner has advanced and is standing on third base when the runner in a run-down is called out for offensive interference, the umpire shall send the runner standing on third base back to second base. This same principle applies if there is a run-down between second and third base and succeeding runner has reached second (the reasoning is that no runner shall advance on an interference play and a runner is considered to occupy a base until he legally has reached the next succeeding base).

Runner is Tagged

(c)   He is tagged, when the ball is alive, while off his base. EXCEPTION: A batter-runner cannot be tagged out after overrunning or oversliding first base if he returns immediately to the base;

APPROVED RULING: (1) If the impact of a runner breaks a base loose from its position, no play can be made on that runner at that base if he had reached the base safely.

APPROVED RULING: (2) If a base is dislodged from its position during a play, any following runner on the same play shall be considered as touching or occupying the base if, in the umpire's judgment, he touches or occupies the point marked by the dislodged bag.

Failure to Retouch Base

(d)   He fails to retouch his base after a fair or foul ball is legally caught before he, or his base, is tagged by a fielder. He shall not be called out for failure to retouch his base after the first following pitch, or any play or attempted play. This is an appeal play;

Runners need not "tag up" on a foul tip. They may steal on a foul tip. If a so-called tip is not caught, it becomes an ordinary foul. Runners then return to their bases.

Force Play

(e)   He fails to reach the next base before a fielder tags him or the base, after he has been forced to advance by reason of the batter becoming a runner. However, if a following runner is put out on a force play, the force is removed and the runner must be tagged to be put out. The force is removed as soon as the runner touches the base to which he is forced to advance, and if he overslides or overruns the base, the runner must be tagged to be put out. However, if the forced runner, after touching the next base, retreats for any reason towards the base he had last occupied, the force play is reinstated, and he can again be put out if the defense tags the base to which he is forced;

PLAY. Runner on first and three balls on batter: Runner steals on the next pitch, which is fourth ball, but after having touched second he overslides or overruns that base. Catcher's throw catches him before he can return. Ruling is that runner is out. (Force out is removed.)

Oversliding and overrunning situations arise at bases other than first base. For instance, before two are out, and runners on first and second, or first, second and third, the ball is hit to an infielder who tries for the double play. The runner on first beats the throw to second base but overslides the base. The relay is made to first base and the batter-runner is out. The first baseman, seeing the runner at second base off the bag, makes the return throw to second and the runner is tagged off the base. Meanwhile runners have crossed the plate. The question is: Is this a force play? Was the force removed when the batter-runner was out at first base? Do the runs that crossed the plate during this play and before the third out was made when the runner was tagged at second, count? Answer: The runs score. It is not a force play. It is a tag play.

Runner Touched by Fair Ball

(f) He is touched by a fair ball in fair territory before the ball has touched or passed an infielder. The ball is dead and no runner may score, nor runners advance, except runners forced to advance. EXCEPTION: If a runner is touching his base when touched by an Infield Fly, he is not out, although the batter is out;

If two runners are touched by the same fair ball, only the first one is out because the ball is instantly dead.

If runner is touched by an Infield Fly when he is not touching his base, both runner and batter are out.

(g) He attempts to score on a play in which the batter interferes with the play at home base before two are out. With two out, the interference puts the batter out and no score counts;

(h) He passes a preceding runner before such runner is out;

Running Bases in Reverse

(i) After he has acquired legal possession of a base, he runs the bases in reverse order for the purpose of confusing the defense or making a travesty of the game. The umpire shall immediately call "Time" and declare the runner out;

If a runner touches an unoccupied base and then thinks the ball was caught or is decoyed into returning to the base he last

The Runner

touched, he may be put out running back to that base, but if he reaches the previously occupied base safely he cannot be put out while in contact with that base.

Overrunning
First Base

(j) He fails to return at once to first base after overrunning or oversliding that base. If he attempts to run to second he is out when tagged. If, after overrunning or oversliding first base he starts toward the dugout, or toward his position, and fails to return to first base at once, he is out, on appeal, when he or the base is tagged;

Runner who touches first base in overrunning and is declared safe by the umpire has, within the intent of Rule 4.09 (a) "reached first base" and any run which scores on such a play counts, even though the runner subsequently becomes the third out for failure to return "at once," as covered in Rule 7.08 (j).

Missing
Home Base

(k) In running or sliding for home base, he fails to touch home base and makes no attempt to return to the base, when a fielder holds the ball in his hand, while touching home base, and appeals to the umpire for the decision.

This rule applies only where runner is on his way to the bench and the catcher would be required to chase him. It does not apply to the ordinary play where the runner misses the plate and then immediately makes an effort to touch the plate before being tagged. In that case, runner must be tagged.

RUNNER FAILING TO TOUCH HOME PLATE

Should a runner in scoring fail to touch the home plate and continue on his way to the bench, he may be put out by the fielder touching the home plate and appealing to the umpire for a decision.

Should a batter-runner be prevented by fans who have rushed onto the field from touching a base, or home plate, the umpire shall award the base because of the obstruction of the fans.

THIRD STRIKE NOT CAUGHT

When a batter becomes a base runner on a third strike not caught by the catcher and starts for the dugout, or his position, and then realizes his situation and attempts then to reach first base, he is not out unless he or first base is tagged before he reaches first base. If, however, he actually reaches the dugout or dugout steps, he may not then attempt to go to first base and shall be out.

ABANDONING BASE PATHS

Any runner after reaching first base who leaves the baseline heading for his dugout or his position believing that there is no further play, may be declared out if the umpire judges the act of the runner to be considered abandoning his efforts to run the bases. Even though an out is called, the ball remains in play in regard to any other runner.

This rule also covers the following and similar plays: Less than two out, score tied last of ninth inning, runner on first, batter hits a ball out of park for winning run, the runner on first passes second and thinking the home run automatically wins the game, cuts across the diamond toward his bench as batter-runner circles bases. In this case, the base runner would be called out "for abandoning his effort to touch the next base" and batter-runner permit-ted to continue around the bases to make his home run valid. If there are two out, home run would not count (see Rule 7.1). **This is not an appeal play.**

PLAY - Runner believing he is called out on a tag at first or third base starts for the dugout and progresses a reasonable distance still indicating by his actions that he is out, shall be declared out for abandoning the bases.

In the above two plays the runners are considered actually abandoning their base paths and are treated dif-ferently than the batter who struck out as described. APPROVED RUL-ING of 7.08(a).

BATTER OUT WHEN HE REACHES DUGOUT

Approved Ruling. When a batter becomes a base runner on a third strike not caught by a catcher and starts for the dugout or his position and then realizes the situation and attempts to reach first base, he is not out unless he or first base is tagged before he reaches first base. If, however, he actually reaches the dugout or the steps he may not then attempt to go on to first base and shall be out.

RUNNER OVERSLIDING BASES

PLAY - Runner on first and three balls on batter: Runner steals on the next pitch, which is fourth ball, but after having touched second he overslides or over-runs that base. Catcher's throw catches him before he can return. Ruling is that runner is out. (Force out is removed).

DECOYED RUNNER MAY RETURN

If a runner touches an unoccupied base and then thinks the ball was caught or is decoyed into returning to the base he last touched, he may be put out running back to that base, but if he reaches the previously occupied base safely he cannot be put out while in contact with that base. Under these circumstances he is not to be considered as running bases in reverse order to confuse the defense—but he may **not** return to a previously occupied base after the pitcher has assumed his pitching motion.

INTERPRETATION OF "AT ONCE"

Umpires are instructed to interpret "at once" as meaning "with reason-able speed". If a player running to first base makes his turn toward the dugout, or goes toward his position or otherwise gives indication of not being alert to the situation, then the appeal shall be allowed if asked for. A player under such circumstances, must return to first base, and once such appeal is asked for, cannot break for second.

Runner who touches first base in overrunning and is declared safe by the umpire, has within the intent of Rule 4.09(a) "reached first base" and

any run which scores on such play counts, even though the runner subsequently becomes the third out for failure to return "at once", as covered in Rule 7.08(j).

RUNNER MISSING PLATE MAY RETURN

Runner is coming home and passes the catcher but fails to touch the plate: On an appeal by the fielder on such play, the runner should be declared out if the fielder touches home plate with the ball. This applies only where runner is on his way to the bench and the catcher would be required to chase him. It does not apply to the ordinary play where the runner misses the plate and then immediately makes an effort to touch the plate before being tagged. In that case, the runner must be tagged.

Interference 7.09   It is interference by a batter or a runner when—

(a)   After a third strike he hinders the catcher in his attempt to field the ball;

(b)   After hitting or bunting a fair ball, his bat hits the ball a second time in fair territory. The ball is dead and no runners may advance. If the batter-runner drops his bat and the ball rolls against the bat in fair territory and, in the umpire's judgment, there was no intention to interfere with the course of the ball, the ball is alive and in play;

(c)   He intentionally deflects the course of a foul ball in any manner;

(d)   Before two are out and a runner on third base, the batter hinders a fielder in making a play at home base; the runner is out;

Confusing Fielders   (e)   Any member or members of the offensive team stand or gather around any base to which a runner is advancing, to confuse, hinder or add to the difficulty of the fielders. Such runner shall be declared out for the interference of his teammate or teammates;

(f)   Any batter or runner who has just been put out hinders or impedes any following play being made on a runner. Such runner shall be declared out for the interference of his teammate;

If the batter or a runner continues to advance after he has been put out, he shall not by that act alone be considered as confusing, hindering or impeding the fielders.

(g)   If, in the judgment of the umpire, a base runner willfully and deliberately interferes with a batted ball or a fielder in the act of fielding a batted ball with the obvious intent to break up a double play, the ball is dead. The umpire shall call the runner out for interference and also call out the batter-runner because of the action of his teammate. In no event may bases be run or runs scored because of such action by a runner.

(h)   If, in the judgment of the umpire, a batter-runner willfully and deliberately interferes with a batted ball or a fielder in the act of fielding a batted ball, with the obvious intent to break up a double play, the ball is dead; the umpire shall call the batter-runner out for interference and shall also call out the runner who had advanced closest to the home plate regardless where the double play might have been possible. In no event shall bases be run because of such interference.

*Coach
Assists
Runner*

(i)   In the judgment of the umpire, the base coach at third base, or first base, by touching or holding the runner, physically assists him in returning to or leaving third base or first base.

(j)   With a runner on third base, the base coach leaves his box and acts in any manner to draw a throw by a fielder;

(k)   In running the last half of the distance from home base to first base while the ball is being fielded to first base, he runs outside (to the right of) the three-foot line, or inside (to the left of) the foul line and, in the umpire's judgment, interferes with the fielder taking the throw at first base, or attempting to field a batted ball;

The lines marking the three foot lane are a part of that "lane" but the interpretation to be made is that a runner is required to have both feet within the three foot "lane" or on the lines marking the "lane."

(l)   He fails to avoid a fielder who is attempting to field a batted ball, or intentionally interferes with a thrown ball, provided that if two or more fielders attempt to field a batted ball, and the runner comes in contact with one or more of them, the umpire shall determine which fielder is entitled to the benefit of this rule, and shall not declare the runner out for coming in contact with a fielder other than the one the umpire determines to be entitled to field such a ball;

When a catcher and batter-runner going to first base have contact when the catcher is fielding the ball, there is generally no violation and nothing should be called. "Obstruction" by a fielder

131

attempting to field a ball should be called only in very flagrant and violent cases because the rules give him the right of way, but of course such "right of way" is not a license to, for example, intentionally trip a runner even though fielding the ball. If the catcher is fielding the ball and the first baseman or pitcher obstructs a runner going to first base "obstruction" shall be called and the base runner awarded first base.

(m) A fair ball touches him on fair territory before touching a fielder. If a fair ball goes through, or by, an infielder, and touches a runner immediately back of him, or touches the runner after having been deflected by a fielder, the umpire shall not declare the runner out for being touched by a batted ball. In making such decision the umpire must be convinced that the ball passed through, or by, the fielder, and that no other infielder had the chance to make a play on the ball. If, in the judgment of the umpire, the runner deliberately and intentionally kicks such a batted ball on which the infielder has missed a play, then the runner shall be called out for interference.

PENALTY FOR INTERFERENCE: The runner is out and the ball is dead.

OFFENSIVE INTERFERENCE

If, in a run-down play between third base and home plate, the succeeding runner has advanced and is standing on third base when the runner in a run-down is called out for offensive interference, the umpire shall send the runner standing on third base back to second base. This same principle applies if there is a run-down between second and third base and a succeeding runner has reached second (the reasoning is that no runner shall advance on an interference play and a runner is considered to occupy a base until he legally has reached the next succeeding base).

Rule 7.09(g) and (h) were inserted in the Official Playing Rules to add an additional penalty when a base runner or a batter-runner deliberately and intentionally interferes with a batted ball or a fielder in the act of fielding a batted ball, to deprive the defensive team of an opportunity to complete a possible double play. Keep in mind the rules provide that the runner or batterrunner must interfere **with the obvious attempt to break up a double play.** A runner from third willfully running into the catcher fielding a pop fly ball, or a runner on second base deliberately running into a ground ball or allowing the ball to hit him to prevent a double play are examples that require the call of double play under Rule 7.09(g).

INTENTIONALLY DEFLECTING COURSE OF FOUL BALL

Rule 7.09(c) Provides the runner or batter is out for interference if he intentionally "deflects the course of a foul ball." While picking up a foul ball or otherwise touching it may not by

that act itself actually deflect the course of the ball, yet if, in the umpire's judgment, the ball might become a fair ball had it not been touched, he would judge the act as deflecting the course of the ball.

It will be better if no member of the offensive team picks up or otherwise touches a foul ball. There is no objection to a coach returning a foul ball to the umpire after it has passed first or third base, but the coach should not touch a ball that possibly may go fair.

THREE FOOT LANE

The lines marking the three foot lane are a part of that "lane" but the interpretation to be made is that a runner is required to have **both** feet within the three foot "lane" or on the lines marking the "lane", which is bounded by the foul line on the left and a white line three feet to the right of the foul line the last 45 feet between home base and first base. If the runner straddles either boundary line running the last 45 feet to first base he is outside the "lane". If the runner's right foot is on the foul line and the other foot to the left of the foul line, he is outside the "lane". If the runner is **outside** the "lane" he may be called out for interference, if, in the umpire's judgment, he interferes with a fielder taking a throw at first base or a fielder attempting to field a batted ball. Either the plate or base umpire may call this infraction.

Appeal Plays 7.10 Any runner shall be called out, on appeal, when—

(a) After a fly ball is caught, he fails to retouch his original base before he or his original base is tagged;

"Retouch," in this rule, means to tag up and start from a contact with the base after the ball is caught. A runner is not permitted to take a flying start from a position in back of his base.

(b) With the ball in play, while advancing or returning to a base, he fails to touch each base in order before he, or a missed base, is tagged.

APPROVED RULING: (1) No runner may return to touch a missed base after a following runner has scored. (2) When the ball is dead, no runner may return to touch a missed base or one he has left after he has advanced to and touched a base beyond the missed base.

PLAY. (a) Batter hits ball out of park or ground rule double and misses first base (ball is dead) he may return to first base to correct his mistake before he touches second but if he touches second he may not return to first and if defensive team appeals he is declared out at first.

PLAY. (b) Batter hits ball to shortstop who throws wild into stand (ball is dead) batter-runner misses first base but is awarded second base on the overthrow. Even though the umpire has awarded the runner second base on the overthrow, the runner must touch first base before he proceeds to second base.

These are appeal plays.

(c)   He overruns or overslides first base and fails to return to the base immediately, and he or the base is tagged;

(d)   He fails to touch home base and makes no attempt to return to that base, and home base is tagged.

Any appeal under this rule must be made before the next pitch, or any play or attempted play. If the violation occurs during a play which ends a half-inning, the appeal must be made before the defensive team leaves the field.

An appeal is not to be interpreted as a play or an attempted play.

Successive Appeals

Successive appeals may not be made on a runner at the same base. If the defensive team on its first appeal errs, a request for a second appeal on the same runner at the same base shall not be allowed by the umpire. (Intended meaning of the word "err" is that the defensive team in making an appeal threw the ball out of play. For example, if the pitcher threw to first base to appeal and threw the ball into the stands, no second appeal would be allowed.)

"Fourth Out"

Appeal plays may require an umpire to recognize an apparent "fourth out." If the third out is made during a play in which an appeal play is sustained on another runner, the appeal play decision takes precedence in determining the out. If there is more than one appeal during a play that ends a half-inning, the defense may elect to take the out that gives it the advantage. For the purpose of this rule, the defensive team has "left the field" when the pitcher and all infielders have left fair territory on their way to the bench or clubhouse.

If two runners arrive at home base about the same time and the first runner misses home plate but a second runner legally touches the plate, the runner is tagged out on his attempt to come back and touch the base or is called out, on appeal, then he shall be considered as having been put out before the second runner scored and being the third out. Second runner's run shall not count, as provided in Rule 7.12.

If a pitcher balks when making an appeal, such act shall be a play. An appeal should be clearly intended as an appeal, either by a verbal request by the player or an act that unmistakably indicates an appeal to the umpire. A player, inadvertently stepping on the base with a ball in his hand, would not constitute an appeal. Time is not out when an appeal is being made.

APPEAL PLAYS— CONTINUOUS ACTION

Some approved rulings follow:

1. Runner on 1st, one out. The batter doubles. R-1 runs the bases and tries for home. On the play at the plate, the catcher misses the tag and R-1 misses the plate as he slides by. As the catcher begins to chase R-1 to apply a tag, the batter-runner as he slides by. As the catcher begins to chase R-1 to apply a tag, the batter-runner tries for third base. Seeing this, the catcher throws to the 3rd baseman, who retires the batter-runner. Can the defensive team still appeal at home on R-1? **ANSWER:** Yes. The catcher's play on the batter-runner at 3rd base was still part of the continuous action created by and following the batted ball. Therefore, the defensive team would not lose its rights to make its appeal by playing on R-1 at home or the batter-runner at 3rd, and may still appeal at home. NOTE: To rule otherwise would be to require the catcher to follow a totally unnatural instinct. His natural instinct upon seeing the batter-runner tries for 3rd base is to try to prevent his advance. To require the catcher to refrain from throwing while a runner is attempting to advance in order to preserve his right to make an appeal on R-1 would be unnatural and unfair, and not in keeping with the intent of the rule.

2. Runner on 1st base, one out. The pitcher attempts a pick off, but throws the ball past the 1st baseman down the right field line. R-1 misses 2nd base, but tries for 3rd.

The right fielder's throw to get R–1 at 3rd base is too late, although he is tagged by the 3rd baseman. Can the defense appeal at 2nd base that R-1 missed it? **ANSWER:** Yes. The 3rd baseman's attempted play on R-1 at 3rd base was still part of the continuous action created by and following the aborted pick off throw. Therefore, the defensive team does not lose its right to make its appeal by playing on R-1 at 3rd base and may still appeal.

3. Runners on 1st and 3rd, 2 outs. The pitcher's next pitch is a wild pitch back to the screen. While the ball is being chased down, R-3 crosses the plate. R-1 misses 2nd base, but tries for 3rd. The catcher's throw to 3rd base gets past the 3rd baseman and R-1 tries for 3rd. The catcher's throw to 3rd base gets past the 3rd baseman and R-1 tries to score. The shortstop, backing up 3rd base attempts to throw R-1 out at the plate, but the catcher's tag is too late and R-1 is ruled safe. Can the defensive team still appeal on R-1 at 2nd base? **ANSWER:** Yes. The defensive team's attempted plays on R-1 at 3rd and home were still part of the continuous action created by and following the wild pitcher ball. Therefore, the defensive team does not lose its right to make its appeal by attempting these plays, and may still appeal on R-1 at 2nd base.

4. Runner on 1st, one out. The batter singles. R-1 misses 2nd base and advances to 3rd without a play. The ball comes into the infield and is returned to the pitcher. The pitcher stretches and comes to a set position and then legally steps off the rubber to

start an appeal at 2nd base. The original runner from 1st (now on 3rd) breaks for home as the defense starts its appeal. The pitcher, instead of completing his appeal play, throws home to get the runner, but the tag is too late and he is ruled safe. Can the defensive team still appeal at 2nd base? **ANSWER:** No. the defensive team's attempt to retire the original runner at home occurred after a definite break in the original continuous action that was created by and followed the batted ball. Therefore, the defensive team lost its right to make any appeals once it made the play at home and may not appeal.

5. Runner on 1st, one out. R-1 goes to 3rd on a single, but misses 2nd base. R-1 is safe at 3rd on a sliding tag play. The ball is returned to the pitcher, who steps on the rubber, stretches and comes to a set position. The defense intends to appeal but the pitcher balks as he steps off the rubber. After the penalty is enforced, can the defense still appeal at 2nd base on the original R-1? **ANSWER:** No. The defense did not lose its right to appeal by playing on R-1 at 3rd base; that play was still part of the continuous action created by and following the batted ball. However, a balk is considered a play for the purpose of this section of the appeal rule. Since the defensive team cannot appeal following a play or attempted play, the pitcher's balk cost the defensive team its right to make an appeal.

6. Runner on 2nd, one out R-2 attempts to score on a single, but misses 3rd base. R-2 is safe at home on a sliding tag play. On the throw home, the batter-runner tries to take 2nd and is safe there on a sliding play, as the catcher's throw is too late to retire him.

Time is called. The pitcher steps on the rubber, stretches and comes to a set position. The defense intends to appeal at 3rd on the original R-2. The pitcher legally steps back off the rubber, checks the runner at 2nd base and steps to throw to 3rd for the appeal. The pitcher's throw, however, is wild and goes into dead territory beyond the 3rd baseman. The runner on 2nd is properly awarded home. Can the defense still make its intended appeal at 3rd on the original R-2 when a new ball is put into play? **ANSWER:** No. The attempted plays to retire the original R-2 at home and the batter-runner at 2nd occurred during the continuous action which was created by and followed the batted ball, and do not nullify the defensive team's right to make an appeal. However, once the defensive team "errs" (i.e., throws the ball out of play) in its attempt to appeal at 3rd on the original R-2, it loses its right to make the appeal. Throwing the ball out of play in this situation is considered an attempted play which occurred after a definite break in the continuous action play.

7. No runners. The batter doubles, but misses 1st base. Time is called. The pitcher steps on the rubber, stretches and comes to a set position. The defense intends to appeal at 1st base. The pitcher legally steps off the rubber and checks the runner at 2nd base. The pitcher's throw for the appeal gets past the 1st baseman, but remains in play. The runner advances to 3rd, as the ball is being retrieved. Can the defensive team still make its intended appeal at 1st base? **ANSWER:** Yes. Since the ball is live and in play, if the ball is retrieved and thrown back to 1st base immediately.

8. Runner on 1st, one out. The batter singles. R-1 misses 2nd base, but is was safe at 3rd on a sliding tag play. Time is called. The pitcher steps on the rubber, stretches and comes to a set position. The defense intends to appeal at 2nd base. The pitcher legally steps off the rubber. Seeing this, the original R-1 (now on 3rd) bluffs as if to go home. The pitcher, now off the rubber, steps toward 3rd and cocks his arm as if to throw, but does not throw. Can the defensive team still make its intended appeal at 2nd base on the original R-1? **ANSWER:** Yes. The attempted play on the original R-1 at 3rd was still part of the continuous action created by and following the batted ball and therefore did not nullify the defensive team's right to make an appeal. The bluff by the pitcher (steps and cocked arm) to check the runner at 3rd is not considered a play or attempted play. A play or attempted play was defined at the American League umpires meeting on February 18, 1981, at the Sheraton Hotel in New York City as "...a legitimate effort by a defensive player who has possession of the ball to actually retire a runner. This may include an actual attempt to tag a runner, a fielder running toward a base with the ball in an attempt to force or tag a runner, or actually throwing to another defensive player in an attempt to retire a runner. A fake or feint to throw shall not be deemed a play or an attempted play. (The fact that the runner is not out is not relevant)." Therefore, the defensive team may still attempt its intended appeal at 2nd base.

RUNNER FAILING TO TOUCH HOME PLATE

Should a runner in scoring fail to touch the home plate and continue on his way to the bench, he may be put out by the fielder touching the home plate and appealing to the umpire for a decision.

Should a batter-runner be prevented by fans who have rushed onto the field from touching a base, or home plate, the umpire shall award the base because of the obstruction of the fans.

RETURNING TO MISSED BASE

APPROVED RULING. A runner may not return to a missed base when ball is dead if he has already touched a base in advance of the missed base. The reasoning in this rule is that the runner should not be permitted to take action advantageous to him when the defensive team (because of ball being dead) is unable to prevent it. A runner may, of course, return to any missed base while ball is in play, unless a following runner has scored.

He may return to a missed base when the ball is dead if he has not touched the next base.

PLAY - (a) Batter hits ball out of park or ground rule double and misses first base (ball is dead) - he may return to first base to correct his mistake before he touches second but if he touches second he may not return to first, and if defensive team appeals he is declared out at first.

PLAY - (b) Batter hits ball to shortstop who throws wild into stand (ball is dead), batter-runner misses first base but is awarded second base on the over-throw. Even though the umpire has awarded the runner second base on the over-throw, the runner must touch first base before he proceeds to second base.

The Runner

Fielders' Space   7.11   The players, coaches or any member of an offensive team shall vacate any space (including both dugouts) needed by a fielder who is attempting to field a batted or thrown ball.

PENALTY: Interference shall be called and the batter or runner on whom the play is being made shall be declared out.

Following Runner Status   7.12   Unless two are out, the status of a following runner is not affected by a preceding runner's failure to touch or retouch a base. If, upon appeal, the preceding runner is the third out, no runners following him shall score. If such third out is the result of a force play, neither preceding nor following runners shall score.

PLAY —

*Bases full, two out, batter hits a home run and misses second base. Appeal is made and the umpire sustains the appeal. All runners, except batter, score if they have crossed the home plate before appeal is **sustained.***

The Pitcher

8.00 The Pitcher.

Legal Pitching Delivery

8.01 Legal pitching delivery. There are two legal pitching positions, the Windup Position and the Set Position, and either position may be used at any time.

Pitchers shall take signs from the catcher while standing on the rubber.

Pitchers may disengage the rubber after taking their signs but may not step quickly onto the rubber and pitch. This may be judged a quick pitch by the umpire. When the pitcher disengages the rubber, he must drop his hands to his sides.

Pitchers will not be allowed to disengage the rubber after taking each sign.

The Windup Position

(a) The Windup Position. The pitcher shall stand facing the batter, his entire pivot foot on, or in front of and touching and not off the end of the pitcher's plate, and the other foot free. From this position any natural movement associated with his delivery of the ball to the batter commits him to the pitch without interruption or alteration. He shall not raise either foot from the ground, except that in his actual delivery of the ball to the batter, he may take one step backward, and one step forward with his free foot.

When a pitcher holds the ball with both hands in front of his body, with his entire pivot foot on, or in front of and touching but not off the end of the pitcher's plate, and his other foot free, he will be considered in the Windup Position.

The pitcher may have one foot, not the pivot foot, off the rubber and any distance he may desire back of a line which is an extension to the back edge of the pitcher's plate, but not at either side of the pitcher's plate.

With his "free" foot the pitcher may take one step backward and one step forward, but under no circumstances, to either side, that is to either the first base or third base side of the pitcher's rubber.

If a pitcher holds the ball with both hands in front of his body, with his entire pivot foot on or in front of and touching but not off the end of the pitcher's plate, and his other foot free, he will be considered in a windup position.

The Pitcher

From this position he may:

(1) deliver the ball to the batter, or

(2) step and throw to a base in an attempt to pick-off a runner, or

(3) disengage the rubber (if he does he must drop his hand to his sides).

In disengaging the rubber the pitcher must step off with his pivot foot and not his free foot first.

He may not go into a set or stretch position: if he does it is a balk.

The Set Position

(b) The Set Position. Set Position shall be indicated by the pitcher when he stands facing the batter with his entire pivot foot on, or in front of, and in contact with, and not off the end of the pitcher's plate, and his other foot in front of the pitcher's plate, holding the ball in both hands in front of his body and coming to a complete stop. From such Set Position he may deliver the ball to the batter, throw to a base or step backward off the pitcher's plate with his pivot foot. Before assuming Set Position, the pitcher may elect to make any natural preliminary motion such as that known as "the stretch." But if he so elects, he shall come to Set Position before delivering the ball to the batter. After assuming Set Position, any natural motion associated with his delivery of the ball to the batter commits him to the pitch without alteration or interruption. Preparatory to coming to a set position, the pitcher shall have one hand on his side; from this position he shall go to his set position as defined in Rule 8.01 (b) without interruption and in one continuous motion.

The whole width of the foot in contact with the rubber must be on the rubber. A pitcher cannot pitch from off the end of the rubber with just the side of his foot touching the rubber.

Complete Stop

The pitcher, following his stretch, must (a) hold the ball in both hands in front of his body and (b) come to a complete stop. This must be enforced. Umpires should watch this closely. Pitchers are constantly attempting to "beat the rule" in their efforts to hold runners on bases and in cases where the pitcher fails to make a complete "stop" called for in the rules, the umpire should immediately call a "Balk."

(c) At any time during the pitcher's preliminary movements and until his natural pitching motion commits him to the pitch, he may throw to any base provided he steps directly toward such base before making the throw.

The pitcher shall step "ahead of the throw." A snap throw followed by the step directly toward the base is a balk.

Illegal Pitch

(d) If the pitcher makes an illegal pitch with the bases unoccupied, it shall be called a ball unless the batter reaches first base on a hit, an error, a base on balls, a hit batter or otherwise.

A ball which slips out of a pitcher's hand and crosses the foul line shall be called a ball; otherwise it will be called no pitch. This would be a balk with men on base.

(e) If the pitcher removes his pivot foot from contact with the pitcher's plate by stepping backward with that foot, he thereby becomes an infielder and if he makes a wild throw from that position, it shall be considered the same as a wild throw by any other infielder.

The pitcher, while off the rubber, may throw to any base. If he makes a wild throw, such throw is the throw of an infielder and what follows is governed by the rules covering a ball thrown by a fielder.

THE PITCHER: THE SET POSITION

Preparatory to coming to a set position, the pitcher shall have one hand by his side.

Set position is assumed by the pitcher when he stands facing the batter with his entire pivot foot on, and parallel to the pitcher's plate. The pivot foot may not extend beyond the end of the pitcher's plate. The non-pivot foot must be on the ground in front of the pitcher's plate. The pitcher must be holding the ball in both hands in front of his body and come to a single complete and discernible stop before throwing the ball. A complete stop shall not be construed as occurring because of a change in the direction of the hands and arms.

From such set position he must deliver the ball to the batter, throw to a base or step backward off the pitcher's plate with his pivot foot.

Before assuming the set position the pitcher may elect to make any natural preliminary motion such as that known as the "stretch". But if he so elects, he shall come to the set position before delivering the ball to the batter. After assuming the set position any natural motion associated with his delivery of the ball to the batter commits him to the pitch without alteration or interruption.

The pitcher, following his stretch, must (a) hold the ball in both hands in front of his body and (b) come to a complete and discernible stop with both feet on the ground. This must be enforced. Umpires should watch

The Pitcher

this closely and should immediately call a "balk" for any violation.

It is permissible for a pitcher with no one on base to pitch to a batter from the set position.

PITCHERS TAKE SIGN WHILE ON RUBBER

The pitcher must take the sign from the catcher while standing in his position on the rubber. Umpires will enforce this rule, the purpose of which is to avoid unnecessary delays in the progress of the game.

PICK-OFFS: FROM THE WIND UP POSITION

From the windup position a pitcher may step and throw to any base to attempt to pick off a runner. The pitcher doesn't have to step off the rubber with his pivot foot in this instance. The basis for this interpretation is to allow the pitcher to step and throw to a base from the windup position as specified in 8.01 (a)(2). The pitcher cannot make any motion associated with his motion to home or it will be called a balk.

EXAMPLE: Bases loaded. Pitcher in windup position. Before making any motion associated with his pitch to home he turns and throws to second in one motion in an attempt to pick off the runner at second base.

ANSWER: Legal. The pitcher should be allowed to step and throw to a base in an attempt to retire a runner from a windup position in accordance with 8.01(a)(2).

PITCHER MUST TAKE SIGNS WHILE ON THE RUBBER

National League pitchers must take signs from the catcher while standing on the rubber. Signs shall not be taken while the pitcher is straddling or standing behind the rubber.

Pitchers may disengage the rubber after taking their signs but may not step quickly onto the rubber and pitch. This may be judged as a quick pitch by the umpire. When the pitcher disengages the rubber, he must drop his hands to his sides.

Pitchers will not be allowed to disengage the rubber after taking each sign. This will defeat the purpose of Official Baseball Rule 8.01 which was put into the rules to establish uniformity in taking signs while on the rubber in all professional leagues.

Wind-up Position. The pitcher must have both feet squarely on the ground and his entire pivot foot must be on, or in front of and in contact with, the front edge of the **pitcher's** **rubber** preliminary to pitching.

The rules permit the pitcher to have one foot, not the pivot foot, off the rubber and any distance he may desire back of a line which is an extension of the back edge of the pitcher's plate, but not at either side of the pitcher's plate.

With his "free" foot the pitcher may take **one step** backward and **one step** forward, but under no circumstances, to either side, that is to either the first base or third base side of the pitcher's rubber.

IF PITCHER HOLDS BALL WITH BOTH HANDS IN FRONT OF BODY

NOTE. If a pitcher holds the ball **with both hands in front of his body,** with his entire pivot foot on or in front of and touching but not off the end of the pitcher's plate, and his other foot free, he will be considered in a windup position.

From this position he may:

(1) deliver the ball to the batter, or

(2) step and throw to a base in an attempt to pick-off a runner, or

(3) disengage the rubber (if he does he must drop his hands to his sides).

In disengaging the rubber the pitcher first must step off with his pivot foot and not his free foot first.

He may not go into a set or stretch position—if he does it is a balk.

SET POSITION

At the end of the 1987 season Rule 8.01(b) was clarified by the Official Playing Rules

Committee. This new language is in effect for the 1988 season, on a one-year trial basis, with determination for future use to be made at the end of the 1988 season.

Set position. Preparatory to coming to a set position, the pitcher shall have one hand by his side.

Set position is assumed by the pitcher when he stands facing the batter with his entire pivot foot on, and parallel to the pitcher's plate, or in front of, parallel to and in contact with, the pitcher's plate. The pivot foot may not extend beyond the end of the pitcher's plate. The non-pivot foot must be on the ground in the front of the

pitcher's plate. The pitcher must hold the ball in both hands in front of his body and come to a single complete and discernible stop before throwing the ball. A complete stop shall not be construed as occurring because of a change in direction of the hands and arms.

From such Set Position he must deliver the ball to the batter, throw to a base or step backward off the pitcher's plate with his pivot foot.

Before assuming Set Position, the pitcher may elect to make any natural preliminary motion such as that known as "the stretch". But if he so elects, he shall come to Set Position before delivering the ball to the batter. After assuming Set Position, any natural motion associated with his delivery of the ball to the batter commits him to the pitch without alteration or interruption.

The pitcher, following his stretch, must (a) hold the ball in both hands in front of his body, and (b) come to a single complete and discernible stop, with both feet on the ground. This must be enforced. Umpires should watch this closely and should immediately call a "balk" for any violation.

Pitcher's Prohibitions 8.02 The pitcher shall not—

(a) (1) Bring his pitching hand in contact with his mouth or lips while in the 18 foot circle surrounding the pitching rubber. EXCEPTION: Provided it is agreed to by both managers, the umpire prior to the start of a game played in cold weather, may permit the pitcher to blow on his hand.

PENALTY: For violation of this part of this rule the umpires shall immediately call a ball. However, if the pitch is made and a batter reaches first base on a hit, an error, a hit batsman or otherwise, and no other runner is put out before advancing at least one base, the play shall proceed without reference to the violation.

Repeated offenders shall be subject to a fine by the league president.

(2)   Apply a foreign substance of any kind to the ball;

(3)   expectorate on the ball, either hand or his glove;

(4)   rub the ball on his glove, person or clothing;

(5)   deface the ball in any manner;

(6)   deliver what is called the "shine" ball, "spit" ball, "mud" ball or "emery" ball. The pitcher, of course, is allowed to rub the ball between his bare hands.

PENALTY: For violation of any part of this rule 8.02 (a) (2 to 6) the umpire shall:

(a)   Call the pitch a ball, warn the pitcher and have announced on the public address system the reason for the action.

(b)   In the case of a second offense by the same pitcher in the same game, the pitcher shall be disqualified from the game.

(c)   If a play follows the violation called by the umpire, the manager of the offense may advise the plate umpire that he elects to accept the play. Such election shall be made immediately at the end of the play. However, if the batter reaches first base on a hit, an error, a base on balls, a hit batsman, or otherwise, and no other runner is put out before advancing at least one base, the play shall proceed without reference to the violation.

(d)   Even though the offense elects to take the play, the violation shall be recognized and the penalties in (a) and (b) will still be in effect.

(e)   The umpire shall be sole judge on whether any portion of this rule has been violated.

All umpires shall carry with them one official rosin bag. The umpire-in-chief is responsible for placing the rosin bag on the ground back of the pitcher's plate. If at any time the ball hits the rosin bag it is in play. In the case of rain or wet field, the umpire may instruct the pitcher to carry the rosin bag in his hip pocket. A pitcher may use the rosin bag for the purpose of applying rosin to his bare hand or hands. Neither the pitcher nor any other player shall dust the ball with the rosin bag; neither shall the pitcher nor any other player be permitted to apply rosin from the bag to his glove or dust any part of his uniform with the rosin bag.

Foreign Substances

(b) Have on his person, or in his possession, any foreign substance. For such infraction of this section (b) the penalty shall be immediate ejection from the game.

(c) Intentionally delay the game by throwing the ball to players other then the catcher, when the batter is in position, except in an attempt to retire a runner.

PENALTY: If, after warning by the umpire, such delaying action is repeated, the pitcher shall be removed from the game.

(d) Intentionally Pitch at the Batter.

If, in the umpire's judgment, such a violation occurs, the umpire may elect either to:

1. Expel the pitcher, or the manager and the pitcher, from the game, or

2. may warn the pitcher and the manager of both teams that another such pitch will result in the immediate expulsion of that pitcher (or a replacement) and the manager.

If, in the umpire's judgment, circumstances warrant, both teams may be officially "warned" prior to the game or at any time during the game.

(League Presidents may take additional action under authority provided in Rule 9.05)

To pitch at a batter's head is unsportsmanlike and highly dangerous. It should be and is condemned by everybody. Umpires should act without hesitation in enforcement of this rule.

SCUFFED BASEBALLS

The procedure in handling this is in the normal prescribed way. The umpire will examine the ball if requested by a player, or if the umpire detects something unusual in the flight of the ball. If the ball has been defaced and there is no natural event to explain it (ball bounced into the dirt, ball hitting an object, etc.), the pitcher shall be warned. The warning shall remain in place for the rest of the season. If that pitcher throws another ball that has been defaced, the pitcher will be ejected.

The Pitcher

Ejection of a pitcher for defacing a ball carries with it an automatic ten-day suspension.

It should be noted that the responsibility for pitching a defaced ball rests solely with the pitcher.

Pitchers will not be harassed needlessly—**do not conduct searches.** The pitcher assumes full responsibility for throwing a defaced ball. Who defaces it or cuts it, or how, is relatively important.

FOREIGN SUBSTANCE ON THE BALL

This rule legislates against the application of foreign substances on the ball by the pitcher. The umpires have the responsibility of detecting the application of foreign substances before the ball is pitched and also when the ball is pitched to the batter. If the umpire detects or suspects that a foreign substance has been applied to the ball he should request the pitcher (or catcher) to give him the ball. If, upon examination he is firmly convinced that the pitcher has applied a foreign substance such as a grease, lubricant, tar, etc. or has expectorated on the ball, he should warn the pitcher and have such warning announced over the public address system. On second such infraction the umpire shall remove the pitcher from the game.

Enforcement under this rule should be uniform by all umpires. In calling an infraction, umpires must be certain in their own mind of a foreign substance being applied to the ball. Managers may come out of the dugout to question the umpire's call, but no protest or arguments should be tolerated as enforcement is an act of judgment on the part of the umpire.

When the umpire issues a warning he should signal the call to the press box by raising his left hand high above his head.

If a pitcher is disqualified, the substitute pitcher should have time for a full warm-up similar to the time allowed when an injured pitcher is removed from the game.

Under this Rule the umpires have the responsibility to apply a penalty of immediate ejection from the game if the pitcher has on his person, or in his possession, any foreign substance that would affect the flight of the ball.

We are not desirous of having umpires examine pitchers for foreign substances on their person or in their possession, and such procedures will not be necessary if pitchers, managers, coaches and club management regulate against such illegal practices. We are asking the umpires, however, if they feel warranted, to ask the player for equipment they wish to inspect, and the player should consent. Continuous refusal to consent may be reason for ejection. At no time should umpires place their hands on the player's person or use physical force to obtain his equipment.

Warm-Up Pitches   8.03   When a pitcher takes his position at the beginning of each inning, or when he relieves another pitcher, he shall be permitted to pitch not to exceed eight preparatory pitches to his catcher during which play shall be suspended. A league by its own action may limit the number of preparatory pitches to less than eight preparatory pitches. Such preparatory pitches shall not consume more than one minute of time. If a sudden emergency causes a pitcher to be summoned into the game without any opportunity to warm up, the umpire-in-chief shall allow him as many pitches as the umpire deems necessary.

WARM-UP PITCHES	RELIEF PITCHER
When a pitcher takes his position at the beginning of each inning, or when he relieves another pitcher he shall be permitted to pitch not to exceed eight preparatory pitches to his catcher during which play shall be suspended. Such preparatory pitches shall not consume more than one minute of time.	When a pitcher warming up in the "bull pen" has been designated to the umpire as a relief pitcher, at the call of the umpire, he must take his position on the rubber promptly. Any extra pitches thrown in the bull pen may be subtracted from the eight permissible from the mound.

RELIEF PITCHER MUST COME IN IMMEDIATELY	WARM-UP PITCHES
Umpires will insist that the relief pitcher in the bull pen come immediately to the pitching mound and be allowed not more than eight preparatory pitches which shall not consume more than one minute. Umpires shall not only motion for the relief pitcher to come into the game, but shall move toward the bull pen if the pitcher is slow responding.	Provides that umpires allow 8 preparatory pitches between innings and when a relief pitcher comes into a game. The home club pitcher may not warm up on the mound prior to the start of the game. He may take only his 8 preparatory pitches. This could give the home club pitcher some advantage and since pre-game practice conditions should be equal for both starting pitchers, both pitchers should warm-up where pitchers normally warm-up.

Delay by Pitcher   8.04   When the bases are unoccupied, the pitcher shall deliver the ball to the batter within 20 seconds after he receives the ball. Each time the pitcher delays the game by violating this rule, the umpire shall call "Ball."

The intent of this rule is to avoid unnecessary delays. The umpire shall insist that the catcher return the ball promptly to the pitcher, and that the pitcher take his position on the rubber promptly. Obvious delay by the pitcher should instantly be penalized by the umpire.

Balk by Pitcher 8.05 If there is a runner, or runners, it is a balk when—

(a) The pitcher, while touching his plate, makes any motion naturally associated with his pitch and fails to make such delivery;

If a left handed or right handed pitcher swings his free foot past the back edge of the pitcher's rubber, he is required to pitch to the batter except to throw to second base on a pick-off-play.

(b) The pitcher, while touching his plate, feints a throw to first base and fails to complete the throw;

(c) The pitcher, while touching his plate, fails to step directly toward a base before throwing to that base;

Requires the pitcher, while touching his plate, to step directly toward a base before throwing to that base. If a pitcher turns or spins off of his free foot without actually stepping or if he turns his body and throws before stepping, it is a balk.

A pitcher is to step directly toward a base before throwing to that base but does not require him to throw (except to first base only) because he steps. It is possible, with runners on first and third, for the pitcher to step toward third and not throw, merely to bluff the runner back to third; then seeing the runner on first start for second, turn and step toward and throw to first base. This is legal. However, if, with runners on first and third, the pitcher, while in contact with the rubber, steps toward third and then immediately and in practically the same motion "wheels" and throws to first base, it is obviously an attempt to deceive the runner at first base, and in such a move it is practically impossible to step directly toward first base before the throw to first base, and such a move shall be called a balk. Of course, if the pitcher steps off the rubber and then makes such a move, it is not a balk.

(d)   The pitcher, while touching his plate, throws, or feints a throw to an unoccupied base, except for the purpose of making a play;

Illegal Pitch

(e)   The pitcher makes an illegal pitch;

A quick pitch is an illegal pitch. Umpires will judge a quick pitch as one delivered before the batter is reasonably set in the batter's box. With runners on base the penalty is a balk; with no runners on base, it is a ball. The quick pitch is dangerous and should not be permitted.

(f)   The pitcher delivers the ball to the batter while he is not facing the batter;

(g)   The pitcher makes any motion naturally associated with his pitch while he is not touching the pitcher's plate;

(h)   The pitcher unnecessarily delays the game;

Feinting Pitch

(i)   The pitcher, without having the ball, stands on or astride the pitcher's plate or while off the plate, he feints a pitch;

(j)   The pitcher, after coming to a legal pitching position, removes one hand from the ball other than in an actual pitch, or in throwing to a base;

(k)   The pitcher, while touching his plate, accidentally or intentionally drops the ball;

(l)   The pitcher, while giving an intentional base on balls, pitches when the catcher is not in the catcher's box;

(m) The pitcher delivers the pitch from Set Position without coming to a stop.

PENALTY: The ball is dead, and each runner shall advance one base without liability to be put out, unless the batter reaches first on a hit, an error, a base on balls, a hit batter, or otherwise, and

all other runners advance at least one base, in which case the play proceeds without reference to the balk.

APPROVED RULING: In cases where a pitcher balks and throws wild, either to a base or to home plate, a runner or runners may advance beyond the base to which he is entitled at his own risk.

APPROVED RULING: A runner who misses the first base to which he is advancing and who is called out on appeal shall be considered as having advanced one base for the purpose of this rule.

Intent of Pitcher

Umpires should bear in mind that the purpose of the balk rule is to prevent the pitcher from deliberately deceiving the base runner. If there is doubt in the umpire's mind, the "intent" of the pitcher should govern. However, certain specifics should be borne in mind:

(a) Straddling the pitcher's rubber without the ball is to be interpreted as intent to deceive and ruled a balk.

(b) With a runner on first base the pitcher may make a complete turn, without hesitating toward first, and throw to second. This is not to be interpreted as throwing to an unoccupied base.

SPECIAL BALK REGULATIONS

With a runner on first or on second base and the pitcher indulges in a preliminary stretch by raising his arms over his head or out in front, he must return to a natural pitching position and STOP before starting his delivery of the ball to the batsman. Failure to STOP and separate his preliminary stretch or motion from his regular pitching motion shall be declared a balk.

If a pitcher's free foot passes the plane of the rubber, he is committed to pitch.

It is a balk if the pitcher throws to the 1st baseman back of and off the bag or moving in for a possible bunt and not within a reasonable proximity of the bag when he catches the ball.

Managers, coaches, and players may not come on the field to protest a balk if it is called against the pitcher for failure to step toward 1st base.

The umpire should point to his foot in this instance.

ILLEGAL PITCH

At the time an umpire calls a ball for an illegal pitch, he shall turn around and notify the press of such action by making a throwing motion and then giving the count to the press box. (Playing Rule 8.07 (a)).

LEFTHANDED PITCHER'S FREE FOOT CROSSING PLANE OF RUBBER

A lefthanded pitcher's free leg is permitted to swing backward when pitching from the set position (with men on base) before he is committed to pitch to the batter. If any part of the free foot extends beyond the back edge of the pitcher's rubber the

pitcher must pitch the ball to the batter except if he throws the ball or aborts a throw to second base on a pick-off play. If the knee of his free leg extends beyond the back edge of the pitcher's rubber and his free foot does not, he will be permitted to throw to first bast without a balk being called.

BALK

Any umpire may call a balk. Base umpires are sometimes in a better position to call a balk than the plate umpire. A balk shall be called audibly and with hands raised over head, as is done when calling "Time".

Umpires should bear in mind that the purpose of the balk rule is to prevent the pitcher from deliberately deceiving the base runner. If there is doubt in the umpire's mind, the "intent" of the pitcher should govern. However, certain specifics should be borne in mind:

(a) Straddling the pitcher's rubber without the ball is to be interpreted as intent to deceive and ruled a balk.

(b) With a runner on first base the pitcher may make a complete turn, without hesitating, toward first, and throw to second. This is not to be interpreted as throwing to an unoccupied base.

When a pitcher swings his free foot past the back edge of the pitcher's rubber, it is a balk if he does not pitch to the batter, unless he throws to second base on a pick-off play.

Requires the pitcher, while touching his plate, to step directly toward a base **before** throwing to that base. If a pitcher turns or spins off of his free foot without actually stepping or if he turns his body and throws **before** stepping, it is a balk.

A pitcher is to step directly toward a base before throwing to that base but does not require him to throw (except to first base only) because he steps. It is possible, with runners on first and third, for the pitcher to step toward third and not throw, merely to bluff the runner back to third; then seeing the runner on first start for second, turn and step toward and throw to first base. This is legal. However, if, with runners on first and third, the pitcher, while in contact with the rubber, steps toward third and then immediately and **in practically the same motion** "wheels" and throws to first base, it is obviously an attempt to deceive the runner at first base, and in such a move it is practically impossible to step directly toward first base before the throw to first base, and such a move shall be called a balk. Of course, if the pitcher steps off the rubber and then makes such a move, it is not a balk.

A manager or coach may not protest the call of a balk as defined in 8.05(c). If such protest is made, the manager or coach shall be ejected from the game.

A pitcher must come to a stop with his front foot on the ground.

Penalty under Rule 8.05 provides that if a batter reaches first base safely on a hit or error, bases on balls, or otherwise, on a pitch on which a balk is called, he shall be entitled to first base only if all other runners have advanced one base **or more** on the play, in which case the balk is disregarded. If the runner or **all** runners do not advance, the balk penalty should prevail and the batter must return to the batter's box and runners advanced one base as the penalty for the balk. When a balk is

made on a pitch which is a fourth ball it shall be ruled the same as when the batter hits a balk pitch and is safe on a hit or error, provided all runners advance at least one base on the play. Therefore, with a runner on first, first and second, or first, second and third, when a balk is called on the fourth ball, the batter goes to first base and all runners advance at least one base. If they attempt to advance more than one base, they do so at their own risk.

However, if first base is not occupied and all other runners do not advance at least one base on the play, the balk penalty prevails, with the ball dead, batter returning to the batter's box assuming the same ball and strike count as before the balk pitch and all runners allowed to advance one base as penalty for the balk.

STEALING BASE ON BALL 4 BALK SITUATION

Ball three on batter, on next pitch, which is ball four, a balk is called, runner on second is attempting to steal third on the pitch; N.L. ruling:

Batter goes to first on ball four, runner safe at third stays there. Because a runner from second advanced one base on the pitch the balk is disregarded and base on balls prevails.

Visit to the Mound

8.06 A professional league shall adopt the following rule pertaining to the visit of the manager or coach to the pitcher:

(a) This rule limits the number of trips a manager or coach may make to any one pitcher in any one inning;

(b) A second trip to the same pitcher in the same inning will cause this pitcher's automatic removal;

(c) The manager or coach is prohibited from making a second visit to the mound while the same batter is at bat, but

(d) if a pinch-hitter is substituted for this batter, the manager or coach may make a second visit to the mound, but must remove the pitcher.

Visit Concluded

A manager or coach is considered to have concluded his visit to the mound when he leaves the 18-foot circle surrounding the pitcher's rubber.

If the manager or coach goes to the catcher or infielder and that player then goes to the mound or the pitcher comes to him at his position before there is an intervening play (a pitch or other play) that will be the same as the manager or coach going to the mound.

Any attempt to evade or circumvent this rule by the manager or coach going to the catcher or an infielder and then that player going to the mound to confer with the pitcher shall constitute a trip to the mound.

If the coach goes to the mound and removes a pitcher and then the manager goes to the mound to talk with the new pitcher, that will constitute one trip to that new pitcher that inning.

In a case where a manager has made his first trip to the mound and then returns the second time to the mound in the same inning with the same pitcher in the game and the same batter at bat, after being warned by the umpire that he cannot return to the mound, the manager shall be removed from the game and the pitcher required to pitch to the batter until he is retired or gets on base. After the batter is retired, or becomes a base runner, then this pitcher must be removed from the game. The manager should be notified that his pitcher will be removed from the game after he pitches to one hitter, so he can have a substitute pitcher warmed up.

The substitute pitcher will be allowed eight preparatory pitches or more if in the umpire's judgment circumstances justify.

TRIPS TO THE MOUND BY MANAGER OR COACH

American League rules limit the number of trips a manager or coach may make to any one pitcher in any one inning. A manager or coach is considered to have concluded his visit to the mound when he crosses the foul line. On a second trip to the mound in the same inning by a manager or coach the relief pitcher shall be designated by the manager or coach when crossing the foul line.

The second trip to the mound in the same inning by a manager or coach will cause the pitcher's automatic removal. (The pitcher may be placed at another position, but under no circumstances will he be permitted to return to pitch again in the game.) In this situation, automatic removal means: the pitcher is automatically removed from the mound, not from the game. If the manager or coach makes an obvious attempt to delay the game, the pitcher must remain in the game until the batter is retired or becomes a base-runner or the side retired. If, however, after the manag-er or coach leaves the mound a batter is substituted for the batter who was at bat when the manager made his first trip to the mound, then the manager may return to the mound to remove the pitcher.

If a manager or coach starts toward the mound and gets as far as the foul line and then realizes he is wrong, he can correct himself and go back to the bench without penalty. Umpires may warn them if they see them start for the mound the second time in an inning.

The catcher or any other player may not go to the dugout and then immediately to the mound. If so, it will be considered a visit to the mound by the manager.

If the manager or coach goes to the catcher or infielder and that player then goes to the mound or the pitcher comes to him at his position before there is an intervening play (a pitch or other play) this will be considered the same as the manager or coach going to the mound.

If the coach goes to the mound to

The Pitcher

remove a pitcher and then the manager goes to the mound to talk with the new pitcher, this will constitute one trip to that pitcher that inning.

If a pitcher is removed and the manager or coach remains to talk to the new pitcher, this is not charged as a visit with the new pitcher.

These regulations apply to playing managers.

This rule was adopted by the clubs to speed up games and managers should abide by the spirit of the rule.

The manager may request permission from the umpire to visit the mound in case of injury to the pitcher and with permission granted it will not be counted as a visit to the mound.

TRIPS TO THE MOUND BY PLAYING MANAGER

Subject to the judgment of the umpire, any visit to the mound will be considered a trip. The umpire shall notify the playing manager and the opposing manager each time a trip is charged.

TRIPS TO THE MOUND BY PLAYING COACH

While playing he will be treated as a player until such time he is considered to have abused the privilege. If, in the judgment of the umpire, the privilege is abused, the playing coach and his manager will be advised that any future visits to the mound will be charged as trips.

INFIELDERS MAY NOT HUDDLE ON MOUND

One infielder and the catcher may approach and talk to the pitcher. All other players must remain in their positions.

MANAGER VISITING MOUND

Official Playing Rules limit the number of trips a manager or coach may make to any one pitcher in any one inning. The second trip to the mound to the same pitcher in the same inning by a manager or coach will cause that pitcher's automatic removal from the game.

The manager or coach is prohibited from making a second visit to the mound while the same hitter is at bat, but if a pinch hitter is substituted for this batter the manager or coach may then make a second visit to the mound but must remove the pitcher.

A manager or coach is considered to have concluded his visit to the mound when he leaves the 18 foot circle surrounding the pitcher's rubber.

If the manager or coach goes to the catcher or infielder and that player then goes to the mound or the pitcher comes to him at his position before there is an intervening play (a pitch or other play) that will be the same as the manager or coach going to the mound.

Any attempt to evade or circumvent this rule by the manager or coach going to the catcher or an infielder and then that player going to the mound to confer with the pitcher shall constitute a trip to the mound.

If the coach goes to the mound and removes a pitcher and then a manager goes to the mound to talk with the new pitcher, that will constitute one trip to that new pitcher that inning.

In a case where a manager has made his first trip to the mound and then returns the second time to the mound in the same inning with the

same pitcher in the game and the **same batter at bat,** after being warned by the umpire that he cannot return to the mound, the **manager** shall be removed from the game and the pitcher required to pitch to the batter until he is retired or gets on base. After the batter is retired, or becomes a base runner, then this pitcher must be removed from the game. The manager should be notified that his pitcher will be removed from the game after he pitches to one hitter, so he can have a substitute pitcher warmed up. The substitute pitcher will be allowed eight preparatory pitches or more if in the umpire's judgment circumstances justify.

The Umpire

9.00   The Umpire.

Umpire   9.01   (a)   The league president shall appoint one or more umpires to
Appointment officiate at each league championship game. The umpires
shall be responsible for the conduct of the game in accordance with these official rules and for maintaining discipline
and order on the playing field during the game.

         (b)   Each umpire is the representative of the league and of pro-
fessional baseball, and is authorized and required to enforce
all of these rules. Each umpire has authority to order a player, coach, manager or club officer or employee to do or
refrain from doing anything which affects the administering
of these rules, and to enforce the prescribed penalties.

Umpire   (c)   Each umpire has authority to rule on any point not specifical-
Authority ly covered in these rules.

         (d)   Each umpire has authority to disqualify any player, coach,
manager or substitute for objecting to decisions or for
unsportsmanlike conduct or language, and to eject such disqualified person from the playing field. If an umpire disquali-
fies a player while a play is in progress, the disqualification
shall not take effect until no further action is possible in that
play.

         (e)   Each umpire has authority at his discretion to eject from the
playing field (1) any person whose duties permit his pres-
ence on the field, such as ground crew members, ushers,
photographers, newsmen, broadcasting crew members,
etc., and (2) any spectator or other person not authorized to
be on the playing field.

NO PHOTOGRAPHERS ON FIELD

League rules prohibit photographers on the playing field during the progress of a championship game. Photographers may be on the field in spring training games.

Procedure When Umpires Fail to Appear.

(a) If none of the umpires assigned to a championship game are on hand at game time, the umpires for the game shall be competent local substitute umpires who have been approved by the League office. If such local substitute umpires are not available, the managers of the contending teams shall each choose two players from the other team who are not in the starting line-up and the four players thus selected shall be the umpires for the game. Such local substitute umpires or player-umpires shall have all of the responsibility and authority of any regular staff umpire. The plate umpire shall be chosen by lot.

(b) If only one umpire should be on hand for a championship game, the additional umpires for the game shall be competent local substitute umpires who have been approved by the League office who shall act as base umpires, subject to the authority of the umpire-in-chief. If such local substitute umpires are not available, the managers of the contending teams shall each choose one player from the other team who is not in the starting line-up, and the two players thus selected shall act as base umpires, subject to the authority of the umpire-in-chief.

(c) If the assigned umpires or local substitute umpires arrive after a game has started with player-umpires officiating under the terms of Rule 15.2(a) or 15.2(b), such umpires shall take over their assigned duties, relieving the player-umpires.

Judgment Decisions 9.02 (a) Any umpire's decision which involves judgment, such as, but not limited to, whether a batted ball is fair or foul, whether a pitch is a strike or a ball, or whether a runner is safe or out, is final. No player, manager, coach or substitute shall object to any such judgment decisions.

> (a) Players leaving their position in the field or on base, or managers or coaches leaving the bench or coaches box, to argue on BALLS AND STRIKES will not be permitted. They should be warned if they start for the plate to protest the call. If they continue, they will be ejected from the game.

(b) If there is reasonable doubt that any umpire's decision may be in conflict with the rules, the manager may appeal the decision and ask that a correct ruling be made. Such appeal shall be made only to the umpire who made the protested decision.

Consulting Another Umpire (c) If a decision is appealed, the umpire making the decision may ask another umpire for information before making a final decision. No umpire shall criticize, seek to reverse or interfere with another umpire's decision unless asked to do so by the umpire making it.

> (c) The manager or the catcher may request the plate umpire to ask his partner for help on a half swing when the plate umpire calls the pitch a ball, but not when the pitch is called a strike. The manager may not complain that the umpire made an improper call, but only that he did not ask his partner for help. Field umpires must be alerted to the request from the plate umpire and quick-

ly respond. Managers may not protest the call of a ball or strike on the pretense they are asking for information about a half swing.

Appeals on a half swing may be made only on the call of ball and when asked to appeal, the home plate umpire must refer to a base umpire for his judgment on the half swing. Should the base umpire call the pitch a strike, the strike call shall prevail. Baserunners must be alert to the possibility that the base umpire on appeal from the plate umpire may reverse the call of a ball to the call of a strike, in which event the runner is in jeopardy of being out by the catcher's throw. Also, a catcher must be alert in a base stealing situation if a ball call is reversed to a strike by the base umpire upon appeal from the plate umpire.

The ball is in play on appeal on a half swing.

On a half swing, if the manager comes out to argue with first or third base umpire and if after being warned he persists in arguing, he can be ejected as he is now arguing over a called ball or strike.

(d) No umpire may be replaced during a game unless he is injured or becomes ill.

CHECKED SWING APPEALS

An appeal may be made when the umpire calls a pitch a ball on a checked swing. In such an instance the umpire shall make an immediate call but must appeal to the appropriate base umpire if requested by the defensive team. The plate umpire may—on his own volition—ask for help from the appropriate base umpire if in doubt on a checked swing.

UMPIRES' JUDGMENT
(No appeals allowed)

There shall be no appeal from any decision of the umpire on the ground that he was not correct in his conclusion as to whether a batted ball was fair or foul, a base-runner safe or out, a pitched ball a strike or a ball, or any other play involving accuracy of judgment; and no decision rendered by him shall be reversed, except that he be convinced that it is in violation of one of the rules.

EXCEPTION:

No manager, player or coach will be permitted to leave the bench (nor can the coach leave his position on the coaching lines) to question an umpire's decision on the calling of balls and strikes. For violation of this rule, the manager, player or coach will be removed from the game.

The Umpire

HALF SWING

The manager or the catcher (but not the pitcher) may request the plate umpire to ask his partner for help on a half swing when the plate umpire **calls the pitch a ball,** but not when the pitch is called a strike. The manager may not complain that the umpire made an improper call, but only that he did not ask his partner for help. Field umpires must be alert to the request from the plate umpire and quickly respond. If the batter is entitled to run on third strike, request should be made instantly. Managers may not protest the call of a ball or strike on the pretense they are asking for information about a half swing.

Calls by umpires on half swings shall be made vocally only by saying "ball" or "strike" and not by commenting, "He didn't swing. He didn't go around," etc. Such comments may lead to confusion on the part of the hitter.

Appeals on a half swing may be made only on the call of ball and when asked to appeal, the home plate umpire must refer to a base umpire for his judgment on the half swing. Should the base umpire call the pitch a strike, the strike call shall prevail.

Baserunners must be alert to the possibility that the base umpire on appeal from the plate umpire may reverse the call of a ball to the call of a strike, in which event the runner is in jeopardy of being put out by the catcher's throw. Also, a catcher must be alert in a base stealing situation if a ball call is reversed to a strike by the base umpire upon appeal from the plate umpire. Managers or coaches may not go onto the field to protest the base umpires responsive call on a half swing. A checked swing on an attempted bunt may not be protested.

The ball is in play on appeal on a half swing.

Jurisdiction of the Umpire 9.03

(a) If there is only one umpire, he shall have complete jurisdiction in administering the rules. He may take any position on the playing field which will enable him to discharge his duties (usually behind the catcher, but sometimes behind the pitcher if there are runners).

(b) If there are two or more umpires, one shall be designated umpire-in-chief and the others field umpires.

Umpire-In-Chief 9.04

(a) The umpire-in-chief shall stand behind the catcher. (He usually is called the plate umpire.) His duties shall be to:

  (1) Take full charge of, and be responsible for, the proper conduct of the game;

  (2) Call and count balls and strike;

  (3) Call and declare fair balls and fouls except those commonly called by field umpires;

  (4) Make all decisions on the batter;

(5) Make all decisions except those commonly reserved for the field umpires;

(6) Decide when a game shall be forfeited;

(7) If a time limit has been set, announce the fact and the time set before the game starts;

(8) Inform the official scorer of the official batting order, and any changes in the lineups and batting order, on request;

(9) Announce any special ground rules, at his discretion.

Field Umpires

(b) A field umpire may take any position on the playing field he thinks best suited to make impending decisions on the bases. His duties shall be to:

(1) Make all decisions on the bases except those specifically reserved to the umpire-in-chief;

(2) Take concurrent jurisdiction with the umpire-in-chief in calling "Time," balks, illegal pitches, or defacement or discoloration of the ball by any player.

(3) Aid the umpire-in-chief in every manner in enforcing the rules, and excepting the power to forfeit the game, shall have equal authority with the umpire-in-chief in administering and enforcing the rules and maintaining discipline.

Final Determination

(c) If different decisions should be made on one play by different umpires, the umpire-in-chief shall call all the umpires into consultation, with no manager or player present. After consultation, the umpire-in-chief (unless another umpire may have been designated by the league president) shall determine which decision shall prevail, based on which umpire was in best position and which decision was most likely correct. Play shall proceed as if only the final decision had been made.

WORKING AGREEMENT

1. We will position the second base umpire inside at all times even with two out, and then allow the individual crew chiefs two options as to how they want to cover fly balls;

(1) by sending the second base umpire positioned in the middle of the infield, or

(2) by sending the "wing umpire" (1st or 3rd base umpires).

EXCEPTION: With a runner on second only or runners on 2nd

and 3rd the second base umpire may work behind the runner on the third base side only.

REASON: In the event of a line drive or possible trapped ball, this system presents less movement. If a line drive should occur and the third base umpire goes out, this system now prevents the plate umpire from covering 3rd or 2nd base umpire sliding over to take a play. Again, this is the only exception to our working agreement. At all other times the second base umpire will remain inside. this is contingent upon the crew chief's discretion.

2. NO RUNNERS ON BASE—The 2nd base umpire is behind 2nd base and has the responsibility of the entire outfield, except for the ball hit down the foul lines for a fair or foul ruling. Remember that when an umpire goes out you revert to a three-man system.

3. RUNNER ON FIRST BASE—The 2nd base umpire will be positioned in the infield for a possible steal or force play. On fly balls to the outfield, however, the 2nd base umpire may proceed to the outfield to render a decision with the remaining umpires reverting to the three-man system.

EXCEPTION: On fly balls or line drives that force the left or right fielder in or out, the 3rd and 1st base umpires will proceed to the outfield to make the decision. The 3rd and 1st base umpires will proceed to the outfield to make the decision.the 3rd and 1st base umpires will also render all decisions on balls hitting or near the foul lines. If the 3rd base umpire has proceeded to the outfield, decisions at 3rd base and home plate will be rendered by the home plate and 1st base umpires respectively.

The crew chief may choose to use option (2) where the 1st and 3rd base umpires split the responsibilities for the decisions in the outfield. The 3rd base umpire has responsibility from center field to the left field line, and the 1st base umpire is responsible from center field to the right field line. In these cases the 2nd base umpire will slide over to cover possible plays depending on which "wing umpire" (1st or 3rd) goes out, or rotate depending on the crew chief's preference.

4. RUNNERS ON FIRST AND THIRD—Same two options as above with the exception being on option (1) on any routine fly from center to the left field line the 2nd base umpire (who is positioned in the infield) will go out to make a decision on the catch. The 1st base umpire has the responsibility of any plays at 1st and 2nd. Using this option (1) the only time the 3rd base umpire would go out is if the play looks like the left fielder is coming in to make a shoestring catch (a trap ball) or when the 3rd base umpire has to make a fair or foul ruling on a ball down the line. If the 3rd base umpire goes out, the plate umpire has the responsibility for the tag up at 3rd or a play at 3rd. If there is a possibility of a play at 3rd, then the 1st base umpire must go home for a possible play.

With runners on 1st and 3rd and less than two outs, the 1st base umpire will proceed to the outfield and make the decision on all balls hit from center field to right field. If the ball is hit in the are from center field to left field the 2nd base umpire will proceed to the outfield to render the decision.

IF THE FIRST BASE UMPIRE GOES OUT for any reason, the 2nd base umpire must hustle into the infield to make a decision at 2nd or 1st. The plate umpire can help in certain situations. IF THE THIRD BASE UMPIRE GOES OUT to make a decision on a fair or foul ball or on a catch, the plate umpire must come up to cover 3rd and the 1st base umpire must drift toward home.

THERE ARE SITUATIONS such as a man on 2nd with less than two outs when we allow the 1st base umpire to go out from center to the right field line so the 2nd base umpire can position himself to watch for the possible tag at 2nd base.

5. When the second base umpire is positioned behind second base, he has responsibility for all the outfield plays, EXCEPT FOR FAIR AND FOUL DECISIONS DOWN THE LINE OR CATCHES ON THE LINE. (When the second base umpire goes out, always revert to the three-man system.)

UMPIRE IN CHIEF

The Umpire In Chief is the umpire working the plate. He is in charge of the game and shall be responsible for conduct of the game under Official Playing Rule 9.04 (a).

The Umpire In Chief shall be the sole judge of fitness of the playing field for resumption of play after "time" is called and play suspended because of weather conditions, or other unusual circumstances that could result in a forfeiture, such as inadequate crowd control, etc.

Between games of a double-header, or whenever a game is suspended because of unfitness of the playing field, the Umpire In Chief shall have control of ground keepers and assistants for the purpose of making the field suitable for play.

Every member of the American league staff is qualified as a Major League umpire and when he acts as Umpire In Chief, he will assume all the responsibilities attendant upon that assignment; particularly the calling off of a game because of weather conditions, or the supervision of the ground crew in getting the field into shape to continue a game that has been halted by rain.

CREW CHIEF

Each umpiring crew shall have a crew chief. The crew chief shall intervene and assist in the resolution of any problem.

CREW CHIEFS

Crew Chiefs are supervisors of their team and the League office will work through them in their responsibilities of generally supervising the work of the umpires assigned to their team.

The League President will designate crew chiefs and if the crew chief is unable to work for any reason, the President shall name a temporary crew chief. During the vacation of a crew chief, the League President will designate which member of the crew will assume the responsibilities of the crew chief.

The crew chief shall, when he is the plate umpire, assume all the duties of the "umpire-in-chief" as shown in Rule 9.04(a):

In addition, he shall, whether plate umpire or base umpire:

1. Rotate the umpires, including himself, so that two umpires are in the stands near the playing field one hour and thirty minutes before the starting time of the game to

observe that "fraternizing" does not occur between members of the opposing teams and that players do not bunt toward the stands after the gates are opened.

2. **Enforce League rule prohibiting visitors in umpires' dressing room.**

3. Check with the ground keeper to determine where he will be located in the event it is necessary to bring out the ground crew to cover the field or to turn on the lights.

4. Check with the plate umpire to be certain he rubs the proper number of baseballs for the game.

5. Make final decision in case of conflicting decisions on one play, as provided in Rule 9.04(c) and League instructions (even though he may have made one of the conflicting decisions).

6. Approve with the plate umpire the final calling of any game. When anyone but the crew chief is working at home plate he shall (by signal) ask crew chief working the bases before suspending play because of weather.

7. Discuss controversial matters with the press, radio and television representatives as covered in umpire instructions.

8. Give approval before any game may be forfeited.

9. Encourage and require a review of each day's work after each game or before the start of the next game and encourage periodic reviews and discussions of rules either at hotel or at the park. This helps to generate a strong team spirit.

10. Generally supervise the work of other umpires on his team and put particular emphasis on having uniformity in dealing with situations which arise so that all members of his team will, insofar as possible, handle ejections of players, bench jockeying, as uniformly as possible.

11. Be certain that the second base umpire has a stop watch with him to apply the 20 second rule.

12. When an umpire is assigned to "fill in" temporarily in another crew due to injury or illness, this umpire shall start work at third base unless directed otherwise by the League office. Umpires called up from the minor leagues as vacation replacements will always begin their assignments at third base.

WORKING ON INFIELD WITH MEN ON BASES

The second base umpire will take his position on the infield grass inside the baseline with runners on first, first and second, on second base only, or with bases full. Only when there is no runner on base or a runner on third base is the umpire to take his position behind the skinned part of the infield at second base.

In addition, umpires shall position themselves in fair territory in calling plays at first base unless the play develops so quickly that an umpire cannot comfortably arrive in this position. **The calling of all plays in foul territory at first base is not the proper mechanics for National League umpires when time permits the umpire to get into fair territory to make his call.**

Umpires are not to drift into the outfield when routine fly balls are hit in these areas, This instruction is particularly to be followed when there are runners on base.

These instructions cannot regulate the "proper position" for all plays, but you are advised to move quickly and alertly to the proper position on each call. To lag in attaining a good position brings on trouble. We hear more criticism about the position of an umpire on a call than any other complaint, and that is the reason we are urging you to work on a good position on all base calls.

Reporting 9.05 (a) The umpire shall report to the league president within twelve
Violations hours after the end of a game all violations of rules and other
incidents worthy of comment, including the disqualification
of any trainer, manager, coach or player, and the reasons
therefore.

(b) When any trainer, manager, coach or player is disqualified for
a flagrant offense such as the use of obscene or indecent
language, or an assault upon an umpire, trainer, manager,
coach or player, the umpire shall forward full particulars to
the league president within four hours after the end of the
game.

Penalties (c) After receiving the umpire's report that a trainer, manager,
coach or player has been disqualified, the league president
shall impose such penalty as he deems justified, and shall
notify the person penalized and the manager of the club of
which the penalized person is a member. If the penalty
includes a fine, the penalized person shall pay the amount of
the fine to the league within five days after receiving notice
of the fine. Failure to pay such fine within five days shall
result in the offender being debarred from participation in
any game and from sitting on the players' bench during any
game, until the fine is paid.

General GENERAL INSTRUCTIONS TO UMPIRES
Instructions

Umpires, on the field, should not indulge in conversation with
players. Keep out of the coaching box and do not talk to the
coach on duty.

Keep your uniform in good condition. Be active and alert on the
field.

Be courteous, always, to club officials; avoid visiting in club
offices and thoughtless familiarity with officers or employees of
contesting clubs. When you enter a ball park your sole duty is to
umpire a ball game as the representative of baseball.

Do not allow criticism to keep you from studying out bad situations that may lead to protested games. Carry your rule book. It is
better to consult the rules and hold up the game ten minutes to
decide a knotty problem than to have a game thrown out on
protest and replayed.

Keep the game moving. A ball game is often helped by energetic
and earnest work of the umpires.

You are the only official representative of baseball on the ball field. It is often a trying position which requires the exercise of much patience and good judgment, but do not forget that the first essential in working out of a bad situation is to keep your own temper and self-control.

You no doubt are going to make mistakes, but never attempt to "even up" after having made one. Make all decisions as you see them and forget which is the home or visiting club.

Keep your eye everlastingly on the ball while it is in play. It is more vital to know just where a fly ball fell, or a thrown ball finished up, than whether or not a runner missed a base. Do not call the plays too quickly, or turn away too fast when a fielder is throwing to complete a double play. Watch out for dropped balls after you have called a man out.

Do not come running with your arm up or down, denoting "out" or "safe." Wait until the play is completed before making any arm motion.

Each umpire team should work out a simple set of signals, so the proper umpire can always right a manifestly wrong decision when convinced he has made an error. If sure you got the play correctly, do not be stampeded by players' appeals to "ask the other man." If not sure, ask one of your associates. Do not carry this to extremes, be alert and get your own plays. But remember! The first requisite is to get decisions correctly. If in doubt don't hesitate to consult your associate. Umpire dignity is important but never as important as "being right."

A most important rule for umpires is always "BE IN POSITION TO SEE EVERY PLAY." Even though your decision may be 100% right, players still question it if they feel you were not in a spot to see the play clearly and definitely. Finally, be courteous, impartial and firm, and so compel respect from all.

UNWARRANTED ATTACK ON FIELD

A player guilty of an unwarranted attack on another player is subject to discipline and may be fined, suspended, or suspended without pay.

Any player who deliberately throws a bat or other object with the intention of engaging in any physical attack or other violence upon any player, manager, coach or umpire during or in connection with any game, shall be subject to suspension without salary or a fine, or both, as the case may warrant, in the judgment of the League President.

PROCEDURE FOR REPORTING TROUBLE

When an umpire has any difficulty on the field, involving removal of a player, he must wire League Headquarters full details immediately after the game and follow this wire with a full, written report by special delivery or air mail, when possible. When the trouble is serious all members of the crew working in that game must make a report on the occurrence in the same manner.

Anything that is **not** "routine" should be called into the League Office the morning after the occurrence. The identical report should then be mailed to the League Office. Extreme care should be taken in preparing the reports as they may be made available to the Players Association.

In case the incident is very offensive, all umpires should file reporters in the same manner.

FRATERNIZATION

Umpires must not carry on idle conversations with coaches or players during the progress of a championship game, or with other umpires unless proper officiating of the game requires it.

DEPORTMENT

Skillful mechanics are of primary importance but good deportment is also essential, and basic judgment of an umpire will include consideration of his attitude and disposition and the respect he commands from those playing and observing the game for his demeanor and its effect on his ability to "handle", the game. Each umpire should frequently ponder his way and manner of doing his job and diligently strive for improvement.

The following maxims have been applied with success for many years and are still considered sound:

1. Cooperate with the other umpires working with you. Help each other. Don't hesitate to ask for assistance from each other if you are blocked on a play. The main objective is to have all decisions ultimately correct.

2. Keep all personalities out of your work. You must be able to forgive and forget. Every game is a new game.

3. Avoid sarcasm. Don't insist on the last word. If, after an argument, a player is walking away—let him go!

4. Never charge a player, or follow him if he is moving away—and no pointing your finger or violent gestures during an argument.

5. As concerns umpiring, there is a very old adage and a wise one:— "Hear only the things you should hear—be deaf to the others."

6. Keep your temper. A decision or an action taken in anger is never sound.

7. Watch your language! For an umpire to act or use, toward a player, coach or manager, language which, if used toward the umpire, would result in the player, coach or manager being disciplined—will not be condoned.

8. If the manager or captain has a legitimate point to argue under the rules, it is your duty to listen to him. An umpire can do this with dignity and no loss of respect. **Be understanding**—remember, the players are engaged in a heated contest. You are impartial judges and should **maintain a calm dignity** becoming the authority you have.

9. Review your work after every game. Only by self examination will you improve.

CONDUCT

Any umpire who shall bet any sum whatsoever upon any baseball game in connection with which the bettor has no duty to perform, shall be declared ineligible for one year.

Any umpire who shall bet any sum whatsoever upon any baseball game in connection with which the bettor has a duty to perform shall be declared permanently ineligible.

If an umpire is contacted either in person or by telephone by anyone outside the baseball framework for the purpose of influencing him to do an improper act that would affect the outcome of a game, he shall advise the League President immediately of this conversation. Umpires must not comment on physical conditions of ball players, such as a player has a sore arm, or sprained ankle, or reveal any information to outsiders that might be helpful in "betting" on the outcome of the game. Umpires must be alert to these possibilities.

ON GIFTS TO UMPIRES

Any player or person connected with a Club, who shall give, or offer to give, any gift or reward to an umpire for services rendered or supposed to be or to have been rendered, in defeating or attempting to defeat a competing Club, or for the umpire's decision on anything connected with the playing of a baseball game; and any umpire who shall render, or promise or agree to render, any such decision otherwise than on its merits, or who shall solicit or accept such gift or reward for any such service or decision or who, having been offered any such gifts or reward, or having been solicited to render any such decision otherwise than on its merits, shall fail to inform the League President or the Commissioner

immediately of such offer or solicitation, and all facts and circumstances connected there with, shall be declared permanently ineligible.

CALL PLAYS DECISIVELY

Call all plays decisively, but not too quickly. If decisions are not called too quickly, there will be very little reason to reverse a decision but sometimes this may be necessary. If an umpire is blocked out and his partner has a better view of the play, the umpire should solicit his partner's help to make sure the play is called correctly. The main objective is to have all decisions ultimately correct.

An umpire should call plays decisively enough so they are clearly indicated to coaches, players and fans alike. The safe call should be clearly distinctive from the out call, and out calls are best understood when an umpire raises a closed fist above his head. The proper verbal calls to be used to avoid confusion are "safe", or "out", "ball" or "strike". Do not say "yes" or "no" or other words that might confuse the players. Increased TV coverage and larger stadiums require umpires to leave no doubt in the fan's mind that the player is out or safe.

Do not call plays at the bases hurriedly. This rushes your timing and rhythm. Be certain that the runner is safe or out before you call the play.

The main objective is to have all decisions ultimately correct. It will not be the correct call if the first baseman comes off the bag before he catches the ball, or the baseman on a double play at second base comes off the bag or has not reached the bag before he has caught the relay throw. Your instructions are to get these plays right.

When a pitch hits the batter after hitting his bat, the umpire shall indicate

clearly and decisively that it was a foul tip.

When a batter is awarded first base because of being hit with a pitched ball or for catcher's interference, point decisively to first base, leaving no doubt that the batter is awarded first base.

INDICATING FAIR OR FOUL BALLS

Batted balls hit down the foul lines should be called in a very decisive manner as follows: If the umpire is facing the plate when the call is made, foul balls will be called by throwing hands up in the air to indicate a halt in play, then pointing toward foul territory with the left arm if on the right field line and the right arm if on the left field line. If the umpire has his back to the plate when the call is made, **throw hands up in the air to indicate a halt in play, then point toward foul territory with the right arm on the right field line and with the left arm if on the left field line.** Do not cross your body with your arm in calling fair or foul balls. In calling fair balls, the arm motion is just the opposite as it is when foul balls are called. Give your signal decisively and yell fair or foul ball so that the fielder can hear as he chases the ball.

Batted balls hit out of the park near the foul lines should also be called very decisively, so there can be no question about the umpire's decision on the play. Umpires should move down the line when balls are hit almost to or over the fence near the foul lines.

Umpires are cautioned to judge balls hit for distance directly down the foul lines fair or foul as the ball passes the point where the outfield fence or barrier and the foul pole join. The umpires are not to judge the ball fair or foul before it reaches this point unless it is obvious that the ball will land foul.

The home plate umpire shall decide whether any bunted ball or any slowly hit ball is fair or foul between home plate and first or third base. The base umpire shall decide whether any batted ball is fair or foul after it passes first or third base. The base umpire shall also decide whether any line drive or hard hit balls are fair or foul, whether it be between home plate and first or third, or beyond first or third base. The umpire should clearly signal that it is a fair or a foul ball.

NO VISITORS

Umpire Rooms. No visitors shall be permitted at any time in the umpires' dressing rooms. The term "visitors" shall include club officers and employees, newspaper, radio and television representatives, photographers, friends, relatives and ex-umpires. No one except the umpires, League officers, members of Baseball Commissioner's staff and the clubhouse attendant assigned to the umpires' room shall be permitted in these rooms before, during or after a ball game. <u>There are no exceptions to this rule.</u> The umpire crew chief shall be responsible for its enforcement, and for reporting any violations to the President.

Clubhouse and Bench. No persons shall be admitted to the team clubhouse or permitted to enter or visit the bench except accredited photographers and accredited representatives of the press, radio and television. Such authorized visitors shall not be permitted in the dugout during a game. The League has furnished each club with printed copies of League Rule 8, and the clubs shall keep a copy posted in the umpires' rooms, in the home and visitors' clubhouses and in the home and visitors' dugouts.

TICKET REQUESTS

Each umpire may request a maximum of four reserved seats each day for use by his immediate family **and** two reserve seats each for use by his friends or relatives (not immediate family).

KEEP THE GAME MOVING

Players, managers, and coaches have the primary responsibility of keeping the action alive and moving in the game. The delivery by the pitcher, batters in the box ready to hit, managers quickly changing pitchers, teams changing sides rapidly all speed up the time of the games. Umpires, too, have the responsibility of keeping the action alive in the game. The fans do not want dead spots. The following procedures shall be in effect:

Whether or not a ball remains in play is up to be sole judgment of the umpire.

Likewise, the umpire has the final judgment of whether the batter may step out of the batter's box.

Pinch hitters should be on the benches when called upon to substitute for another batter. Only two catchers and a staff of relief pitchers will be allowed in the bull pen. If a club has only one catcher, another player—either an infielder or outfielder—may be allowed in the bull pen.

When the catcher is the next batter, he shall have his shin-guards off when he enters the on-deck circle.

All batters, including pitchers, are required to be in the on-deck circle when it is their turn to bat. A substitute player about to enter the game may warm up in the bull pen.

Umpires shall deliver a new ball to the catcher or directly to the pitcher. The toss should be accurate. Coaches should throw foul balls directly back to the pitcher.

"Time" should not be called during any play where further action in that play appears possible, unless in the umpire's judgment, a particular situation requires "Time" being called. "Time" should not be called when the so-called "hidden ball" trick is being attempted.

CONVERSATION WITH CREW AND PLAYERS

Umpires are requested not to make "social visits" to other crew members unless the conversation actually affects the playing of the day's game. There is absolutely too much conversation between the umpires, and these talks must be minimized to official business.

Umpires have been criticized by club management because they talk with the ball players or coaches. The clubs' protests are valid when such conversations are made while the ball is in play. It is difficult for the League office to ask the players not to fraternize and then the umpires absorb the players' time talking with them.

HITTER MOVING TOWARD PITCHER

Any player who charges the mound—that is, runs to the mound with the intention of challenging or fighting with the pitcher—**shall be automatically ejected from the game** and a fine will be assessed in such instances, case by case. Any instances of a hitter moving toward a pitcher and **retaining his bat as he moves will be the subject of severe disciplinary action** and should be reported immediately by the umpires to the League Office.

PUBLIC ADDRESS ANNOUNCER

League rules require the public address announcer to make all announcements which are directed by the plate umpire pertaining to the lineups and the Official Playing and

League Rules. The public address announcer shall make such announcements immediately as directed by the umpire.

It is of the utmost importance that the clubs give the patrons who attend ball games as much information as they can about what goes on in a game, because the radio and TV announcers are giving the non-paying "at home" fan detailed information. Umpires can help by giving the public address announcer full information on any decisions made on unusual plays, so the announcer can give the information to the fans.

All this is designed to help keep the fans informed.

The home club should notify the umpires whom to contact near the playing surface (coach, trainer, public address announcer, etc.), who can then transmit the information to someone to notify the media and the public.

RULES SECTION

The Official Playing Rules, League Rules and these Umpire Instructions and bulletins issued by the League President shall govern the playing of all National League games.

All umpires should understand these Rules and Instructions and any differences in interpretation between umpires should be resolved between them before the playing of a championship game.

A thorough knowledge of the Rules and a common sense application is expected of all umpires. Consistency in performance should be an individual goal and a staff objective.

LIMITATIONS ON VISITORS

Umpires' Rooms. No visitors shall be permitted at any time in the umpires' dressing rooms. The term visitors shall include club officers and employees, newspaper, radio and television representatives, photographers, friends and relatives. No one save the umpires, League officers and the clubhouse attendant assigned to the umpires' room shall be permitted to these rooms before, during or after a ball game. There are no exceptions to this rule. The umpire team captain shall be responsible for its enforcement, and for reporting any violations to the President.

Additional American League and National League Guidelines for Umpires

PLAYER-UMPIRE PHOTOGRAPHS AND ENDORSEMENTS

Under American League Resolutions, no player, manager or umpire shall permit his picture in uniform to be published in connection with the sponsorship or advertising of any medical, tobacco, or alcoholic product. Any player, manager or umpire who violates this rule shall be subject to penalty.

TICKET ALLOWANCE

Upon request to Traveling Secretary:

Each player and coach will be allowed 4 reserve seats for his immediate family free of all service charges.

Each player and coach will also be allowed 2 daily reserved seats free of all service charges. Provisions have been made to allow each umpire not more than six (6) reserved seats per game.

BASEBALL PROMOTION

In addition to his services in connection with the actual playing of baseball, the player agrees to cooperate with the club and participate in any and all promotional activities of the club and its League, which, in the opinion of the club, will promote the welfare of the club or professional baseball, and to observe and comply with all requirements of the club respecting conduct and service of its team and its players, at all times, whether on or off the field.

PAYMENT OF FINES

Any fine assessed by the President of the American League against any manager, player, scorer or other employee must be paid personally by the manager, player, scorer, or employee and under no circumstances is the fine to be refunded to the manager, player, scorer or employee by any club. If any club reimburses any manager, player, scorer or other employee for any fine, then the club making such reimbursement shall be assessed a sum of not over five thousand dollars ($5,000).

In any instance wherein a fine or suspension is imposed upon a manager, coach, or player, notification of action by the League President shall not be released to the press, etc., until ample time has been given for notification of the manager, coach, or player involved.

Any fines assessed by the League President must be paid within ten days (10) of notification or the manager, coach, or player shall be eligible for suspension.

A manager, coach, or player fined or suspended by the League President may request a hearing by the President, and such request shall be granted in all instances.

SMOKING

Once gates are open, players must not smoke in view of public. After a warning, violators should be reported.

CONTRACT

Clubs and players will abide by the provisions and regulations of the Uniform Players' Contract.

BASIC AGREEMENT

Clubs and players will be guided by the articles and provisions of the Basic Agreement between the American and National Leagues and the Major League Baseball Players Association relating to scheduling, salaries, expenses and allowances, termination pay, post season play, grievances, and other matters covered therein.

ORGANS/AUDIO

Clubs should instruct their organists not to play when the ball is about to be put in play. The organ should stop playing as soon as the hitter is in the batter's box and the pitcher is on the rubber.

AUDIO: All music, chants, noise, cheers, etc. should cease when the batter initially steps into the batter's box. Music, noise, messages, exhortations, etc. can be used at the following times:

1. Before the start of the game
2. Between innings
3. During pitching changes
4. As the batter is proceeding toward the batter's box
5. After the game has ended.

SCOREBOARD GUIDELINES

Scoreboards, particularly with TV replay capabilities, should not be used in a manner which might incite fan violence, intentionally reflect upon the judgment call of an umpire or denigrate the visiting club, visiting club officials or official scorers. The home club is responsible for the requisite monitoring of its scoreboard operation and shall abide by any guidelines or directives issued by the League Office.

Listed below are the guidelines and regulations to be followed by the operators of your video boards and sound systems. These entities should be operated for the enjoyment and interest of your fans and should not be used to incite crowds or distract players. These guidelines and regulations also apply to the television monitors that can be viewed by the spectators.

(a) The video boards and monitors should not be used to display replays of controversial plays that could reflect on the judgment of the umpire. Such replays can incite the crowd.

    1. Replays of balls and strikes are prohibited.

    2. Close plays that could cause a club (either home or visitor) to argue or harass the umpire and hence affect crowd behavior should not be shown.

    3. The video screens should not be used when the batter is in the batter's box. Preferably the screen should be blank so that there is no chance of distracting the hitter.

    4. If there is any doubt as to whether or not a replay be shown, don't show it.

(b) Any fights involving uniformed personnel or fans should not be shown.

(c) Any episode or event that could denigrate an umpire, visiting club members, visiting club officials, or official scorers should not be displayed.

(d) Do not display the likenesses of the umpires nor use their names in any way to embarrass them.

(e) Do not show fans running on the field or display them if they are inappropriately dressed or drinking alcoholic beverages.

(f) Live game action is not to be shown. Close-ups of the batter while in the on-deck circle are permitted, but when the batter initially steps into the batter's box, all live action must cease. A blank screen, still shots, statistics, or other non-moving pictures may be shown until the batter finishes his turn at bat. Batters hitting home runs can be shown as they circle the bases.

(g) Arguments between umpires and players should never be shown.

(h) Live shots of fans are permitted, but good judgment should be employed. Don't show fans doing anything that does not conform to acceptable behavior.

NO VISITORS IN DRESSING ROOM

No visitors are permitted in the Umpires' Dressing Room.

If visitors should be present, they must leave 15 minutes before the start of the game or sooner, if the crew chief wishes.

There should also be a 15-minute cooling off period after the game.

Note the Commissioner's rules for security in the clubhouses. All umpires will adhere to them without exception. Immediate family will be allowed to visit the clubhouse at the previously stated time, which is up to 30 minutes before game time. Immediate family is defined as

grandfather, father, brothers, sons. If the home team has special rules covering visitors and immediate family and a common entrance is used both personnel and umpires, then the umpires must adhere to the special regulations of the home club in addition to the Commissioner's regulations.

All playing fields, dugouts, clubhouses and related facilities and areas are off-limits to all but essential personnel. This applies to facilities for both home and visiting clubs and to all spring training, exhibition, All-Star, regular season and post-season games and club practices.

The application of this rule and related concerns shall be as follows:

(a) The areas of limited access shall include the following: playing fields, dugouts, clubhouses, managers' offices, shower rooms, trainers and doctors' rooms, players' lounges, video, weight or exercise rooms, laundry and equipment rooms and umpires' dressing rooms. Clubs are free to designate other limited access areas or restrictions.

(b) Only the following groups shall be granted full or partial access to the areas listed above: players, representatives of the Players Association, managers, coaches, umpires and their union representatives, trainers, team physicians, accredited media, appropriate club, league and central office officials and employees and those persons necessary for the normal conduct of club operations (e.g., clubhouse attendants, equipment men, security personnel). Immediate family members are also permitted if approved by the club.

Each club is to clearly post its policy on immediate family access and provide a copy to all players, employees

and to the Office of the Commissioner. Other groups or persons (e.g., special guests on Old Timer's Days, Baseball Chapel, etc.), where appropriate and with the prior approval of the club, will be allowed access to restricted areas on a limited basis.

These areas are accordingly closed to all other individuals including friends, business associates, agents, attorneys, equipment salesmen or other vendors, unauthorized doctors or therapists, etc. Where possible, clubs should minimize the need for delivery of equipment, food and supplies to clubhouses while in use by players.

(c) Enforcement of these provisions is the responsibility of each club's general manager, field manager and security director or stadium operations manager. A copy of this notice is to be distributed to all uniformed personnel plus other appropriate club personnel and posted in each clubhouse. All individuals responsible for clubhouse access control **must** be familiar with this notice and be aware that NO EXCEPTIONS ARE PERMITTED.

A security guard, familiar with these regulations and authorized credentials, should be posted at each clubhouse entrance when in use prior to, during and after games and practices. Each entrance door to any restricted area should have a sign posted clearly stating that entrance is limited to players and authorized club personnel only. Other security checkpoints should also be reviewed so as to stop unauthorized personnel at the earliest possible time.

(d) Clubs are hereby advised to continue enforcement of the rule prohibiting public telephones in any of these restricted areas.

(e) All clubs are to undertake a careful review of their policies with

respect to team travel. Only appropriate club personnel, player, immediate family members and accredited and authorized media should ordinarily utilize chartered air or bus services. Friends, associates, agents, attorneys, etc. should not be transported by charter. Further, club personnel should not make any hotel, bus or commercial flight arrangements for these persons without the approval of the club's chief operating officer. The Umpire In Chief of that day is responsible for the enforcement of this rule.

BALL PARK FACILITIES

Dressing Rooms. Each club shall provide its park with suitable clubhouses for its own players, for the visiting club's players, and for the umpires. These clubhouses shall be supplied with adequate toilet facilities, hot and cold water, shower baths or shower rooms adequate for the number of men using each clubhouse, uniform driers and sufficient suitable lockers. These clubhouses shall be properly heated and cared for. The visiting players' clubhouse shall be subject to the control of the visiting club during each series.

Public Address Announcer. The public address announcer of each National League park shall, during the progress of the game, make all announcements which are directed by the plate umpire pertaining to lineups and the rules.

Visiting Club's Schedule Responsibility. The visiting club shall arrange to arrive in each city where it is scheduled to play not less than three hours before the scheduled starting time of the first game of a series. The visiting club shall not schedule an arrival which does not conform to this rule without consent of the home club and the approval of the President.

MISCELLANEOUS

Exhibition Games. Any exhibition game played by League clubs, for which an admission is charged, shall be played according to the Official Playing Rules, except that, where other adequate space is not available, players may run in the outfield during the playing of the game provided there is not interference with play.

Restrictions on Use of Photographs. No player, manager, coach, trainer or umpire shall permit the use of his picture in uniform in connection with the advertising or endorsement of any tobacco products (which includes cigarettes, cigars, smoking tobacco, or smokeless tobacco such as snuff, chewing tobacco, etc.) or alcoholic beverages (which includes whiskey, beers, wines, brandies and liquors.

The Official Scorer

10.00   The Official Scorer.

Official Scorer Appointment   10.01   (a)   The league president shall appoint an official scorer for each league championship game. The official scorer shall observe the game from a position in the press box. The scorer shall have sole authority to make all decisions involving judgment, such as whether a batter's advance to first base is the result of a hit or an error. He shall communicate such decisions to the press box and broadcasting booths by hand signals or over the press box loud-speaker system, and shall advise the public address announcer of such decisions if requested.

Scorer Judgement Calls   The Official Scorer must make all decisions concerning judgment calls within twenty-four (24) hours after a game has been officially concluded. No judgment decision shall be changed thereafter except, upon immediate application to the League President, the scorer may request a change, citing the reasons for such. In all cases, the official scorer is not permitted to make a scoring decision which is in conflict with the scoring rules.

After each game, including forfeited and called games, the scorer shall prepare a report, on a form prescribed by the league president, listing the date of the game, where it was played, the names of the competing clubs and the umpires, the full score of the game, and all records of individual players compiled according to the system specified in these Official Scoring Rules. He shall forward this report to the league office within thirty-six hours after the game ends. He shall forward the report of any suspended game within thirty-six hours after the game has been completed, or after it becomes an official game because it cannot be completed, as provided by the Official Playing Rules.

Scorer's Authority   (b)   (1)   To achieve uniformity in keeping the records of championship games, the scorer shall conform strictly to the Official Scoring Rules. The scorer shall have authority to rule on any point not specifically covered in these rules.

(2)   If the teams change sides before three men are put out, the scorer shall immediately inform the umpire of the mistake.

(3)   If the game is protested or suspended, the scorer shall make a note of the exact situation at the time of the protest or suspension, including the score, the number

of outs, the position of any runners, and the ball and strike count on the batter.

> NOTE: It is important that a suspended game resume with exactly the same situation as existed at the time of suspension. If a protested game is ordered replayed from the point of protest, it must be resumed with exactly the situation that existed just before the protested play.

(4) The scorer shall not make any decision conflicting with the Official Playing Rules, or with an umpire's decision.

(5) The scorer shall not call the attention of the umpire or of any member of either team to the fact that a player is batting out of turn.

Respect and Dignity

(c) (1) The scorer is an official representative of the league, and is entitled to the respect and dignity of his office, and shall be accorded full protection by the league president. The scorer shall report to the president any indignity expressed by any manager, player, club employee or club officer in the course of, or as the result of, the discharge of his duties.

RECORDS

Drawn, tie, suspended or postponed games shall not count in the series as games, but must be played off, if possible, as provided in these regu-

lations. The individual performances of players in any game of five or more innings shall be included in the official averages.

Official Scorer Report

10.02 The official score report prescribed by the league president shall make provisions for entering the information listed below, in a form convenient for the compilation of permanent statistical records:

(a) The following records for each batter and runner:

(1) Number of times he batted, except that no time at bat shall be charged against a player when

(i) He hits a sacrifice bunt or sacrifice fly

(ii) He is awarded first base on four called balls

(iii) He is hit by a pitched ball

(iv)   He is awarded first base because of interference or obstruction.

(2)   Number of runs scored

(3)   Number of safe hits

(4)   Number of runs batted in

(5)   Two-base hits

(6)   Three-base hits

(7)   Home runs

(8)   Total bases on safe hits

(9)   Stolen bases

(10)   Sacrifice bunts

(11)   Sacrifice flies

(12)   Total number of bases on balls

(13)   Separate listing of any intentional bases on balls

(14)   Number of times hit by a pitched ball

(15)   Number of times awarded first base for interference or obstruction. (16) Strikeouts

Fielder Records

(b)   The following records for each fielder:

(1)   Number of putouts

(2)   Number of assists

(3)   Number of errors

(4)   Number of double plays participated in

(5)   Number of triple plays participated in

Pitcher Records

(c)   The following records for each pitcher:

(1)   Number of innings pitched.

> NOTE: In computing innings pitched, count each putout as one-third of an inning. If a starting pitcher is replaced with one out in the sixth inning, credit that pitcher with 5 1/3 innings. If a starting pitcher is replaced

with none out in the sixth inning, credit that pitcher with 5 innings, and make the notation that he faced ____ batters in the sixth. If a relief pitcher retires two batters and is replaced, credit that pitcher with 2/3 inning pitched.

(2)   Total number of batters faced

(3)   Number of batters officially at bat against pitcher computed according to 10.02 (a) (1).

(4)   Number of hits allowed

(5)   Number of runs allowed

(6)   Number of earned runs allowed

(7)   Number of home runs allowed

(8)   Number of sacrifice hits allowed

(9)   Number of sacrifice flies allowed

(10)   Total number of bases on balls allowed

(11)   Separate listing of any intentional bases on balls allowed

(12)   Number of batters hit by pitched balls

(13)   Number of strikeouts

(14)   Number of wild pitches

(15)   Number of balks

(d)   The following additional data:

(1)   Name of the winning pitcher

(2)   Name of the losing pitcher

(3)   Names of the starting pitcher and the finishing pitcher for each team.

(4)   Name of pitcher credited with save.

Passed Balls   (e)   Number of passed balls allowed by each catcher.

(f)   Name of players participating in double plays and triple plays.

EXAMPLE: Double Plays—Jones, Roberts and Smith (2). Triple Play—Jones and Smith.

(g) Number of runners left on base by each team. This total shall include all runners who get on base by any means and who do not score and are not put out. Include in this total a batter-runner whose batted ball results in another runner being retired for the third out.

Grand Slam

(h) Names of batters who hit home runs with bases full.

(i) Names of batters who ground into force double plays and reverse force double plays.

(j) Names of runners caught stealing.

(k) Number of outs when winning run scored, if game is won in last half-inning.

(l) The score by innings for each team.

Umpire Names

(m) Names of umpires, listed in this order (1) plate umpire, (2) first base umpire, (3) second base umpire, (4) third base umpire.

(n) Time required to play the game, with delays for weather or light failure deducted.

Player Listing

10.03 (a) In compiling the official score report, the official scorer shall list each player's name and his fielding position or positions in the order in which the player batted, or would have batted if the game ends before he gets to bat.

NOTE: When a player does not exchange positions with another fielder but is merely placed in a different spot for a particular batter, do not list this as a new position.

EXAMPLES: (1) Second baseman goes to the outfield to form a four-man outfield. (2) Third baseman moves to a position between shortstop and second baseman.

(b) Any player who enters the game as a substitute batter or substitute runner, whether or not he continues in the game thereafter, shall be identified in the batting order by a special symbol which shall refer to a separate record of substitute batters and runners. Lower case letters are recommended as symbols for substitute batters, and numerals as symbols for substitute runners. The record of substitute batters shall describe what the substitute batter did.

EXAMPLES—a-Singled for ___ in third inning; b-Flied out for ___ in sixth inning; c-Forced ___ for ___ in seventh inning; d-Grounded out for ___ in ninth inning; 1-Ran for ___ in ninth inning.

The record of substitute batters and runners shall include the name of any such substitute whose name is announced, but who is removed for a second substitute before he actually gets into the game. Such substitution shall be recorded as "e-Announced as substitute for ___ in seventh inning." Any such second substitute shall be recorded as batting or running for the first announced substitute.

HOW TO PROVE A BOX SCORE

Box Score

(c)   A box score is in balance (or proved) when the total of the team's times at bat, bases on balls received, hit batters, sacrifice bunts, sacrifice flies and batters awarded first base because of interference or obstruction equals the total of that team's runs, players left on base and the opposing team's putouts.

WHEN PLAYER BATS OUT OF TURN

Batting Out of Turn

(d)   When a player bats out of turn, and is put out, and the proper batter is called out before the ball is pitched to the next batter, charge the proper batter with a time at bat and score the putout and any assists the same as if the correct batting order had been followed. If an improper batter becomes a runner and the proper batter is called out for having missed his turn at bat, charge the proper batter with a time at bat, credit the putout to the catcher, and ignore everything entering into the improper batter's safe arrival on base. If more than one batter bats out of turn in succession score all plays just as they occur, skipping the turn at bat of the player or players who first missed batting in the proper order.

CALLED AND FORFEITED GAMES

(e)   (1)   If a regulation game is called, include the record of all individual and team actions up to the moment the game ends, as defined in Rules 4.10 and 4.11. If it is a tie game, do not enter a winning or losing pitcher.

        (2)   If a regulation game is forfeited, include the record of all individual and team actions up to the time of forfeit.

If the winning team by forfeit is ahead at the time of forfeit, enter as winning and losing pitchers the players who would have qualified if the game had been called at the time of forfeit. If the winning team by forfeit is behind or if the score is tied at the time of forfeit, do not enter a winning or losing pitcher. If a game is forfeited before it becomes a regulation game, include no records. Report only the fact of the forfeit.

RUNS BATTED IN

Runs Batted In

10.04   (a)   Credit the batter with a run batted in for every run which reaches home base because of the batter's safe hit, sacrifice bunt, sacrifice fly, infield out or fielder's choice; or which is forced over the plate by reason of the batter becoming a runner with the bases full (on a base on balls, or an award of first base for being touched by a pitched ball, or for interference or obstruction).

(1)   Credit a run batted in for the run scored by the batter who hits a home run. Credit a run batted in for each runner who is on base when the home run is hit and who scores ahead of the batter who hits the home run.

(2)   Credit a run batted in for the run scored when, before two are out, an error is made on a play on which a runner from third base ordinarily would score.

(b)   Do not credit a run batted in when the batter grounds into a force double play or a reverse force double play.

(c)   Do not credit a run batted in when a fielder is charged with an error because he muffs a throw at first base which would have completed a force double play.

Scorer's Judgment

(d)   Scorer's judgment must determine whether a run batted in shall be credited for a run which scores when a fielder holds the ball, or throws to a wrong base. Ordinarily, if the runner keeps going, credit a run batted in; if the runner stops and takes off again when he notices the misplay, credit the run as scored on a fielder's choice.

Base Hits

BASE HITS

10.05   A base hit shall be scored in the following cases:

(a)   When a batter reaches first base (or any succeeding base) safely on a fair ball which settles on the ground or touches a fence before being touched by a fielder, or which clears a fence;

(b) When a batter reaches first base safely on a fair ball hit with such force, or so slowly, that any fielder attempting to make a play with it has no opportunity to do so;

> NOTE: A hit shall be scored if the fielder attempting to handle the ball cannot make a play, even if such fielder deflects the ball from or cuts off another fielder who could have put out a runner.

Unnatural Bounce

(c) When a batter reaches first base safely on a fair ball which takes an unnatural bounce so that a fielder cannot handle it with ordinary effort, or which touches the pitcher's plate or any base, (including home plate), before being touched by a fielder and bounces so that a fielder cannot handle it with ordinary effort;

(d) When a batter reaches first base safely on a fair ball which has not been touched by a fielder and which is in fair territory when it reaches the outfield unless in the scorer's judgment it could have been handled with ordinary effort;

(e) When a fair ball which has not been touched by a fielder touches a runner or an umpire. EXCEPTION: Do not score a hit when a runner is called out for having been touched by an Infield Fly;

(f) When a fielder unsuccessfully attempts to put out a preceding runner, and in the scorer's judgment the batter-runner would not have been put out at first base by ordinary effort.

> NOTE: In applying the above rules, always give the batter the benefit of the doubt. A safe course to follow is to score a hit when exceptionally good fielding of a ball fails to result in a putout.

No Base Hits

10.06 A base hit shall not be scored in the following cases:

(a) When a runner is forced out by a batted ball, or would have been forced out except for a fielding error;

(b) When the batter apparently hits safely and a runner who is forced to advance by reason of the batter becoming a runner fails to touch the first base to which he is advancing and is called out on appeal. Charge the batter with a time at bat but no hit;

(c)   When the pitcher, the catcher or any infielder handles a batted ball and puts out a preceding runner who is attempting to advance one base or to return to his original base, or would have put out such runner with ordinary effort except for a fielding error. Charge the batter with a time at bat but no hit;

(d)   When a fielder fails in an attempt to put out a preceding runner, and in the scorer's judgment the batter-runner could have been put out at first base.

> NOTE: This shall not apply if the fielder merely looks toward or feints toward another base before attempting to make the putout at first base;

Runner Interference

(e)   When a runner is called out for interference with a fielder attempting to field a batted ball, unless in the scorer's judgment the batter-runner would have been safe had the interference not occurred.

DETERMINING VALUE OF BASE HITS

Safe Hits   10.07   Whether a safe hit shall be scored as one-base hit, two-base hit, three-base hit or home run when no error or putout results shall be determined as follows:

(a)   Subject to the provisions of 10.07 (b) and (c), it is a one-base hit if the batter stops at first base; it is a two-base hit if the batter stops at second base; it a three-base hit if the batter stops at third base; it is a home run if the batter touches all bases and scores.

(b)   When, with one or more runners on base, the batter advances more than one base on a safe hit and the defensive team makes an attempt to put out a preceding runner, the scorer shall determine whether the batter made a legitimate two-base hit or three-base hit, or whether he advanced beyond first base on the fielder's choice.

> NOTE: Do not credit the batter with a three-base hit when a preceding runner is put out at the plate, or would have been out but for an error. Do not credit the batter with a two-base hit when a preceding runner trying to advance from first base is put out at third base, or would have been out but for an error. However, with the exception of the above, do not determine the value of base-hits by the number of

The Official Scorer

bases advanced by a preceding runner. A batter may deserve a two-base hit even though a preceding runner advances one or no bases; he may deserve only a one-base hit even though he reaches second base and a preceding runner advances two bases.

EXAMPLES: (1) Runner on first, batter hits to right fielder, who throws to third base in unsuccessful attempt to put out runner. Batter takes second base. Credit batter with one-base hit. (2) Runner on second. Batter hits fair fly ball. Runner holds up to determine if ball is caught, and advances only to third base, while batter takes second. Credit batter with two-base hit. (3) Runner on third. Batter hits high fair fly. Runner takes lead, then runs back to tag up, thinking ball will be caught. Ball falls safe, but runner cannot score, although batter has reached second. Credit batter with two-base hit.

Oversliding Base

(c) When the batter attempts to make a two-base hit or a three-base hit by sliding, he must hold the last base to which he advances. If he overslides and is tagged out before getting back to the base safely, he shall be credited with only as many bases as he attained safely. If he overslides second base and is tagged out, he shall be credited with a one-base hit; if he overslides third base and is tagged out, he shall be credited with a two-base hit.

NOTE: If the batter overruns second or third base and is tagged out trying to return, he shall be credited with the last base he touched. If he runs past second base after reaching that base on his feet, attempts to return and is tagged out, he shall be credited with a two-base hit. If he runs past third base after reaching that base on his feet, attempts to return and is tagged out, he shall be credited with a three-base hit.

Last Base Safely Touched

(d) When the batter, after making a safe hit, is called out for having failed to touch a base, the last base he reached safely shall determine if he shall be credited with a one-base hit, a two-base hit or a three-base hit. If he is called out after missing home base, he shall be credited with a three-base hit. If he is called out for missing third base, he shall be credited with a two-base hit. If he is called out for missing second base, he shall be credited with a one-base hit. If he is called out for missing first base, he shall be charged with a time at bat, but no hit.

(e)   When the batter-runner is awarded two bases, three bases or a home run under the provisions of Playing Rules 7.05 or 7.06 (a), he shall be credited with a two-base hit, a three-base hit or a home run, as the case may be.

GAME-ENDING HITS

Game Ending Hits

(f)   Subject to the provisions of 10.07 (g), when the batter ends a game with a safe hit which drives in as many runs as are necessary to put his team in the lead, he shall be credited with only as many bases on his hit as are advanced by the runner who scores the winning run, and then only if the batter runs out his hit for as many bases as are advanced by the runner who scores the winning run.

> NOTE: Apply this rule even when the batter is theoretically entitled to more bases because of being awarded an "automatic" extra-base hit under various provisions of Playing Rules 6.09 and 7.05.

(g)   When the batter ends a game with a home run hit out of the playing field, he and any runners on base are entitled to score.

STOLEN BASES

Stolen Bases

10.08   A stolen base shall be credited to a runner whenever he advances one base unaided by a hit, a putout, an error, a force-out, a fielder's choice, a passed ball, a wild pitch or a balk, subject to the following:

(a)   When a runner starts for the next base before the pitcher delivers the ball and the pitch results in what ordinarily is scored a wild pitch or passed ball, credit the runner with a stolen base and do not charge the misplay. EXCEPTION: If, as a result of the misplay, the stealing runner advances an extra base, or another runner also advances, score the wild pitch or passed ball as well as the stolen base.

Wild Throw

(b)   When a runner is attempting to steal, and the catcher, after receiving the pitch, makes a wild throw trying to prevent the stolen base, credit a stolen base. Do not charge an error unless the wild throw permits the stealing runner to advance one or more extra bases, or permits another runner to advance, in which case credit the stolen base and charge one error to the catcher.

(c)   When a runner, attempting to steal, or after being picked off base, evades being put out in a run-down play and advances to the next base without the aid of an error, credit the runner with a stolen base. If another runner also advances on the play, credit both runners with stolen bases. If a runner advances while another runner, attempting to steal, evades being put out in a run-down play and returns safely, without the aid of an error, to the base he originally occupied, credit a stolen base to the runner who advances.

Double or Triple Steal

(d)   When a double or triple steal is attempted and one runner is thrown out before reaching and holding the base he is attempting to steal, no other runner shall be credited with a stolen base.

(e)   When a runner is tagged out after oversliding a base, while attempting either to return to that base or to advance to the next base, he shall not be credited with a stolen base.

Muffed Throw

(f)   When in the scorer's judgment a runner attempting to steal is safe because of a muffed throw, do not credit a stolen base. Credit an assist to the fielder who made the throw; charge an error to the fielder who muffed the throw, and charge the runner with "caught stealing."

(g)   No stolen base shall be scored when a runner advances solely because of the defensive team's indifference to his advance. Score as a fielder's choice.

Caught Stealing

CAUGHT STEALING

(h)   A runner shall be charged as "Caught Stealing" if he is put out, or would have been put out by errorless play when he

   (1)   Tries to steal.

   (2)   Is picked off a base and tries to advance (any move toward the next base shall be considered an attempt to advance).

   (3)   Overslides while stealing.

> NOTE: In those instances where a pitched ball eludes the catcher and the runner is put out trying to advance, no caught stealing shall be charged. No caught stealing should be charged when a runner is awarded a base due to obstruction.

SACRIFICES

Sacrifice Bunt 10.09 (a) Score a sacrifice bunt when, before two are out, the batter advances one or more runners with a bunt and is put out at first base, or would have been put out except for a fielding error. (b) Score a sacrifice bunt when, before two are out, the fielders handle a bunted ball without error in an unsuccessful attempt to put out a preceding runner advancing one base. EXCEPTION: When an attempt to turn a bunt into a putout of a preceding runner fails, and in the scorer's judgment perfect play would not have put out the batter at first base, the batter shall be credited with a one-base hit and not a sacrifice.

(c) Do not score a sacrifice bunt when any runner is put out attempting to advance one base on a bunt. Charge the batter with a time at bat.

(d) Do not score a sacrifice bunt when, in the judgment of the scorer, the batter is bunting primarily for a base hit and not for the purpose of advancing a runner or runners. Charge the batter with a time at bat.

> NOTE: In applying the above rule, always give the batter the benefit of the doubt.

Sacrifice Fly (e) Score a sacrifice fly when, before two are out, the batter hits a fly ball or a line drive handled by an outfielder or an infielder running in the outfield which

(1) is caught, and a runner scores after the catch, or

(2) is dropped, and a runner scores, if in the scorer's judgment the runner could have scored after the catch had the fly been caught.

> NOTE: Score a sacrifice fly in accordance with 10.09 (e) (2) even though another runner is forced out by reason of the batter becoming a runner.

PUTOUTS

Putouts 10.10 A putout shall be credited to each fielder who (1) catches a fly ball or a line drive, whether fair or foul; (2) catches a thrown ball which puts out a batter or runner, or (3) tags a runner when the runner is off the base to which he legally is entitled.

(a) Automatic putouts shall be credited to the catcher as follows:

(1) When the batter is called out for an illegally batted ball;

(2) When the batter is called out for bunting foul for his third strike; (Note exception in 10.17 (a)(4).

(3) When the batter is called out for being touched by his own batted ball;

(4) When the batter is called out for interfering with the catcher.

(5) When the batter is called out for failing to bat in his proper turn; (See 10.03 (d).

(6) When the batter is called out for refusing to touch first base after receiving a base on balls;

(7) When a runner is called out for refusing to advance from third base to home with the winning run.

Other Automatic Putouts

(b) Other automatic putouts shall be credited as follows (Credit no assists on these plays except as specified):

(1) When the batter is called out on an Infield Fly which is not caught, credit the putout to the fielder who the scorer believes could have made the catch;

(2) When a runner is called out for being touched by a fair ball (including an Infield Fly), credit the putout to the fielder nearest the ball;

(3) When a runner is called out for running out of line to avoid being tagged, credit the putout to the fielder whom the runner avoided;

(4) When a runner is called out for passing another runner, credit the putout to the fielder nearest the point of passing;

(5) When a runner is called out for running the bases in reverse order, credit the putout to the fielder covering the base he left in starting his reverse run;

(6) When a runner is called out for having interfered with a fielder, credit the putout to the fielder with whom the runner interfered, unless the fielder was in the act of throwing the ball when the interference occurred, in which case credit the putout to the fielder for whom

the throw was intended, and credit an assist to the fielder whose throw was interfered with;

(7) When the batter-runner is called out because of interference by a preceding runner, as provided in Playing Rule 6.05 (m), credit the putout to the first baseman. If the fielder interfered with was in the act of throwing the ball, credit him with an assist, but credit only one assist on any one play under the provisions of 10.10 (b) (6) and (7).

ASSISTS

Assists   10.11   An assist shall be credited to each fielder who throws or deflects a batted or thrown ball in such a way that a putout results, or would have resulted except for a subsequent error by any fielder. Only one assist and no more shall be credited to each fielder who throws or deflects the ball in a run-down play which results in a putout, or would have resulted in a putout, except for a subsequent error.

> NOTE: Mere ineffective contact with the ball shall not be considered an assist. "Deflect" shall mean to slow down or change the direction of the ball and thereby effectively assist in putting out a batter or runner.

(a) Credit an assist to each fielder who throws or deflects the ball during a play which results in a runner being called out for interference, or for running out of line.

(b) Do not credit an assist to the pitcher on a strikeout. EXCEPTION: Credit an assist if the pitcher fields an uncaught third strike and makes a throw which results in a putout.

(c) Do not credit an assist to the pitcher when, as the result of a legal pitch received by the catcher, a runner is put out, as when the catcher picks a runner off base, throws out a runner trying to steal, or tags a runner trying to score.

(d) Do not credit an assist to a fielder whose wild throw permits a runner to advance, even though the runner subsequently is put out as a result of continuous play. A play which follows a misplay (whether or not it is an error) is a new play, and the fielder making any misplay shall not be credited with an assist unless he takes part in the new play.

The Official Scorer

DOUBLE PLAYS—TRIPLE PLAYS

Double and Triple Plays

10.12 Credit participation in the double play or triple play to each fielder who earns a putout or an assist when two or three players are put out between the time a pitch is delivered and the time the ball next becomes dead or is next in possession of the pitcher in pitching position, unless an error or misplay intervenes between putouts.

> NOTE: Credit the double play or triple play also if an appeal play after the ball is in possession of the pitcher results in an additional putout.

ERRORS

Errors

10.13 An error shall be charged for each misplay (fumble, muff or wild throw) which prolongs the time at bat of a batter or which prolongs the life of a runner, or which permits a runner to advance one or more bases.

> NOTE (1) Slow handling of the ball which does not involve mechanical misplay shall not be construed as an error.
>
> NOTE (2) It is not necessary that the fielder touch the ball to be charged with an error. If a ground ball goes through a fielder's legs or a pop fly falls untouched and in the scorer's judgment the fielder could have handled the ball with ordinary effort, an error shall be charged.
>
> NOTE (3) Mental mistakes or misjudgments are not to be scored as errors unless specifically covered in the rules.

(a) An error shall be charged against any fielder when he muffs a foul fly, to prolong the time at bat of a batter whether the batter subsequently reaches first base or is put out.

(b) An error shall be charged against any fielder when he catches a thrown ball or a ground ball in time to put out the batter-runner and fails to tag first base or the batter-runner.

(c) An error shall be charged against any fielder when he catches a thrown ball or a ground ball in time to put out any runner on a force play and fails to tag the base or the runner.

Wild Throws

(d) (1) An error shall be charged against any fielder whose wild throw permits a runner to reach a base safely, when in the scorer's judgment a good throw would have put out the runner. EXCEPTION: No error shall be charged under this section if the wild throw is made attempting to prevent a stolen base.

(2)   An error shall be charged against any fielder whose wild throw in attempting to prevent a runner's advance permits that runner or any other runner to advance one or more bases beyond the base he would have reached had the throw not been wild.

(3)   An error shall be charged against any fielder whose throw takes an unnatural bounce, or touches a base or the pitcher's plate, or touches a runner, a fielder or an umpire, thereby permitting any runner to advance.

NOTE: Apply this rule even when it appears to be an injustice to a fielder whose throw was accurate. Every base advanced by a runner must be accounted for.

(4)   Charge only one error on any wild throw, regardless of the number of bases advanced by one or more runners.

Missed Throw   (e)   An error shall be charged against any fielder whose failure to stop, or try to stop, an accurately thrown ball permits a runner to advance, providing there was occasion for the throw. If such throw be made to second base, the scorer shall determine whether it was the duty of the second baseman or the shortstop to stop the ball, and an error shall be charged to the negligent player.

NOTE: If in the scorer's judgment there was no occasion for the throw, an error shall be charged to the fielder who threw the ball.

(f)   When an umpire awards the batter or any runner or runners one or more bases because of interference or obstruction, charge the fielder who committed the interference or obstruction with one error, no matter how many bases the batter, or runner or runners, may be advanced.

NOTE: Do not charge an error if obstruction does not change the play in the opinion of the scorer.

No Error Charged

10.14   No error shall be charged in the following cases:

(a)   No error shall be charged against the catcher when after receiving the pitch, he makes a wild throw attempting to prevent a stolen base, unless the wild throw permits the stealing runner to advance one or more extra bases, or permits any other runner to advance one or more bases.

Double or Triple Play

(b)   No error shall be charged against any fielder who makes a wild throw if in the scorer's judgment the runner would not have been put out with ordinary effort by a good throw, unless such wild throw permits any runner to advance beyond the base he would have reached had the throw not been wild.

(c)   No error shall be charged against any fielder when he makes a wild throw in attempting to complete a double play or triple play, unless such wild throw enables any runner to advance beyond the base he would have reached had the throw not been wild.

> NOTE: When a fielder muffs a thrown ball which, if held, would have completed a double play or triple play, charge an error to the fielder who drops the ball and credit an assist to the fielder who made the throw.

(d)   No error shall be charged against any fielder when, after fumbling a ground ball or dropping a fly ball, a line drive or a thrown ball, he recovers the ball in time to force out a runner at any base.

Letting Foul Fly Fall

(e)   No error shall be charged against any fielder who permits a foul fly to fall safe with a runner on third base before two are out, if in the scorer's judgment the fielder deliberately refuses the catch in order that the runner on third shall not score after the catch.

Pitcher and Catcher

(f)   Because the pitcher and catcher handle the ball much more than other fielders, certain misplays on pitched balls are defined in Rule 10.15 as wild pitches and passed balls. No error shall be charged when a wild pitch or passed ball is scored.

(1)   No error shall be charged when the batter is awarded first base on four called balls or because he was touched by a pitched ball, or when he reaches first base as the result of a wild pitch or passed ball.

(i) When the third strike is a wild pitch, permitting the batter to reach first base, score a strikeout and a wild pitch.

(ii) When the third strike is a passed ball, permitting the batter to reach first base, score a strikeout and a passed ball.

(2) No error shall be charged when a runner or runners advance as the result of a passed ball, a wild pitch or a balk.

(i) When the fourth called ball is a wild pitch or a passed ball, and as a result (a) the batter-runner advances to a base beyond first base; (b) any runner forced to advance by the base on balls advances more than one base, or (c) any runner, not forced to advance, advances one or more bases, score the base on balls, and also the wild pitch or passed ball, as the case may be;

(ii) When the catcher recovers the ball after a wild pitch or passed ball on the third strike, and throws out the batter-runner at first base, or tags out the batter-runner, but another runner or runners advance, score the strikeout, the putout and assists, if any, and credit the advance of the other runner or runners as having been made on the play.

WILD PITCHES—PASSED BALLS

Wild Pitches and Passed Balls   10.15   (a) A wild pitch shall be charged when a legally delivered ball is so high, or so wide, or so low that the catcher does not stop and control the ball by ordinary effort, thereby permitting a runner or runners to advance.

(1) A wild pitch shall be charged when a legally delivered ball touches the ground before reaching home plate and is not handled by the catcher, permitting a runner or runners to advance.

(b) A catcher shall be charged with a passed ball when he fails to hold or to control a legally pitched ball which should have been held or controlled with ordinary effort, thereby permitting a runner or runners to advance.

BASES ON BALLS

Bases on Balls   10.16   (a)   A base on balls shall be scored whenever a batter is awarded first base because of four balls having been pitched outside the strike zone, but when the fourth such ball touches the batter it shall be scored as a "hit batter." (See 10.18 (h) for procedure when more than one pitcher is involved in giving a base on balls: Also see 10.17 (b) relative to substitute batter who receives base on balls.)

(b)   Intentional base on balls shall be scored when the pitcher makes no attempt to throw the last pitch to the batter into the strike zone but purposely throws the ball wide to the catcher outside the catcher's box.

     (1)   If a batter awarded a base on balls is called out for refusing to advance to first base, do not credit the base on balls. Charge a time at bat.

STRIKEOUTS

Strikeouts   10.17   (a)   A strikeout shall be scored whenever:

     (1)   A batter is put out by a third strike caught by the catcher;

     (2)   A batter is put out by a third strike not caught when there is a runner on first before two are out;

     (3)   A batter becomes a runner because a third strike is not caught;

     (4)   A batter bunts foul on third strike. EXCEPTION: If such bunt on third strike results in a foul fly caught by any fielder, do not score a strikeout. Credit the fielder who catches such foul fly with a putout.

(b)   When the batter leaves the game with two strikes against him, and the substitute batter completes a strikeout, charge the strikeout and the time at bat to the first batter. If the substitute batter completes the turn at bat in any other manner, including a base on balls, score the action as having been that of the substitute batter.

EARNED RUNS

Earned Runs   10.18   An earned run is a run for which the pitcher is held accountable. In determining earned runs, the inning should be reconstructed without the errors (which include catcher's interference) and passed balls, and the benefit of the doubt should always be given to the pitcher in determining which bases would have been reached by errorless play. For the purpose of determining earned runs, an intentional base on balls, regardless of the circumstances, shall be construed in exactly the same manner as any other base on balls.

(a) An earned run shall be charged every time a runner reaches home base by the aid of safe hits, sacrifice bunts, a sacrifice fly, stolen bases, putouts, fielder's choices, bases on balls, hit batters, balks or wild pitches (including a wild pitch on third strike which permits a batter to reach first base) before fielding chances have been offered to put out the offensive team. For the purpose of this rule, a defensive interference penalty shall be construed as a fielding chance.

   (1) A wild pitch is solely the pitcher's fault, and contributes to an earned run just as a base on balls or a balk.

No Earned Run

(b) No run shall be earned when scored by a runner who reaches first base (1) on a hit or otherwise after his time at bat is prolonged by a muffed foul fly; (2) because of interference or obstruction or (3) because of any fielding error.

(c) No run shall be earned when scored by a runner whose life is prolonged by an error, if such runner would have been put out by errorless play.

(d) No run shall be earned when the runner's advance is aided by an error, a passed ball, or defensive interference or obstruction, if the scorer judges that the run would not have scored without the aid of such misplay.

(e) An error by a pitcher is treated exactly the same as an error by any other fielder in computing earned runs.

(f) Whenever a fielding error occurs, the pitcher shall be given the benefit of the doubt in determining to which bases any runners would have advanced had the fielding of the defensive team been errorless.

Relief Pitcher

(g) When pitchers are changed during an inning, the relief pitcher shall not be charged with any run (earned or unearned) scored by a runner who was on base at the time he entered the game, nor for runs scored by any runner who reaches base on a fielder's choice which puts out a runner left on base by the preceding pitcher.

NOTE: It is the intent of this rule to charge each pitcher with the number of runners he put on base, rather than with the individual runners. When a pitcher puts runners on base, and is relieved, he shall be charged with all runs subsequently scored up to and including the number of runners he left on base when he left the game, unless such runners are put out without action by the batter, i.e., caught stealing, picked off base, or called out for interference when a batter-runner does not reach first base on the play. EXCEPTION: see example 7.

EXAMPLES:

(1) P1 walks A and is relieved by P2. B grounds out, sending A to second. C flies out. D singles, scoring A. Charge run to P1.

(2) P1 walks A and is relieved by P2. B forces A at second. C grounds out, sending B to second. D singles, scoring B. Charge run to P1.

(3) P1 walks A and is relieved by P2. B singles, sending A to third. C grounds to short, and A is out at home, B going to second. D flies out. E singles, scoring B. Charge run to P1.

(4) P1 walks A and is relieved by P2. B walks. C flies out. A is picked off second. D doubles, scoring B from first. Charge run to P2.

(5) P1 walks A and is relieved by P2. P2 walks B and is relieved by P3. C forces A at third. D forces B at third. E hits home run, scoring three runs. Charge one run to P1; one run to P2, one run to P3.

(6) P1 walks A, and is relieved by P2, P2 walks B. C singles, filling the bases. D forces A at home. E singles, scoring B and C. Charge one run to P1 and one run to P2.

(7) P1 walks A, and is relieved by P2. P2 allows B to single, but A is out trying for third. B takes second on the throw. C singles, scoring B. Charge run to P2.

Count on Batter

(h) A relief pitcher shall not be held accountable when the first batter to whom he pitches reaches first base on four called balls if such batter has a decided advantage in the ball and strike count when pitchers are changed.

(1) If, when pitchers are changed, the count is
2 balls, no strike,
2 balls, 1 strike,
3 balls, no strike,
3 balls, 1 strike,
3 balls, 2 strikes,
and the batter gets a base on balls, charge that batter and the base on balls to the preceding pitcher, not to the relief pitcher.

(2) Any other action by such batter, such as reaching base on a hit, an error, a fielder's choice, a force-out, or being touched by a pitched ball, shall cause such a batter to be charged to the relief pitcher.

NOTE: The provisions of 10.18 (h) (2) shall not be construed as affecting or conflicting with the provisions of 10.18 (g).

(3) If, when pitchers are changed, the count is
2 balls, 2 strikes,
1 ball, 2 strikes,
1 ball, 1 strike,
1 ball, no strike,
no ball, 2 strikes,
no ball, 1 strike,
charge that batter and his actions to the relief pitcher.

(i) When pitchers are changed during an inning, the relief pitcher shall not have the benefit of previous chances for outs not accepted in determining earned runs.

NOTE: It is the intent of this rule to charge relief pitchers with earned runs for which they are solely responsible. In some instances, runs charged as earned against the relief pitcher can be charged as unearned against the team.

EXAMPLES: (1) With two out, P1 walks A. B reaches base on an error. P2 relieves P1. C hits home run, scoring three runs. Charge two unearned runs to P1, one earned run to P2.

(2) With two out, P1 walks A and B and is relieved by P2. C reaches base on an error. D hits home run, scoring four runs. Charge two unearned runs to P1, two unearned runs to P2.

(3) With none out, P1 walks A. B reaches base on an error. P2 relieves P1. C hits home run, scoring three runs. D and E strike out. F reaches base on an error. G hits home run, scoring two runs. Charge two runs, one earned, to P1. Charge three runs, one earned, to P2.

WINNING AND LOSING PITCHER

Winning and Losing Pitchers

10.19 (a) Credit the starting pitcher with a game won only if he has pitched at least five complete innings and his team not only is in the lead when he is replaced but remains in the lead the remainder of the game.

(b) The "must pitch five complete innings" rule in respect to the starting pitcher shall be in effect for all games of six or more innings. In a five-inning game, credit the starting pitcher with a game won if he has pitched at least four complete innings and his team not only is in the lead when he is replaced but remains in the lead the remainder of the game.

Multiple Relievers

(c) When the starting pitcher cannot be credited with the victory because of the provisions of 10.19 (a) or (b) and more than one relief pitcher is used, the victory shall be awarded on the following basis:

(1) When, during the tenure of the starting pitcher, the winning team assumes the lead and maintains it to the finish of the game, credit the victory to the relief pitcher judged by the scorer to have been the most effective;

(2) Whenever the score is tied the game becomes a new contest insofar as the winning and losing pitcher is concerned;

(3) Once the opposing team assumes the lead all pitchers who have pitched up to that point are excluded from being credited with the victory except that if the pitcher against whose pitching the opposing team gained the lead continues to pitch until his team regains the lead, which it holds to the finish of the game, that pitcher shall be the winning pitcher;

(4) The winning relief pitcher shall be the one who is the pitcher of record when his team assumes the lead and maintains it to the finish of the game. EXCEPTION: Do not credit a victory to a relief pitcher who is ineffective in a brief appearance, when a succeeding relief pitcher

pitches effectively in helping his team maintain the lead. In such cases, credit the succeeding relief pitcher with the victory.

(d) When a pitcher is removed for a substitute batter or substitute runner, all runs scored by his team during the inning in which he is removed shall be credited to his benefit in determining the pitcher of record when his team assumes the lead.

(e) Regardless of how many innings the first pitcher has pitched, he shall be charged with the loss of the game if he is replaced when his team is behind in the score, or falls behind because of runs charged to him after he is replaced, and his team thereafter fails either to tie the score or gain the lead.

Shutout

(f) No pitcher shall be credited with pitching a shutout unless he pitches the complete game, or unless he enters the game with none out before the opposing team has scored in the first inning, puts out the side without a run scoring and pitches all the rest of the game. When two or more pitchers combine to pitch a shutout a notation to that effect should be included in the league's official pitching records.

(g) In some non-championship games (such as the Major League All-Star Game) it is provided in advance that each pitcher shall work a stated number of innings, usually two or three. In such games, it is customary to credit the victory to the pitcher of record, whether starter or reliever, when the winning team takes a lead which it maintains to the end of the game, unless such pitcher is knocked out after the winning team has a commanding lead, and the scorer believes a subsequent pitcher is entitled to credit for the victory.

SAVES FOR RELIEF PITCHERS

Saves   10.20   Credit a pitcher with a save when he meets all three of the following conditions:

(1) He is the finishing pitcher in a game won by his club; and

(2) He is not the winning pitcher; and

(3) He qualifies under one of the following conditions:

(a) He enters the game with a lead of no more than three runs and pitches for at least one inning; or

(b)   He enters the game, regardless of the count, with the potential tying run either on base, or at bat, or on deck (that is, the potential tying run is either already on base or is one of the first two batsmen he faces); or

(c)   He pitches effectively for at least three innings.

No more than one save may be credited in each game.

STATISTICS

Statistics 10.21   The league president shall appoint an official statistician. The statistician shall maintain an accumulative record of all the batting, fielding, running and pitching records specified in 10.02 for every player who appears in a league championship game.

The statistician shall prepare a tabulated report at the end of the season, including all individual and team records for every championship game, and shall submit this report to the league president. This report shall identify each player by his first name and surname, and shall indicate as to each batter whether he bats righthanded, lefthanded or both ways; as to each fielder and pitcher, whether he throws righthanded or lefthanded.

When a player listed in the starting lineup for the visiting club is substituted for before he plays defensively, he shall not receive credit in the defensive statistics (fielding), unless he actually plays that position during a game. All such players, however, shall be credited with one game played (in "batting statistics") as long as they are announced into the game or listed on the official lineup card.

Any games played to break a divisional tie shall be included in the statistics for that championship season.

DETERMINING PERCENTAGE RECORDS

Percentage 10.22   To compute
Records

(a)   Percentage of games won and lost, divide the number of games won by the total games won and lost;

(b)   Batting average, divide the total number of safe hits (not the total bases on hits) by the total times at bat, as defined in 10.02 (a);

(c)   Slugging percentage, divide the total bases of all safe hits by the total times at bat, as defined in 10.02 (a);

(d)   Fielding average, divide the total putouts and assists by the total of putouts, assists and errors;

(e)   Pitcher's earned-run average, multiply the total earned runs charged against his pitching by 9, and divide the result by the total number of innings he pitched.

> NOTE: Earned-run average shall be calculated on the basis of total innings pitched including fractional innings. EXAMPLE: 9 1/3 innings pitched and 3 earned runs is an earned-run average of 2.89 (3 ER times 9 divided by 9 1/3 equals 2.89).

(f)   On-base percentage, divide the total of hits, all bases on balls, and hit by pitch by the total of at bats, all bases on balls, hit by pitch and sacrifice flies.

> NOTE: For the purpose of computing on-base percentage, ignore being awarded first base on interference or obstruction.

MINIMUM STANDARDS FOR INDIVIDUAL CHAMPIONSHIPS

Minimum 10.23
Standards

To assure uniformity in establishing the batting, pitching and fielding championships of professional leagues, such champions shall meet the following minimum performance standards:

(a)   The individual batting champion or slugging champion shall be the player with the highest batting average or slugging percentage, provided he is credited with as many or more total appearances at the plate in League Championship games as the number of games scheduled for each club in his league that season, multiplied by 3.1 in the case of a major league player. EXCEPTION: However, if there is any player with fewer than the required number of plate appearances whose average would be the highest, if he were charged with the required number of plate appearances or official at bats, then that player shall be awarded the batting championship or slugging championship.

> EXAMPLE: If a major league schedules 162 games for each club, 502 plate appearances qualify (162 times 3.1 equals 502). If a National Association league schedules 140 games for each club, 378 plate appearances qualify (140 times 2.7 equals 378).

Total appearances at the plate shall include official times at bat, plus bases on balls, times hit by pitcher, sacrifice hits, sacrifice flies and times awarded first base because of interference or obstruction.

(b)   The individual pitching champion shall be the pitcher with the lowest earned-run average, provided that he has pitched at least as many innings as the number of games scheduled for each club in his league that season. EXCEPTION: However, pitchers in National Association leagues shall qualify for the pitching championship by having the lowest earned-run average and having pitched at least as many innings as 80% of the number of games scheduled for each club in his league that season.

(c)   The individual fielding champions shall be the fielders with the highest fielding average at each position, provided:

(1)   A catcher must have participated as a catcher in at least one-half the number of games scheduled for each club in his league that season;

(2)   An infielder or outfielder must have participated at his position in at least two-thirds of the number of games scheduled for each club in his league that season;

(3)   A pitcher must have pitched at least as many innings as the number of games scheduled for each club in his league that season. EXCEPTION: If another pitcher has a fielding average as high or higher, and has handled more total chances in a lesser number of innings, he shall be the fielding champion.

GUIDELINES FOR CUMULATIVE PERFORMANCE RECORDS

Hitting Streaks   10.24   CONSECUTIVE HITTING STREAKS.

(a)   A consecutive hitting streak shall not be terminated if the plate appearance results in a base on balls, hit batsman, defensive interference or a sacrifice bunt. A sacrifice fly shall terminate the streak.

(b)   CONSECUTIVE-GAME HITTING STREAKS.
A consecutive-game hitting streak shall not be terminated if all the player's plate appearances (one or more) result in a base on balls, hit batsman, defensive interference or a sacrifice bunt. The streak shall terminate if the player has a sacrifice fly and no hit.

The player's individual consecutive-game hitting streak shall be determined by the consecutive games in which the player appears and is not determined by his club's games.

(c) CONSECUTIVE PLAYING STREAK.
A consecutive-game playing streak shall be extended if the player plays one half-inning on defense, or if he completes a time at bat by reaching base or being put out. A pinch-running appearance only shall not extend the streak. If a player is ejected from a game by an umpire before he can comply with the requirements of this rule, his streak shall continue.

(d) SUSPENDED GAMES.
For the purpose of this rule, all performances in the completion of a suspended game shall be considered as occurring on the original date of the game.

Index

Listed by Official Rule numbers.

Accident to Player or Umpire   5.10 (c) and (h).

Appeals   6.07 (b), 7.10.

Balk Ball Dead   5.09 (c), 8:05;
     Penalty   7.04 (a), 7.07, 8.05;
     Penalty waived   8.05.

Ball Called Ball   2.00;
     Dead Ball   3.12, 5.02, 5.09, 5.10;
     Live Ball   5.02, 5.11;
     Official Game Balls   3.01 (c).

Base Coaches Number   4.05;
     Restrictions   3.17, 4.05 (b).
     Interference   5.09 (g), 7.09 (i-j).
     Accidental Interference   5.08.

Batter Becomes Runner   6.08, 6.09;
     Batter Interference   6.05 (h), 6.06 (c), 7.08 (g), 7.09;
     Batter Out   6.02 (c), 6.05, 6.06, 6.07, 7.09, 7.11
     Penalty; Interference with Batter   6.08 (c), 7.04 (d).

Batter's Box   2.00, 6.03, 6.06 (b).

Batting Order   4.01, 4.04, 6.01, 6.04.

Batting Out of Order   6.07.

Catcher Interference by   6.08 (c), 7.04 (d), 7.07.
     Interference with   6.06 (c).

Catcher's Position   4.03 (a).

Championship Qualifications (Individual)   10.22.

Cumulative Performance Records Guide Lines   10.24.

Defacing, Discoloring Ball   3.02, 8.02 (a).

Definitions   (alphabetically) Rule 2.00.

Deflected Batted Ball   6.09 (g-h), 7.05 (a) and (f).

Delay of Game By Batter   6.02 (c);
     by Pitcher   8.02 (c); 8.04;
     Forfeit for Delays   4.15.

Designated Hitter   6.10.

Discipline of Team Personnel   3.14, 4.06, 4.07, 4.08, 4.15,
     9.01 (b) and (d), 9.05.

Doubleheaders   4.13.

Index

Equipment Ball   1.09;
    Bases   1.06;
    Bats   1.10;
    Benches   1.08;
    Commercialization   1.17;
    Gloves   1.12, 1.13, 1.14, 1.15;
    Helmets   1.16;
    Home Base   1.05;
    Pitcher's   Plate 1.07;
    Toe Plate   1.11 (g);
    Uniforms   1.11.

Equipment Thrown at Ball   7.05 (a-e).

Fair Ball Bounces Out of Play   6.09 (e-f-g), 7.05 (f).

Fielder Falls Into Dugout   5.10 (f), 7.04 (c).

Fielder's Choice   2.00, 10.14 (f) (2) (ii).

Forfeits   4.15, 4.16, 4.17, 4.18.

Ground Rules   3.13, 9.04 (a) (9).

Illegal Pitch   2.00, 8.01 (d), 8.02 (a) (6) 8.05 (e).

Illegally Batted Ball 6.06 (a).

Infield Fly 2.00, 6.05 (e) and (l) Note, 7.08 (f).

Intentionally Dropped Ball   6.05 (l).

Interference Defensive   2.00, 6.08 (c), 7.04 (d), 7.07;
    Offensive   2.00, 5.09 (f), (g), 6.05 (h) (i) (m) and (n), 6.06 (c),
      6.08 (d), 7.08 (b) (f) and (g), 7.09, 7.11;
    Spectator   2.00, 3.16;
    Umpires   2.00, 5.09 (b), (f); 6.08 (d).

Light Failure   4.12 (a-b), 5.10 (b).

Missed Base   7.02, 7.04
    Note,   7.08 (k), 7.10 (b), 7.12, 8.05 Penalty Approved Ruling.

Obstruction   7.06.

Official Scorer Rule   10.00.

Overrunning First Base   7.08 (c) and (j), 7.10 (c).

Penalties   2.00 (See LEAGUE PRESIDENT.)

Pitcher Legal Position   8.01 (a-b);
    Becomes Infielder   8.01 (e);
    Preparatory Pitches   8.03;
    Take Signs While on Rubber   8.01;
    Throwing at Batter   8.02 (d);
    Throwing to a Base   7.05 (h), 8.01 (c);

Visits by Manager or Coach   8.06.

Players' Positions   4.03.

Playing Field   1.04. (Includes Diagrams of Mound and
     Diamond Layout and Playing Lines.)

Police Protection   3.18.

Postponement Responsibility   3.10.

Protested Games   4.19.

Regulation Game   4.10, 4.11.
     (7-inning Games   4.10 (a) Note).

Resuming Play After Dead Ball   5.11.

Restrictions on Players No Fraternizing   3.09;
     Barred from Stands   3.09;
     Confined to Bench   3.17.

Runner Entitled to Base   7.01, 7.03;
     Touch Requirements   7.02, 7.08 (d), 7.10;
     Runners Advance   7.04, 7.05, 7.06;
     Reverse Run Prohibited   7.08 (i);
     Runner Out   7.08, 7.09 (e-m), 7.10, 7.11;

Running Out of Line   6.05 (k), 7.08 (a).

Score of Game   4.11.

Scoring Rules Rule   10.00

Scoring Runs   4.09, 6.05 (n), 7.07, 7.12.

Spectators Barred from Field   3.15;
     Touching Batted or Thrown Ball   3.16.

Strike   2.00 (See STRIKE AND STRIKE ZONE), 6.08 (b).

Substitutions   3.03, 3.04, 3.05, 3.06, 3.07, 3.08, 4.04.

Suspended Games   4.12.

Time Limits   9.04 (a) (7).

Umpire Rule   9.00.
     Inspects Equipment and Playing Lines   3.01;
     Judge of Playing Conditions   3.10 (c-d), 5.10 (a);
     Controls Ground Crew   3.11;
     Controls Lights   4.14;
     Calls "Time"   5.10;
     Controls Newsmen and Photographers   9.01 (e);
     Time Limits   9.04 (a) (7);
     Umpire's Interference   5.09 (b) and (f), 6.08 (d);
     Touched by Pitch or Thrown Ball   5.08, 5.09 (h), 7.05 (i).

Unsportsmanlike Conduct   4.06 (b).

Wild Throws   5.08, 7.05 (g-h-i)

(Note. Where Rule 2.00 is indexed, the definition of the indexed item includes important explanatory matter.)